T0213893

Lecture Notes in Artificial Intelligence   8750

Subseries of Lecture Notes in Computer Science

LNAI Series Editors

Randy Goebel
University of Alberta, Edmonton, Canada
Yuzuru Tanaka
Hokkaido University, Sapporo, Japan
Wolfgang Wahlster
DFKI and Saarland University, Saarbrücken, Germany

LNAI Founding Series Editor

Joerg Siekmann
DFKI and Saarland University, Saarbrücken, Germany

More information about this series at http://www.springer.com/series/1244

Tibor Bosse · Joost Broekens
João Dias · Janneke van der Zwaan (Eds.)

Emotion Modeling

Towards Pragmatic Computational Models
of Affective Processes

 Springer

Editors
Tibor Bosse
VU University Amsterdam
Amsterdam
The Netherlands

Joost Broekens
Delft University of Technology
Delft
The Netherlands

João Dias
University of Lisbon
Porto Salvo
Portugal

Janneke van der Zwaan
Delft University of Technology
Delft
The Netherlands

ISSN 0302-9743   ISSN 1611-3349   (electronic)
Lecture Notes in Artificial Intelligence
ISBN 978-3-319-12972-3   ISBN 978-3-319-12973-0   (eBook)
DOI 10.1007/978-3-319-12973-0

Library of Congress Control Number: 2014955538

LNCS Sublibrary: SL7 – Artificial Intelligence

Springer Cham Heidelberg New York Dordrecht London

Printed on acid-free paper

Springer International Publishing AG Switzerland is part of Springer Science+Business Media (www.springer.com)

Preface

As research on emotion modeling is becoming more mature, the amount of computational models of affective processes is rapidly increasing. Nevertheless, it is important to cut down the complexity of these models, for multiple reasons.

First, cutting down complexity facilitates reuse of models. Many computational models of affective processes are developed primarily for a practical purpose and are therefore embedded in something else (e.g., an adaptive agent, intelligent virtual character, or robot). These models are often developed (a) in an ad hoc way, building on the best practices from earlier research, (b) based on emotional theories that lack necessary computational details, (c) from scratch, using publications of others instead of using components from existing models or (d) using assumptions from others, and finally (e) without a solid validation scheme. This is understandable given the applied nature of many of these models. However, this approach results in computational models of affective processes that are complex, and difficult to understand and validate. A pragmatic approach is easier to understand, build upon, and implement.

Second, limiting complexity facilitates contributions to psychological research. Computational models of emotion are tools for experimental psychologists that can be used to gain insight into emotion. Many of the computational mechanisms needed for developing these models are not available in emotion psychology. Hence, instead of asking for these mechanisms from psychologists, the models should bring insight, and generate testable hypotheses. For this to be possible the model must be fully specified in a form that is understandable for psychologists, and have clear psychological grounding. Simpler models are easier to understand and ground than complex ones.

The goal of this volume is to gain more insight into the knowledge that is used to develop computational models of affective processes. To this end, the book starts with an introduction to the field, written by Eva Hudlicka. After that, it contains extended versions of eight papers that were presented at the workshop on Standards for Emotion Modeling (held in Leiden, the Netherlands, in 2011) and the workshop on Emotional and Empathic Agents (held in Valencia, Spain, in 2012). To assure a high quality, each chapter was reviewed by at least three anonymous referees. The chapters are distributed over two parts: one part on "Generic Models and Frameworks," and the other one on "Evaluations of Specific Models." Nevertheless, the material of each chapter is self-contained, so that readers can select any individual chapter based on their research interests without the need of reading other chapters.

To conclude, we would like to thank all the authors for their interesting contributions, and in particular Eva Hudlicka for writing an excellent introduction chapter. Also, we express our gratitude to the reviewers for their hard work in assuring the high quality of this survey, and to Alfred Hofmann and Anna Kramer at Springer Verlag for providing us the opportunity to publish this volume.

August 2014

Tibor Bosse
Joost Broekens
João Dias
Janneke van der Zwaan

Contents

Introduction

From Habits to Standards: Towards Systematic Design of Emotion Models and Affective Architectures

Eva Hudlicka[(✉)]

Psychometrix Associates and University of Massachusetts Amherst,
Amherst, MA, USA
hudlicka@cs.umass.edu

Abstract. Emotion modeling has been an active area of research for almost two decades now. Yet in spite of the growing and diverse body of work, designing and developing emotion models remains an art, with few standards and systematic guidelines available to guide the design process, and to validate the resulting models. In this introduction I first summarize some of the existing work attempting to establish more systematic approaches to affective modeling, and highlight the specific contributions to this effort discussed in the papers in this volume. I then propose an analytical computational framework that delineates the core affective processes, *emotion generation* and *emotion effects*, and defines the *abstract computational tasks* necessary to implement these. This framework provides both a common vocabulary for describing the computational requirements for affective modeling, and proposes the building blocks necessary for implementing emotion models. As such, it can serve both as a foundation for developing more systematic guidelines for model design, and as a basis for developing modeling tools. I conclude with a summary and a discussion of some open questions and challenges.

1 Introduction

Emotion modeling has been an active area of research for almost two decades now. Since 1997, when Picard coined the term affective computing (Picard 1997), emotion modeling, and affective computing in general, have blossomed. In the broader area of affective computing there is now a dedicated bi-ennial conference (ACII) and two journals: the International Journal of Synthetic Emotions and IEEE Transactions on Affective Computing, as well as numerous special issues of other journals focusing on some aspect of affective computing (e.g., Intl. Jnl. of Human-Computer Studies, User Modeling and User Adapted Interaction). A number of AAAI symposia have been dedicated to the exploration of specific aspects of emotion modeling (cognition/emotion interaction, affective architectures, emotions in social agents), and numerous workshops have been organized in conjunction with larger conferences, focusing on affective modeling in specific contexts, including agents (IVA, AAMAS), user-adapted interaction (UMUAI), gaming (Foundations of Digital Games), emotion recognition (Automatic Face and Gesture Recognition/FG), and models of affective disorders (Cognitive Science).

© Springer International Publishing Switzerland 2014
T. Bosse et al. (Eds.): Emotion Modeling, LNAI 8750, pp. 3–23, 2014.
DOI: 10.1007/978-3-319-12973-0_1

In spite of the growing and diverse body of work in emotion modeling, designing and developing emotion models remains an art, with few standards and systematic guidelines available to guide the design process, and to validate the resulting models. Few tools exist to support efficient model development. In addition, a lack of terminological clarity in the field continues to persist and hinders cross-disciplinary collaboration. Even the term *affective or emotion modeling* has very distinct meanings. To some, it means developing models of affective processes (the focus of the papers in this volume); that is, models of emotion generation in response to some triggering stimuli, and models of the effects of these emotions on cognition, expression and behavior. To others, affective or emotion modeling means recognition of human emotion: that is, the mapping of sensed data reflecting a particular emotional state onto a recognized emotion. I have addressed this ambiguity in 2008, in a paper titled "What are we modeling when we model emotion?" (Hudlicka 2008a), and suggested that the term emotion modeling should be reserved for modeling affective processes only. This is the meaning assumed in the remainder of this paper.

The lack of standards in emotion modeling stands in contrast with other areas of affective computing, most notably emotion recognition and emotion expression, where standards have begun to emerge. For example, in both emotion recognition and expression, the Facial Action Coding System (FACS), developed by Ekman and Friesen in the 1970's (Ekman and Friesen 1978), has become the de facto standard for analysis and description of facial expressions, and serves as the foundation of both emotion recognition by machines, and the synthesis of emotion expressions in virtual agents and robots. Emotion markup languages are being developed to support emotion expression in agents and robots, and while no markup language has been adopted as a gold standard, the Emotion Markup Language (EmotionML) (Schröder et al. 2011), is emerging as a good candidate.

While affective modeling is of central importance to both basic emotion research and the rapidly growing areas of intelligent virtual agents, social robots, affective gaming, and affective HCI, there has not been as much progress towards standards in this area. In fact, the one conference dedicated solely to affective computing (the biennial ACII) has historically had a predominance of papers on emotion recognition and expression. The majority of ACII papers that do focus on modeling emotion proper do so primarily in the context of applied models - models that control the behavior of virtual agents, social robots or game characters - rather than models whose purpose is to elucidate the underlying mechanisms of affective processes in biological agents.

The lack of standards and guidelines in modeling is perhaps not surprising, considering the complexity of the phenomena addressed and the relatively recent emergence of the affective modeling enterprise. Even disciplines that have devoted much more time to the study of affective processes, most notably psychology, struggle with terminological issues and a lack of adequate theoretical grounding. To make matters even more challenging, computational models of emotion are developed for very distinct purposes: *research models,* developed to emulate affective processes in biological agents to help characterize their mechanisms, and *applied models*, developed as components of a variety of affect-adaptive systems, including virtual agents and social robots, to enhance their believability and effectiveness. Currently, the majority of emotion models fall in the applied category. Finally, the diversity of domains and application areas within which emotion models are being developed (e.g., learning, gaming, decision-support systems, recommender systems) represents yet another challenge for the modeler, since each domain necessitates extensive knowledge engineering to develop the knowledge structures required to implement contextualized affective processing.

An additional, broader, challenge is a clearer understanding of the similarities and differences in the required standards, design principles and pragmatic considerations for research vs. applied models. While some principles and guidelines for these two categories of models clearly overlap (e.g., ability to compare models, theories, and algorithms for particular tasks; re-use of model components), others are quite distinct; e.g., validation approaches and criteria. In addition, an important, but often neglected, aspect of developing applied emotion models is the determination whether a full-fledged emotion model is in fact necessary, or whether the specific context simply requires some particular functionality or task normally associated with affective processing in biological agents. For example, if a synthetic agent needs to display a particular configuration of facial musculature so that its human interlocutor recognizes this configuration as joy (or sadness, or some other emotion), is it in fact necessary to model emotions within this agent, and are the tasks required to produce this configuration appropriately termed emotion? This of course raises the even thornier issue: what is the nature of emotion, and are emotions 'natural kinds' (Feldman-Barrett 2006). Two of the papers in this volume implicitly touch on this topic: van der Zwaan, Dignum and Jonker's paper "Social Support Strategies for Embodied Conversational Agents" and Martínez-Miranda, Bresó and García-Gómez's "Modelling Two Emotion Regulation Strategies as Key Features of Therapeutic Empathy". The former aims to implement social support strategies within an empathic virtual character, and the latter implicitly assumes that implementing empathy in a virtual character requires, first, a full-fledged generation of emotion, which is then followed by appropriate regulation of this emotion to convey an empathic reaction. Gibson's "Affective Processes as Network Hubs" also discusses some of the fundamental adaptive roles of emotions in biological agents, and briefly discusses the constituent underlying processes of emotions. By attempting to model specific functions associated with emotions in biological agents, these papers contribute to a deeper understanding of the nature of emotions: in biological and in virtual agents.

While it is natural that initial progress in new disciplines is necessarily somewhat unsystematic, a number of researchers in affective modeling have increasingly begun to emphasize the need for more systematic approaches to emotion modeling, including consistent terminology, standards and guidelines, as well as model sharing and re-use and the development of modeling tools. These efforts include broader design principles, such as those that have been discussed by Sloman and colleagues since the 1990s, as well as more focused efforts to clarify existing terminology (Hudlicka 2008a), systematically compare existing appraisal theories (Reisenzein 2001; Broekens et al. 2008), develop guidelines for designing affective agent architectures (Canamero 2001) and emotion models (Hudlicka 2011, 2014), and catalog and compare existing methods for particular modeling tasks (e.g., Reilly's comparison of approaches for emotion intensity calculations (Reilly 2006)). The advantages of these efforts are self-evident but bear repeating:

- unambiguous common language to facilitate communication, especially cross-disciplinary communication, which is essential for progress in an interdisciplinary area such as emotion modeling;
- comparison and evaluation of available theories;
- systematic analysis and comparison of existing models;
- principled design of new models;
- construction of theoretically-grounded and practical tools to facilitate model development; and
- more rapid development of emotion models, through model component sharing and re-use.

This volume includes papers from two recent workshops: *SEM 2011*, which focused on the challenges, progress and open questions regarding emotion modeling standards, and a workshop on *Emotional and Empathic Agents*, held in conjunction with AAMAS 2012, which focused on strategies for reducing the complexity of affective models and model re-use. The SEM workshop also addressed the challenges associated with developing more psychologically grounded models, capable of generating testable hypotheses, in part by making explicit the underlying assumptions and rationale for specific design decisions, including the selection of particular theories (e.g., OCC evaluative criteria (Ortony et al. 1988) vs. appraisal variables from componential theories (Scherer 2001)).

The AAMAS workshop aimed to address a number of specific problematic areas in current approaches to modeling:

- ad hoc model development;
- lack of theories that provide sufficient detail to support computational modeling;
- development of models based on descriptions of existing models, rather than re-use of model components;
- unclear assumptions, and lack of complete understanding of the consequences of the assumptions and simplifications made;
- models that are too complex and lack psychological grounding; and
- lack of solid validation schemes.

The papers collected in this volume represent a sampling of the current efforts toward the development of more systematic methods for emotion modeling, toward the development of standards in emotion model design and validation, and toward more pragmatic approaches to model development, including model component sharing and re-use. Given the diversity of the emotion modeling field, it is not surprising that these papers address a broad range of issues, from a variety of theoretical perspectives, and across a variety of contexts. The topics range from efforts to define minimum functionalities for agent emotion models and provide tools for systematic comparisons of alternative approaches (Dias et al.), through approaches to integrating multiple processing levels within an agent architecture (Lowe & Kiryazov and Dias et al.), to papers exploring the best means of generating empathy and supportive behavior in virtual agents (Martínez-Miranda et al. and van der Zwaan et al.), and attempts to address the requirements for realistic modeling of affective expressions across multiple types of social interaction (individual, group and cultural) (Degens et al.). Some papers address more subtle aspects of affective processing, such as approaches to disambiguating the appraisal process via the use of the dominance dimension (van der Ham et al.).

Several papers address modeling of empathy, a central theme of the AAMAS workshop, and the necessary components of emotion models needed to produce empathy-like reactions in synthetic agents: Martínez-Miranda et al.'s paper describes emotion regulation strategies used to generate an appropriately empathic reaction by a virtual agent, and van der Zwaan et al. describe an approach to mapping emotions generated via the OCC model to different supportive strategies provided by an empathic virtual character.

In this paper I first briefly summarize some emerging standards, or perhaps a better term would be patterns and habits, in emotion modeling, and existing work attempting to establish more systematic approaches to modeling. I then suggest that an important component of a pragmatic and principled approach to affective modeling is an analytical computational framework that delineates the core affective processes, those mediating *emotion generation* and those mediating *emotion effects,* and the *abstract computational tasks* necessary to implement these. The framework takes into account the multiple modalities of affective processes, but makes no commitment to a particular modality, theory, representational formalism or reasoning, or a specific algorithm. It outlines a set of abstract computational tasks necessary to model both emotion generation and emotion effects, including the associated affective dynamics, and describes the associated domains that must be defined to implement the affective processes. The objective of the framework is to provide both a common vocabulary to describe the computational requirements for emotion models, and a description of a set of building blocks from which these models can be constructed. The framework can therefore serve both as a foundation for developing more systematic guidelines for model design, and as a basis for developing modeling tools.

The remainder of this paper is organized as follows. Section 2 summarizes existing "patterns and habits" in emotion modeling, as well as emerging efforts at standardization, across several areas of affective modeling, including emotion theories, emotion modalities, cognitive-affective architectures and architecture modules. Section 3 then describes the proposed analytical computational framework, in terms of the core affective processes, emotion generation and emotion effects, and the abstract computational tasks necessary to implement them and the associated domains. Throughout, I make references to the papers in this volume that address a particular topic. Section 4 concludes with a summary and a discussion of some open questions and challenges.

Important caveat: I am focusing here only on psychological models of emotions, typically implemented via some type of a symbolic representational and inferencing formalism, and within the context of a symbolic agent architecture. Numerous models are being developed of affective phenomena at the neural level, in the emerging discipline of affective neuroscience. Since both the scope and the modeling approaches in affective neuroscience are fundamentally different from the psychological models, they are not discussed in this paper.

2 Existing Habits and Emerging Standards

In the discussion below the term 'standards' is used rather loosely. I don't mean standards in a formal sense: as in, an exact set of engineering specifications. Rather, I am discussing emerging defaults and consensus regarding a number of aspects of affective modeling. Specifically, I discuss the dominant theories guiding computational model design (Sect. 2.1), the multiple modalities of emotions (Sect. 2.2), the structure of cognitive-affective architectures, within which models are typically embedded (Sect. 2.3), and the typical modules that such architectures contain (Sect. 2.4). The objective is to provide a summary of the dominant assumptions (patterns, habits) that guide existing modeling efforts, as well as to point out some of the gaps and 'missing links', both in the theories and in the existing models.

2.1 Theories

It is likely that if a group of emotion modelers were asked about the theoretical basis of their models the majority would mention the OCC model: a model of emotion generation via cognitive appraisal proposed by Ortony, Clore and Collins in their seminal book "The Cognitive Structure of Emotions" (Ortony et al. 1988). Numerous versions of this model have been implemented, and the vast majority of existing models of emotion generation use the OCC theory, and its associated categorization of emotions by the type of triggering stimuli (events, actions by other agents, and objects), and evaluative criteria associated with each category (e.g., desirability, praiseworthiness, familiarity). A number of papers in this volume use the OCC model as a basis of emotion generation, including van der Zwaan et al. ("Social Support Strategies for Embodied Conversational Agents"), Martínez-Miranda et al. ("Modelling Two Emotion Regulation Strategies as Key Features of Therapeutic Empathy"), Dias et al. ("FAtiMA Modular: Towards an Agent Architecture with a Generic Appraisal Framework"), and Dastani et al. ("Programming Agents with Emotions").

The OCC model was the first computation-friendly model of cognitive appraisal proposed, and it is therefore not surprising that it has gained prominence as the dominant theoretical framework for models of emotion generation via cognitive appraisal: that is, via evaluation of the match between the agent's goals, needs and preferences and its current situation, comprised of events, actions by other agents and objects.

However, emotion generation is just one aspect of emotion modeling, and cognitive appraisal (or rather cognition in general) represents only one of the several modalities of emotion. In addition, the OCC theory was never intended to account for models of the consequences of emotion: the original aim of the model was to support inferences about other agents' emotions. Thus an exclusive reliance on OCC limits the scope of the resulting model, and/or involves ad hoc approaches to modeling the aspects of affective processing that OCC does not address; most notably the consequences of emotions, or emotion effects: on cognition, on expression and on action selection (behavior).

A noteworthy point about the OCC theory is also the fact that it has remained unchanged since its introduction, and in spite of the many applications, where, one might expect, some of its aspects might have been questioned or modified. One exception is the work of Steunebrink, who has suggested some modifications of the OCC taxonomy of emotions, and pointed out its context dependence (Steunebrink et al. 2009).

Other theoretical perspectives exist to guide emotion modeling, offering varying degrees of support for operationalizing the distinct aspects of complex affective phenomena: the discrete/categorical, dimensional and componential.

Discrete or categorical theories emphasize a small set of fundamental emotions, often termed basic emotions: joy, sadness, fear, anger, and disgust (e.g., Panskepp 1998; Ekman 1992). The existence of dedicated neural circuitry is often assumed, and thus the associated innate, 'hardwired' features. Different emotions are characterized by stable patterns of triggers, behavioral expression, and associated distinct subjective experiences. For modeling purposes, the semantic primitives representing emotions in affective models are the distinct basic emotions themselves.

An alternative method of characterizing affective states is in terms of a small set of underlying dimensions that define a space within which distinct emotions can be located. This *dimensional perspective* describes emotions in terms of two- or three-dimensions. The most frequent dimensional characterization of emotions uses two dimensions: valence and arousal (Russell 2003; Russell and Barrett 1999; Russell and Mehrabian 1977). Valence reflects a positive or negative evaluation, and the associated felt state of pleasure (vs. displeasure), as outlined in the context of undifferentiated affect above. Arousal reflects a general degree of intensity or activation of the organism. The degree of arousal reflects a general readiness to act: low arousal is associated with less energy, high arousal with more energy. Since this 2-dimensional space cannot easily differentiate among emotions that share the same values of arousal and valence, e.g., anger and fear, both characterized by high arousal and negative valence, a third dimension is often added. This is variously termed dominance or stance. The resulting 3-dimensional space is often referred to as the PAD space (Mehrabian et al. 1995) (pleasure (synonymous with valence), arousal, dominance). The representational semantic primitives within this theoretical perspective are thus these 2 or 3 dimensions.

The third view emphasizes the distinct components of emotions, and is often termed the componential view (Leventhal and Scherer 1987). The 'components' referred to in this view are both the distinct modalities of emotions (e.g., cognitive, physiological, behavioral, subjective) and also the components of the cognitive appraisal process. These are referred to as appraisal dimensions or appraisal variables, and include novelty, valence, goal relevance, goal congruence, coping abilities and others. A stimulus, whether real or imagined, is analyzed in terms of its meaning and consequences for the agent, to determine the affective reaction: that is, the generated emotion. The analysis involves assigning specific values to the appraisal variables. Once the appraisal variable values are determined by the agent's evaluative processes, the resulting vector is mapped onto a particular emotion, within the n-dimensional space defined by the n appraisal variables. The semantic primitives for representing emotions within this model are thus these individual appraisal variables. These appraisal variables have much in common with the evaluative criteria proposed by the OCC model, and indeed the OCC model of appraisal fits within the broader componential theoretical perspective. (For a more detailed discussion of the similarities and differences between these two approaches to cognitive appraisal see Hudlicka (2011)).

The majority of emotion models use some combination of these theories, often implicitly. In most models, OCC is used to generate emotions. The emotions are then typically represented as distinct structures, thus implicitly following the discrete/categorical perspective, or as n-tuples representing the PA or PAD dimensions of the dimensional theoretical perspective. For example, Dastani et al. describe the ALMA model of emotion, and its associated EmotionEngine, which uses OCC to derive emotions via cognitive appraisal, and then represents the resulting emotions in terms of 3-tuples corresponding to the PAD dimensions. This (continuous) representation then facilitates the calculation of moods, by combining the PAD representations of multiple emotions over time.

An interesting application of a component of the PAD theory is described in the paper by van der Ham et al., where the dominance dimension is used to determine which of two possible emotions are generated and displayed by an agent in response to a 'blameworthy' act by another agent. Van der Ham and colleagues use existing empirical data from psychology to bias the cognitive appraisal process towards anger (in agents with high dominance, and a corresponding greater sense of control) or sadness (in agents with low dominance, and corresponding lower sense of control). This model in fact combines elements of the OCC cognitive appraisal theoretical perspective, using 'blameworthiness' as one of the evaluation criteria in emotion generation (discussed below), with the dimensional perspective. Interestingly, two alternatives could also be used in place of the dominance dimension of emotion to disambiguate appraisal: the appraisal variable of 'coping potential', from the componential model, discussed below, or a personality trait reflecting general dominance vs. submissiveness, although the latter is obviously a fixed trait rather than a transient state.

Since the different theoretical perspectives were developed for different motivations and to explain different types of data, it is not surprising that they therefore offer different degrees of support for modeling a given component of affective processing. For example, the dimensional theory was developed to characterize felt mood states, and it is therefore not surprising that it offers little support for cognitive appraisal. Similarly, the available empirical data are also associated with distinct perspectives. The bulk of the available data regarding emotion effects on cognition and behavior are available within the discrete theoretical perspective, where specific emotions are associated with particular observed effects; e.g., anger induces aggression, sadness withdrawal, joy approach etc. Less available are data regarding how the specific values of the appraisal variables are related to expressive behavior and behavioral choices. Figure 1 provides a high level overview of the different theoretical perspectives, with respect to the core affective processes necessary to model emotions.

Many open questions remain regarding the most appropriate theory for a particular modeling task, and many opportunities exist for a systematic comparison of the alternative theories, and the associated representational and inferencing requirements, to identify the most appropriate theoretical framework for a particular modeling objective. As is clear from Fig. 1, there are also many opportunities for empirical studies, to collect the necessary data to fully populate the different cells, or to determine that for some cells the theoretically plausible data don't in fact exist.

	Generation	Effects on Cognition	..on Expression	..on Behavior
Discrete	Fixed, simple triggers for basic emotions	Biases on attention, perception & cognitive processes (memory, learning, etc.)	Cross-cultural patterns of expression, esp. facial	Common patterns associated with basic emotions
Dimensional		Some known biases & broad effects on cognitive processes	Some data re: effects of arousal & valence on expressive behavior	Some dimension values associated with trends or broad categories of behavior
Componential (including OCC) (cognitive appraisal)	Evaluative criteria to assess degree of congruence between situation & agent goals	Some data re: effects of appraisal variables on cognition	Some data mapping app. variable values to expression components	

Fig. 1. Summary of the degree of support provided by the distinct theoretical perspectives (row labels) for the different components of affective models (column labels).

2.2 Emotion Modalities

A critical and characteristic aspect of emotions is their multi-modal nature. Emotions in biological agents are manifested across four distinct, but interacting, modalities. The most familiar is the *behavioral/expressive* modality, where the expressive and action-oriented characteristics are manifested; e.g., facial expressions, speech, gestures, posture, and behavioral choices. Closely related is the *somatic/physiological modality* - the neurophysiological substrate making behavior (and cognition) possible (e.g., heart rate, neuroendocrine effects, blood pressure). The *cognitive/interpretive* modality is most directly associated with the evaluation-based definition provided above, and emphasized in the current cognitive appraisal theories of emotion generation, discussed below. The most problematic modality, from a modeling perspective, is the *experiential/subjective* modality: the conscious, and inherently idiosyncratic, experience of emotions within the individual.

While the current emphasis in emotion modeling is on the cognitive modality (involved in appraisal) and the expressive/behavioral modality (manifesting emotions in agents), it is important to recognize that both the physiological, and the experiential modalities, also play critical roles (Izard 1993), although, clearly, represent significant challenges for modelers. Figure 2 provides a summary of the combinations possible when we consider the cross-product of the distinct emotion modalities and the core affective processes, and lists some of the processes that need to be modeled, with the cells containing the most frequently modeled processes highlighted. Clearly, not all of these modalities are relevant for each affective model; e.g., there is little reason to

	Generation	Effects
Cognitive	Cognitive appraisal	Attention, perception, cognitive processes, incl. memory
Physiological Somatic	Environment & physio user factors	Autonomic nervous system manifestations
Expressive / Behavioral	Facial feedback / Feeling theories	Expr: face, speech, gestures, movement Behavior: action selection
Subjective	?	?

Fig. 2. Summary of the processing required for modeling the core affective processes across the distinct emotion modalities (most common processing currently modeled is highlighted in yellow) (Color figure online)

model physiological factors in virtual agents designed to provide empathic support. On the other hand, simulated physiological factors may be important in social robots, for example, to model the effects of fatigue (running out of energy). There are many open questions regarding multi-modal models of emotions, and these models are particularly important in research modeling efforts, that aim to understand the mechanisms of affective processes in biological agents. Our understanding of the cross-modal inter-actions is very limited, and computational modeling has the potential to contribute to elucidating the mechanisms of the multi-modal processes that characterize emotions in biological agents.

2.3   Cognitive-Affective Architecture Structure

A number of researchers have proposed a generic three layer architecture structure to develop agents capable of complex adaptive behavior, and implementing both the cognitive and affective processing necessary to generate a broad range of affective states (Sloman 2003; Sloman et al. 2005; Ortony et al. Ortony et al. 2005; Leventhal and Scherer 1987). This 'triune architecture' framework implements see-think/feel-do processing sequences at three levels of complexity, which are termed (from least to most complex): reactive (also sensorimotor), deliberative (also routine or schematic), and meta-management (also reflective or conceptual). The latter being distinguished by its capability to explicitly represent and reason about structures and processing at the lower levels. Processing occurs in parallel at all three layers, with complex feedback interactions among the layers coordinating the independent processes and influencing the final outcome.

Due to the varying degrees of representational and processing complexity of the distinct layers, different degrees of complexity of affective reactions and affective states can be produced by each layer. Some emotions can be generated at all levels, but vary in the degree of complexity; e.g., some of the basic emotions such as fear can exist at multiple degrees of complexity and cognitive involvement. Other emotions can only exist at the higher levels of complexity; e.g., emotions requiring explicit representations of the self, such as pride, shame and guilt.

Existing cognitive-affective agent architectures typically implement one or both of the lower levels, reactive and deliberative, where the deliberative layer may include some meta-cognitive capabilities. For example, the FAtiMA architecture, which is used in three papers in this volume to implement affective agents (Dias et al., Martínez-Miranda et al., and van der Zwaan et al.), implements two of these layers: reactive and deliberative. The paper by Lowe and Kiryazov, "Utilizing Emotions in Autonomous Robots: An Enactive Approach", represents another attempt at connecting processing at multiple architecture levels to produce adaptive agent behavior, in this case the objective is to "ground" higher-level psychological processes in lower-level processing, the latter simulating physiological processes such as maintaining the necessary energy level.

In terms of the complexity of the resulting emotions, few distinctions currently exist between the same emotion (e.g., fear) being modeled and represented at varying levels of complexity.

The key challenges for emotion modelers, with respect to the architecture structure, is to identify the types of processing necessary to produce particular affective phenomena. Seminal work in this area has been done by Sloman and colleagues, who have asked perhaps the most fundamental question regarding the modeling of emotions in adaptive agents: *"The question of whether an organism or a robot needs emotions or needs emotions of a certain type reduces to the question of what sort of information-processing architecture it has and what needs arise within such an architecture"* (Sloman et al. 2005). This in turn depends on the types of environments within which the agent functions, and on the agent's objectives. A systematic approach to the construction of cognitive-affective architectures following this principle would require the development of taxonomies categorizing environment types and agent tasks, information processing functions, and affective processes. The processes and tasks described in Sect. 3 below represent a modest step in this direction.

2.4 Architecture Modules

The previous section considered the multiple levels of processing complexity within an agent architecture, and the emerging consensus that three levels are usefully delineated. In this Section I discuss some of the actual modules needed to implement the affective/cognitive processing required for modeling emotion generation and emotion effects, and their organization within an architecture. The key question here regards the essential modules, that is, the essential functionalities, necessary to implement the desired affective processing.

Perhaps the most established 'default' architecture in affective modeling is some version of the belief-desire-intention (BDI) architecture (Rao and Georgeff 1998).

By making explicit both the agents' goals and beliefs, each being essential for generation of emotions via cognitive appraisal, the BDI architecture structure lends itself well to supporting emotion modeling, and to being augmented with affective processes. The FAtiMA architecture discussed in several papers in this volume (Dias et al.; Martínez-Miranda et al.) is based on a BDI architecture, which is augmented to include modules required for affective processing. Dias et al. offer the following modules as part of the core FAtiMA architecture: Appraisal Derivation, Affect Derivation and Action Selection, and augment these with additional modules to implement a full-scope agent architecture (e.g., Reactive, Deliberative, Motivational). As the complexity of affective processing increases, additional modules need to be introduced. Thus Martínez-Miranda et al. augment FAtiMA architecture with additional modules to implement multiple emotion regulation strategies: Re-appraisal and Suppression.

Attesting to the broad applicability of the BDI architecture structure, modeling tools have begun to emerge for programming BDI-based affective agents, as discussed by Dastani et al., "Programming Agents with Emotions", who have extended an agent programming language based on the BDI architecture, 2APL, to include affective processing.

The research vs. applied model distinction is also critical when we consider agent architectures and their constituent modules, as well as the notion of minimal functionality and, especially, interchangeable and reusable modules. The challenge of producing a modular architecture is exemplified by the following statement in Dias et al.'s paper, where the authors discuss the challenges associated with managing the complexity of an architecture that evolved over time, and the need to create a new, modular, version of the architecture that reflects the principles of modular design and is thus more amenable to re-use:

> The resulting architecture has become perhaps difficult to use since the complexity of understanding the architecture escalated with the number of existing features. For this reason, a major effort was put in creating a modular version of the architecture, where functionalities and processes are divided into modular independent components."

For applied models, this modular approach is pragmatic, from the architecture design and software engineering perspectives, and necessary for model sharing and re-use. However, for research models, where the purpose is to elucidate the nature of the complex, multi-functional 'components' of biological affective processes, where evolution has created interconnected and tangled layers and components with overlapping functionalities, multi-functional components are the norm, not the exception. Attempting to construct research models via 'modular independent components' may therefore represent a misguided approach for attempting to emulate affective processes in biological agents. It is therefore important to remember that the very criteria for what constitutes pragmatic are likely to be different for different types of models.

3 Computational Analytical Framework

Below I outline a computational analytical framework that provides a basis for systematizing affective model design and analysis by delineating two core affective processes: emotion generation and emotion effects, and identifying the abstract computational tasks necessary to implement these processes. The framework also outlines several abstract domains necessary to implement emotion models, via the suggested computational tasks.

The abstract computational tasks can be thought of as the building blocks of emotion models and represent a candidate set of fundamental generic functions necessary to model the core affective processes. By defining these abstract computational tasks, the proposed framework facilitates systematic comparison of different:

- theories for a particular model component (e.g., OCC appraisal vs. appraisal based on variables defined in the componential models, such as Scherer's);
- representational and inferencing formalisms used to implement a particular theory or a particular task (e.g., logic vs. production rules vs. Bayesian belief nets);
- algorithms for implementing a specific task (e.g., different functions used to model emotion onset and decay).

In addition, defining model structure in terms of these tasks promotes modularity, which in turn facilitates model re-use and model sharing. The proposed framework therefore directly supports the objectives of the two workshops: the development of standards and modeling guidelines, systematic comparison of theories and models, model sharing and re-use, and the development of validation criteria.

3.1 Core Affective Processes

Given the multiple-modalities of emotion, the complexity of the cross-modal interactions, the fact that affective processes exist at multiple levels of aggregation, and our limited existing understanding of these processes, it may seem futile, at best, to speak of 'fundamental processes of emotions'. Nevertheless, for purposes of developing symbolic models of emotions, and for models of emotions in symbolic agent architectures, it is useful to cast the emotion modeling problem in terms of two broad categories of processes: those responsible for the *generation of emotions*, and those which then mediate the *effects of the activated emotions* on cognition, expressive behavior and action selection.

This temporally-based categorization (before and after the 'felt' emotion) provides a useful perspective for computational affective modeling, and helps manage the complexity of the modeling effort, by supporting a systematic deconstruction of these high-level processes into their underlying computational tasks, as discussed below. (There are of course many complex interactions among these categories of processes, which would also need to be represented in order to develop 'valid' models of emotions.)

Note that I am not suggesting that the two core processes, or the associated computational tasks, correspond to distinct, discrete neural processing mechanisms. Rather, they represent useful abstractions, and a means of managing the complexity associated with symbolic affective modeling.

3.2   Abstract Computational Tasks

Below I outline a set of abstract computational tasks required to implement the core processes of emotion generation and emotion effects. I limit the discussion of emotion generation to the cognitive modality, in part because this is the modality best supported by existing theories, and in part because the roles of the non-cognitive modalities in emotion generation are not as well understood. In addition, for the majority of applied models, emotion generation via cognitive appraisal is likely the most appropriate approach.

3.2.1   Modeling Emotion Generation

The following distinct computational tasks are required to implement *emotion generation via cognitive appraisal*:

- Define and implement the {emotion elicitor(s)}–to–{emotion(s)} mapping. Depending on the theoretical perspective adopted, this may involve additional subtasks that map the emotion elicitor(s) onto an intermediate representation (e.g., PAD dimensions; appraisal variables vectors), and the subsequent mapping of these onto the final emotion(s).
- Calculate the intensity of the resulting emotion(s).
- Calculate the decay of these emotions over time.
- Integrate multiple emotions, if multiple emotions were generated.
- Integrate the newly-generated emotion(s) with existing emotion(s) or moods.

Several papers in this volume address many of these computational tasks, and some explicitly state that a motivating factor for their design was to support a systematic comparison of alternative theories or approaches. For example, Dias et al.'s paper ("FAtiMA Modular: Towards an Agent Architecture with a Generic Appraisal Framework") identifies cognitive appraisal as one of the "minimum functionalities" required for emotional agent models, and explicitly focuses on the ability of an architecture to "*allow the implementation and direct comparison of several distinct appraisal theories using the same framework. We believe that such a framework can help us to learn more about emotion theories, and provide a relevant tool for the research community.*" Their paper also outlines a "minimum set of functionalities required to "implement and compare different appraisal theories", and these include many of the generic computational tasks outlined above, handled by distinct modules of the architecture (e.g., distinct components for calculating the different appraisal variable values, integration of multiple emotions derived during appraisal as well as integration of newly-derived emotions with existing moods).

Dias et al. have selected Scherer's theory as the basis of their implementation, correctly pointing out that it is one of the more complex theories proposed for cognitive appraisal, recognizing, for example, the incremental and multi-modal nature of appraisal, the multiple levels at which appraisal takes place (sensory-motor, schematic and conceptual), as well as the numerous feedback interactions among the individual stimulus evaluation checks.

An indirect, and more complex, approach to implementing the emotion intensity calculation tasks is addressed in the paper by Martínez-Miranda, Bresó and García-Gómez's

"Modelling Two Emotion Regulation Strategies as Key Features of Therapeutic Empathy", which explores alternative means of modulating emotion intensity (and thereby implementing coping strategies): reappraisal and suppression.

3.2.2 Modeling Emotion Effects

The multi-modal nature of emotion cannot as easily be ignored when considering models of emotion effects. This is particularly the case in models implemented in the context of embodied agents that need to manifest emotions not only via behavioral choices, but also via expressive manifestations within the channels available in their particular embodiment (e.g., facial expressions, gestures, posture etc.). The multi-modal nature of emotion effects increases both the number and the type of computational tasks necessary to model emotion effects.

The following distinct computational tasks are necessary to implement *the effects of emotions* across multiple modalities:

- Define and implement the emotion/mood–to–effects mappings, for the modalities included in the model (e.g., cognitive, expressive, behavioral, neurophysiological). Depending on the theoretical perspective adopted, this may involve additional subtasks that implement any intermediate steps, and are defined in terms of more abstract semantic primitives provided by the theory (e.g., dimensions, appraisal variables).
- Determine the magnitude of the resulting effect(s) as a function of the emotion or mood intensities.
- Determine the changes in these effects as the emotion or mood intensity decays over time.
- Integrate effects of multiple emotions, moods, or some emotion and mood combinations, if multiple emotions and moods were generated, at the appropriate stage of processing.
- Integrate the effects of the newly-generated emotion with any residual, on-going effects, to ensure believable transitions among states over time.
- Account for variability in the above by both the intensity of the affective state, and by the specific personality of the modeled agent.
- Coordinate the visible manifestations of emotion effects across multiple channels and modalities within a single time frame, to ensure believable manifestations.

The specific tasks necessary for a particular model of course depend on the selected theoretical perspective (e.g., discrete/categorical models don't require a two-stage mapping sequence), and on the specific theory of emotion generation or emotion effects that is implemented in the model. Note also that not all models necessarily require all tasks; e.g., in simpler models, where only one emotion can be generated at a given time, there is no need to integrate multiple emotions.

3.3 Abstract Domains Required for Modeling Emotions

The high-level computational tasks outlined above provide a basis for defining model design guidelines, and for managing the complexity of affective modeling, but they provide only the first step in the top-down deconstruction of modeling requirements. Another example of a computational and design-oriented perspective on emotion modeling, and focusing on emotion generation, is recent work by Broekens and colleagues, who developed a generic set-theoretic formalism, and an abstract framework, for representing, and comparing, appraisal theories.

Building on the work of Reisenzein (Reisenzein 2001), Broekens and colleagues (Broekens et al. 2008) offer a high-level, set-theoretic formalism that depicts the abstract structure of the appraisal process, and represents both the processes involved, and the data manipulated. I have augmented their original framework to also represent modeling of emotion effects. The resulting abstract structure is shown in Fig. 3. The framework illustrates the distinct processes involved in emotion generation and emotion effects modeling, and the data manipulated by these processes (e.g., perception (evaluative processes produce a series of mental objects), appraisal (processes that extract the appraisal variable values from the mental objects), and mediation (processes that map the appraisal values onto the resulting emotion(s)). The distinct processes operate on distinct categories of data: their associated *domains*. Table 1 summarizes these domains and provides examples of their elements: the associated semantic primitives.

This framework thus complements the computational task-based perspective with a set of domains required to implement both emotion generation and emotion effects, and helps define the constituent elements of these domains. These definitions then form a basis for defining the mappings among these domains, necessary to implement emotion generation and emotion effects.

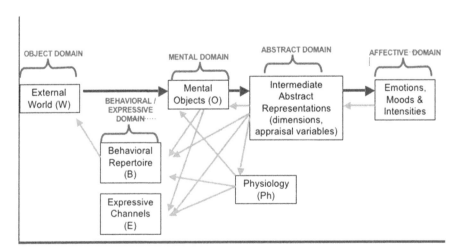

Fig. 3. Distinct abstract domains necessary to implement the abstract computational tasks. *Note that this figure assumes the existence of some intermediate, abstract structures reflecting variables that mediate both emotion generation and emotion effects. Not all affective models necessarily require such an abstract domain. The blue arrows indicate paths mediating emotion generation; the green arrows paths mediating emotion effects* (Color figure online).

Table 1. Domains Required to Implement Affective Models in Agents. *The set of domains in the table represents a superset of possible domains required for emotion modeling. For a given model, and given theoretical foundations, only a subset of these may be necessary.*

Domain name	Description	Examples of domain elements
Object (W)	Elements of the external world (physical, social), represented by cues (agent's perceptual input)	Other agents, events, physical objects
Cognitive (C)	Internal mental constructs necessary to generate emotions, or manifest their influences on cognition	Cues, situations, goals, beliefs, expectations, norms, preferences, attitudes, plans
Abstract (Ab)	Theory-dependent; e.g., dimensions, appraisal variables, OCC evaluative criteria	Pleasure, arousal, dominance; certainty, goal relevance, goal congruence…
Affective (A)	Affective states (emotions, moods) & personality traits	Joy, sadness, fear, anger, pride, envy, jealousy; extraversion
Physiology (Ph)	Simulated physiological characteristics	Level of energy
Expressive Channels (Ex)	Channels within which agent's emotions can be manifested: facial expressions, gestures, posture, gaze & head movement, movement, speech	Facial expressions (smile, frown), speech (sad, excited) gestures (smooth, clumsy), movement (fast, slow) (represented via channel-specific primitives, e.g., FACS)
Behavioral (B)	Agent's behavioral repertoire in its physical and social environment	Walk, run, stand still, pick up object, shake hands w/ another agent

4   Summary, Challenges and Open Questions

In this paper I provided an overview of some of the common practices ("habits") and emerging standards in emotion modeling, focusing on architecture structures and distinct architecture modules, on emotion generation via cognitive appraisal, and on the computational tasks necessary to model both emotion generation and the effects of emotions, across the multiple modalities that characterize affective phenomena. I also highlighted some of the existing gaps in emotion modeling: that is, the aspects of affective processing that are not yet being adequately addressed. These include affective dynamics, the role of the non-cognitive modalities of emotion in emotion generation, and modeling of emotion effects on cognition.

I then described an analytical computational framework consisting two broad categories of affective processes, based on the temporal sequence of emotion generation and consequent emotion effects, and the abstract computational tasks required for their implementation. These tasks can serve as the generic building blocks of affective models, and also as a vocabulary for describing and analyzing theories and models; a vocabulary that could serve as a lingua franca for cross-disciplinary collaborations which are essential for progress in computational affective modeling. By making no commitment to a particular implementation (representation + algorithm), they also facilitate a systematic comparison of alternative implementations, based on different theories.

I suggested that identifying a set of abstract computational tasks necessary for affective modeling, and organizing these within the proposed framework, would facilitate many of the goals of the two workshops summarized in this volume. Specifically: a systematic comparison of existing theories and their adequacy for modeling particular affective processes and phenomena, and a systematic comparison and analysis of existing models, including comparison of alternative approaches to implementing a particular abstract task. This would in turn facilitate more modular approaches to affective modeling, as well as model reuse. In addition, a clear understanding of the constituent computational tasks required for a particular affective phenomenon would also provide a basis for more systematic guidelines for model design and validation. (A more detailed description of this computational framework, and its use to facilitate affective model design, can be found in Hudlicka (2014)). References were made throughout to the contributions in this volume, placing their work in the overall context of the emerging standards, and the proposed computational analytical framework.

Two questions naturally arise regarding the proposed framework and abstract computational tasks. *First*, whether the proposed set of computational tasks is appropriate, and adequate, for the construction of affective models. *Second*, whether a set of minimal functionalities can be defined, without making a commitment to a number of other aspects of the emotion model or an associated agent: e.g., its type (research or applied model); the objective of the associated agent; its embodiment; the theoretical basis for the model. In other words: can a truly abstract, generic set of tasks be defined to support the construction of a broad range of affective models? Assuming that one accepts the notion that identifying abstract computational building blocks of larger models is a useful endeavor, answers to the above questions can only be provided if this approach is tested in practice. And this leads into the larger issue: how do we transition from habits (i.e., common practices) to bona fide standards?

4.1   From Habits to Standards

I believe that four essential components are necessary to establish standards in emotion modeling. The first is the *development of benchmark problems*, which would enable a systematic comparison of alternative approaches to modeling a particular affective process. Given the broad scope and complexity of affective modeling, as well as the distinct objectives of applied vs. research models, clearly a number of such benchmark problems would need to be defined. These benchmark problems would be posed as challenges to the modeling community. Such challenges can often produce significant advances in the associated discipline (e.g., the US DARPA speech initiative). Of course, the challenge with these types of challenges, as it were, is to define them at the appropriate level of resolution, so that useful results are likely to emerge. The DARPA speech challenge was an example of a well-defined problem, which led to significant advances in speech recognition. An example of a challenge that may be too ambitious is the recently introduced Human Brain Project initiative.

The second requirement for standards development, related to the first, is an *emphasis on validation*. Again, given the diversity of model objectives, and the complexity of the domain, a variety of validation criteria are necessary. Furthermore, in the case of research models, the development of validation methods and criteria poses an entirely separate challenge, since our ability to construct detailed symbolic architectures far surpasses our ability to determine whether the corresponding model structures and processes actually exist in the mind. Given the difficulties associated with developing and validating research emotion models, it is likely that progress in the development of emotion modeling standards will be more rapid in the realm of applied models, in the near future.

The third requirement involves *greater collaboration* among (a) different disciplines addressing emotion, most notably psychology, computer science (affective computing, AI, cognitive science, HCI), and cognitive and affective neuroscience, and (b) among emotion modelers working at different levels of model resolution and using different modeling methods. This will require the development of common and consistent terminology, as well as the development of, and adherence to, more formal descriptions. A recent paper by Reisenzein and colleagues (2013) directly addresses this issue.

Finally, the multi-disciplinary, multi-focus, and multi-method collaborations required to advance computational affective modeling will also require a greater *understanding of the distinct levels of analysis of complex information processing systems,* such as those proposed by Pylyshyn (1984) and Marr (1982). Both emphasized the necessity of analyzing the processing within complex systems needs at multiple levels. Pylyshyn termed these semantic, syntactic and physical. Marr termed them computational, algorithmic and implementational. In terms of Marr's terminology: at the highest level of analysis, the computational level attempts to identify the goals and purposes of the computation, and the logic underlying the overall strategy (e.g., sort a list). At the middle level of analysis, the algorithmic level attempts to describe the representational structures, and the algorithmic transformation necessary, to implement the computational tasks that have been identified at the computational level (e.g., sort the list by systematically ordering the adjacent elements according to the sorting criteria). Finally, the implementation level examines how the algorithm can be realized physically (e.g., a digital computer, a brain, a thousand monkeys). The number of levels is not intended to be taken literally, since a system of any significant complexity is likely to have numerous layers of nested virtual machines. Rather, the three levels represent three perspectives on analysis, each affording and emphasizing a distinct set of questions (McClamrock 1991).

Little work has been done to date in analyzing affective processing in terms of the Marr levels. I believe that this type of analysis is essential to address some of the more challenging questions regarding affective processing in biological agents, including the relationship between the symbolic and subsymbolic processing, and the relationships between the three levels of processing proposed for cognitive-affective architectures (discussed in Sect. 2.3), and the Marr levels of analysis.

Perhaps the most significant challenge for emotion modelers, particularly those focused on research models, will be to keep an open mind regarding the fundamental nature of emotions. Two of the most established assumptions about emotions have recently been challenged. First, neuroscientists are increasingly pointing out that the long-established distinction between emotion and cognition is not only inappropriate and unjustified, but may hinder progress in our understanding of these complex modes of information processing. Second, many emotion researchers have pointed out that the term emotion may not refer to a uniform entity (e.g., "Emotion is too broad a class of events to be a single scientific category" (Russell and Barrett 1999, p. 805)).

A more systematic approach to emotion modeling, facilitated by the developments of standards, modeling tools and model re-use, and involving multi-disciplinary collaborations, will help address these fundamental questions regarding the nature of emotions.

References

Broekens, J., De Groot, D., Kosters, W.A.: Formal models of appraisal: theory, specification, and computational model. Cogn. Syst. Res. **9**(3), 173–197 (2008)

Cañamero, L.D.: Building emotional artifacts in social worlds: challenges and perspectives. In: AAAI Fall Symposium "Emotional and Intelligent II: The Tangled Knot of Social Cognition". AAAI Press, Menlo Park (2001)

Ekman, P., Friesen, W.V.: Facial Action Coding System. Consulting Psychologists Press, Palo Alto (1978)

Ekman, P.: An argument for basic emotions. Cogn. Emot. **6**(3–4), 169–200 (1992)

Feldman-Barrett, L.: Are emotions natural kinds? Perspect. Psychol. Sci. **1**(1), 28–58 (2006)

Hudlicka, E.: What are we modeling when we model emotion? In: AAAI Spring Symposium: Emotion, Personality, and Social Behavior (Technical Report SS-08-04, pp. 52–59). Stanford University. AAAI Press, Menlo Park (2008a)

Hudlicka, E.: Guidelines for developing computational models of emotions. Int. J. Synth. Emot. **2**(1), 26–79 (2011)

Hudlicka, E.: Computational analytical framework for affective modeling: towards guidelines for designing computational models of emotions. In: Vallverdú, J. (ed.) Synthesizing Human Emotion in Intelligent Systems and Robotics. IGI Global (2014) (in press)

Izard, C.E.: Four systems for emotion activation: cognitive and noncognitive processes. Psychol. Rev. **100**(1), 68–90 (1993)

Leventhal, H., Scherer, K.R.: The relationship of emotion to cognition. Cogn. Emot. **1**, 3–28 (1987)

Marr, D.: Vision. Freeman, San Francisco (1982)

McClamrock, R.: Marr's three levels: a re-evaluation. Mind. Mach. **1**(2), 185–196 (1991)

Mehrabian, A.: Framework for a comprehensive description and measurement of emotional states. Genet. Soc. Gen. Psychol. Monogr. **121**, 339–361 (1995)

Ortony, A., Clore, G.L., Collins, A.: The Cognitive Structure of Emotions. Cambridge University Press, Cambridge (1988)

Ortony, A., Norman, D., Revelle, W.: Affect and proto-affect in effective functioning. In: Fellous, J.M., Arbib, M.A. (eds.) Who Needs Emotions? Oxford University Press, New York (2005)

Panskepp, J.: Affective Neuroscience: The Foundations of Human and Animal Emotions. Oxford University Press, New York (1998)

Picard, R.: Affective Computing. MIT Press, Cambridge (1997)

Pylyshyn, Z.: Computation and Cognition. MIT Press, Cambridge (1984)

Rao, A.S., Georgeff, M.P.: Decision procedures for BDI logics. J. Logic Comput. **8**(3), 293–342 (1998)

Reilly, W.S.N.: Modeling what happens between emotional antecedents and emotional consequents. Paper Presented at the ACE 2006, Vienna, Austria (2006)

Reisenzein, R.: Appraisal processes conceptualized from a schema-theoretic perspective: contributions to a process analysis of emotions. In: Scherer, K.R., Schorr, A., Johnstone, T. (eds.) Appraisal Processes in Emotion: Theory, methods, research. Oxford University Press, New York (2001)

Reisenzein, R., Hudlicka, E., Dastani, M., Gratch, J., Hindriks, K.V., Lorini, E., Meyer, J.-J.Ch.: Computational modeling of emotion: toward improving the inter- and intradisciplinary exchange. IEEE Trans. Affect. Comput. **4**(3), 246–266 (2013)

Russell, J.: Core affect and the psychological construction of emotion. Psychol. Rev. **110**(1), 145–172 (2003)

Russell, J., Barrett, L.F.: Core affect, prototypical emotional episodes, and other things called emotion: dissecting the elephant. J. Pers. Soc. Psychol. **76**(5), 805–819 (1999)

Russell, J., Mehrabian, A.: Evidence for a three-factor theory of emotions. J. Res. Pers. **11**, 273–294 (1977)

Scherer, K.R.: Appraisal considered as a process of multilevel sequential checking. In: Scherer, K.R., Schorr, A., Johnstone, T. (eds.) Appraisal Processes in Emotion: Theory, Methods, Research. Oxford University Press, New York (2001)

Schröder, M., Baggia, P., Burkhardt, F., Pelachaud, C., Peter, C., Zovato, E.: EmotionML – an upcoming standard for representing emotions and related states. In: D'Mello, S., Graesser, A., Schuller, B., Martin, J.-C. (eds.) ACII 2011, Part I. LNCS, vol. 6974, pp. 316–325. Springer, Heidelberg (2011)

Sloman, A.: How many separately evolved emotional beasties live within us. In: Trappl, R., Petta, P., Payr, S. (eds.) Emotions in Humans and Artifacts? The MIT Press, Cambridge (2003)

Sloman, A., Chrisley, R., Scheutz, M.: The Architectural Basis of Affective States and Processes. In: Fellous, J.-M., Arbib, M.A. (eds.) Who Needs Emotions?. Oxford University Press, New York (2005)

Steunebrink, B.R., Dastani, M., Meyer, J.-J. Ch.: The OCC Model Revisited. In: Reichardt, D. (ed.) Proceedings of the 4th Workshop on Emotion and Computing - Current Research and Future Impact, Paderborn, Germany (2009)

Generic Models and Frameworks

Creating a World for Socio-Cultural Agents

Nick Degens[1]([✉]), Gert Jan Hofstede[1], John Mc Breen[1], Adrie Beulens[1],
Samuel Mascarenhas[2], Nuno Ferreira[2], Ana Paiva[2], and Frank Dignum[3]

[1] Information Technology, Wageningen University, Wageningen, The Netherlands
{nick.degens,gertjan.hofstede,john.mcbreen,adrie.beulens}@wur.nl
[2] Instituto Superior Técnico, Technical University of Lisbon INESC-ID,
Lisbon, Portugal
{samuel.mascarenhas,nuno.ferreira,ana.paiva}@gaips.inesc-id.pt
[3] Information and Computing Sciences, Utrecht University, Utrecht, The Netherlands
f.p.m.dignum@uu.nl

Abstract. Creating agents that are capable of emulating similar socio-cultural dynamics to those found in human interaction remains as one of the hardest challenges of artificial intelligence. This problem becomes particularly important when considering embodied agents that are meant to interact with humans in a believable and empathic manner. In this article, we introduce a conceptual model for socio-cultural agents, and, based on this model, we present a set of requirements for these agents to be capable of showing appropriate socio-cultural behaviour. Our model differentiates between three levels of instantiation: the interaction level, consisting of elements that may change depending on the people involved, the group level, consisting of elements that may change depending on the group affiliation of the people involved, and the society level, consisting of elements that may change depending on the cultural background of those involved. As such, we are able to have culture alter agents' social relationships rather than directly determining actions, allowing for virtual agents to act more appropriately in any social or cultural context.

1 Introduction

Horatio finds himself lost in an unknown city, looking for a place to sleep. Some people are about on the streets, in shops and cafés. What should he do?

Based on the information above, people would have almost no difficulty trying to describe what Horatio could do. This is because we are able to make assumptions about the social relationship between Horatio and the various kinds of people he might try to ask for help. While these assumptions are based on implicit expectations of the context Horatio is in, they do help to make predictions about how others would respond.

For an intelligent agent to be able to make the same assumptions and predictions, it needs operationalized parameters of the social world. What is the relationship between Horatio and people that pass him by on the street? Who

© Springer International Publishing Switzerland 2014
T. Bosse et al. (Eds.): Emotion Modeling, LNAI 8750, pp. 27–43, 2014.
DOI: 10.1007/978-3-319-12973-0_2

would be willing to help him with his predicament? Without being able to discriminate between people, he would expect to be treated the same by every person.

Besides being able to make assumptions about the intentions of the characters, one also needs to consider the difference between 'right' and 'wrong'. Changing just a few elements in an interaction might easily change our perception of right and wrong; what if Horatio demanded of a stranger to take him to a hotel? Without being able to discriminate between actions, he would expect every action to be equally appropriate.

Modelling social behaviour is already quite challenging, as there are many ways in which our behaviour is influenced by our perceptions of the social world (as can be read in Brown's [1] treatise on group dynamics). This modelling exercise becomes even more complicated when you start considering the effect of culture. What if ignoring a stranger is a normal thing to do in the country that Horatio is visiting? Including culture adds an extra level of complexity to the already quite challenging level of social behaviour.

The questions posed above require certain concepts to be present in the mind of an agent. Without them, Horatio has no way to determine what he should do in this foreign place. In this article, we aim to describe how these concepts should be incorporated in the design of a socio-cultural agent. We consider a socio-cultural agent to be one that is able to make assumptions about the social world, and is able to show believable culturally-varying behaviour. Therefore a socio-cultural agent needs a conceptual model of the social world. That model should be as simple as possible, while still being rich enough to allow for short emergent interactions between agents with different cultural configurations. The model presented here will be not be defined in a technical manner, and will still need to be instantiated for specific application domains.

The paper is organized in the following manner. We will start by describing related work on cultural agents. The next section will focus on the notion of rituals, a construct through which behaviour gains social meaning for a group of agents that have shared attention. After that, we focus on different interpretations of these actions by having different social components active in the mind of an agent based on the ritual. In the last part of the paper, we will look at how culture can modify these rituals and moral circles to create culturally-varying behaviour in agents.

Throughout the article, the conceptual model and the concepts therein will be introduced from the perspective of Horatio, who is still in search of directions. He will meet another agent, the elderly Claudius whom he has not met previously, and will interact with him.

2   Related Work

The increasing need for embodied agents to interact in a social and empathic manner has led researchers to address different aspects of social interaction. Particularly related to the work presented in this paper is the Synthetic Group

Dynamics (SGD) model, proposed by Prada and Paiva [2], as it aims to create believable interactions in social groups formed by autonomous agents. In order to achieve this, agents build social relations of power and interpersonal attraction with each other. They also have the notion of belonging to a group in which they are regarded as more or less important, according to their status and/or level of expertise.

Similarly to the SGD model, our proposed model also places a strong emphasis on embedding group dynamics and social relationships in the agent's mind. Differently from SGD, we also address the relationship between culture and the dynamics of groups.

When designing social agents, culture has often been overlooked despite its huge influence on human behaviour [3]. We argue that without taking culture into account, the social richness of agent-based simulations is significantly limited. For instance, it becomes difficult for agents to empathise with users from different cultures if they lack the ability to interpret actions from different cultural perspectives. Moreover, modelling culture has been an essential endeavour when considering agent-based applications for intercultural training such as ORIENT [4], ELECT BiLAT [5], or TLTS [6].

Research on cultural agents is steadily rising. So far, several systems have focused on the adaptation of directly observable features of conversational behaviour to specific cultures. For instance, the work of Jan et al. [7] addresses differences in proxemics, gaze and speech overlap between the North American, Mexican and Arabic cultures. Similarly, the work of Endrass et al. [8] addresses the integration of non-verbal behaviour and communication management aspects, considering differences between the German and Japanese cultures.

While the aforementioned models focus on modelling the effects of culture on communication aspects, the research presented in this paper addresses another important facet of culture, namely, how it influences decision-making and behaviour selection.

In the model proposed in Mascarenhas et al. [9], two of Hofstede's dimensions of culture, individualism and power distance, are directly used to influence the agent's decision-making and appraisal processes. This is done only at the individual level without considering important elements from the social context such as an ongoing ritual, group membership and other relational variables. As a result the agents seem, to the human observer, to be obsessed with their own goals, and to lack social awareness.

Another agent model where culture affects decision-making is the model proposed by Solomon et al. [10], which concerns the definition of specific cultural norms. The model allows defining links between specific actions (e.g. show-picture-of-wife) and one or more cultural norms (e.g. respectful-of-modesty). An association link can either be positive in the case where the action promotes the norm or negative in the opposite case. One drawback of this model is that it requires a great deal of manual configuration as it tries to associate culture directly to individual actions.

One step towards generating culturally appropriate behaviour within an agent model was taken by Mc Breen et al. [11] who propose the concept of cultural meta-norms to operationalize culture. These meta-norms use Hofstede's dimensions of unconscious cultural values to explain how you can create a set of generic rules that give agents a propensity to behave in a certain way in certain relational contexts.

In our proposed model, we follow [12] in arguing that actions are often selected not because of their instrumental effects but because they are an important symbolic step of an ongoing ritual, thus making rituals an essential part of social interaction.

The idea that rituals are important to model cultural differences in embodied agents was also explored in Mascarenhas et al. [12], where a computational model of rituals was implemented and integrated into an affective agent architecture, developed by Dias and Paiva [13]. One limitation of the model proposed by Mascarenhas et al. is that it assumes that agents have a shared knowledge of rituals, which is not true when considering scenarios where agents from different cultures may meet, as exemplified in this paper.

3 Modelling Socio-Cultural Agents

To start discussing the conceptual model for socio-cultural agents, it is necessary to specify in overview the simulated social world in which our agents live. In Fig. 1, we have identified three different levels of instantiation.

They range from the more specified (interaction) to the more abstract (culture):

– The 'interaction' level is comprised mostly of elements that are visible to outsiders, and that may change depending on the people involved;

Conceptual Model for Socio-Cultural Agents

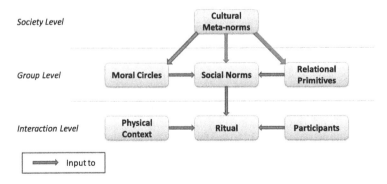

Fig. 1. From culture to actions: a conceptual model for socio-cultural agents

- The 'group' level is comprised mostly of elements that are not necessarily visible to outsiders, and that may change depending on the group affiliation of the people involved;
- The 'society' level is comprised mostly of elements that are invisible to outsiders, and that may change depending on the cultural background of those involved.

In the coming sections, we will discuss each of these three levels in detail, and explain how they relate to each other. Through these explanations, we will specifically name requirements that are necessary to create believable socio-cultural agents.

3.1 'Interaction' Level

...After walking around for a while, Horatio is unsure in which direction to continue and decides that it would be best to ask somebody on the street for more information. At that moment, Claudius, who is on his way to work, is walking in the opposite direction of Horatio. Horatio decides to draw the attention of Claudius...

Some actions may be purely instrumental, e.g. picking up an object that has fallen to the floor. However, in a social world, such actions usually have a symbolic effect as well. For instance, what objects would you pick off the floor, in which places, and with which people present? It is important to be able to understand the social consequences of actions.

These symbolic actions may have some effect on the relationship between yourself and others. However, such an effect only occurs if the other is paying attention; if not, the social meaning of the action might be lost on her.

This process of exchanging symbolic actions can be seen as a ritual, as defined by Rothenbuhler [14]. He states that rituals range from the ceremonial and memorable to the mundane and transient. In fact, any group of people that has a degree of shared attention can be said to be engaged in a ritual. This is reinforced by Bell [15], who claims that rituals are a way through which people can act in the world. We call those people that are part of a ritual its participants and its location the physical context. In our story, the participants would be Claudius and Horatio, and the physical context would be the street.

There are two sides to a ritual, a visible side, i.e. the behaviours of individuals that can be seen by outsiders, and a non-visible side, i.e. the symbolic meaning of the actions as they are being interpreted by participants. This symbolic meaning is impossible to separate from how a community conceives the world [15].

Rituals help mediate changes in social order, and are thus an essential element of social behaviour. As Hofstede et al. [3] say in their work, rituals are "Collective activities that are technically superfluous to reach desired ends but that, within a culture, are considered socially essential."

...In Horatio's mind there is a certain structure to asking a favour of a stranger. First you would politely greet him or her, and after enquiring whether

they know the place, and exchanging pleasantries, you would then proceed to ask the other for help. Doing so would make the stranger feel obliged to help you...

In a further operationalization of the ritual, Hofstede [16] explains that a ritual consists of three elements: a beginning, the body, and an end.

The beginning is characterized by an initiating move and a response. This initiating response carries the social meaning of the ritual. The response can be classified as running along two dimensions: direction (going along or opposing), and strength of the response (ranging from low to high). Depending on the response, a ritual is either initiated or aborted; if the purpose of the ritual is clear to both parties and agreed upon, they proceed to the body of the ritual.

Within the body of the ritual, the actual social change is put into action. For the ritual to be effective, the participants of the ritual must act in an appropriate manner.

The last stage of the ritual would be the end, in which the social change is reinforced in the appropriate manner and the ritual is brought to its conclusion. This will free the agent's attention for other activities.

The first two requirements for socio-cultural agents are:

1. They need to be aware of their physical context, and whether they are taking part in a ritual with other participants;
2. They must be able to decode the social meaning of a perceived ritual;

... On his way to work, Claudius sees a stranger walk up to him with an uncertain look on his face. This kind of behaviour is typical of people who need directions, and need somebody to help them on their way...

A ritual can help to decode the social meaning of certain actions. For example, in the USA, when a long-time boyfriend drops down on one knee in front of his girlfriend, few compatriots would not understand the social meaning of the action.

Not all behaviour will be interpreted in the same manner; the same ritual might mean something different depending on the physical context and the participants. This issue is particularly true when the participants are from different cultures, but even within the same culture, there is no guarantee that you 'speak' the same language. The meaning of a ritual may even change over time [15].

In the example above, Claudius recognizes that when Horatio walks up to him in a certain way, it means that he needs some help. What if somebody did that at night in a shady part of town? What if Horatio and Claudius had been old friends? Would Horatio still have walked up to Claudius in the same manner, and if so, would it have meant the same thing?

The third requirement for socio-cultural agents is:

3. The symbolic meaning of a ritual needs to be able to change depending on the people involved (participants) and the environment (physical context).

3.2 'Group' Level

Tajfel and Turner [17] posit that there is a difference between interpersonal situations (in which behaviour is primarily influenced by personological variables) and group situations (in which behaviour is primarily influenced by category-based processes). As such, on a group level, it becomes important to take into account more elements than just those present in the interaction. Behaviour may be influenced by people that are not present ('would your parents approve of your behaviour?'), and previous interactions may have an impact on your current behaviour. On this level, we discriminate between three different elements: moral circles, relational variables, and social norms.

Moral Circles. In the past section, we talked about the concept of 'social order'. By this we mean that there may be pre-existing social relations between the participants of a ritual. Sometimes there may be a connection between individuals, without having previously met, such as while watching a football match together with other spectators. These relations might not always be visible to all during an interaction between agents; they may only exist in the minds of the individual. To describe these relations, we use the concept of moral circles. A moral circle can be considered "the boundary drawn around those entities in the world deemed worthy of moral consideration" [18]. This concept is similar to what Singer [19] alludes to in his work on the evolution of moral progress and ethics: a large part of social interaction is influenced by who we let into our moral circle. Only then can we build meaningful relationships.

In our work, we formalize a moral circle to consist of three elements: the people to whom it applies, their mutual perceptions of social attributes (or relational primitives), and the social norms that regulate their behaviour. Both relational primitives and social norms are discussed in the following sections.

In Kemper's status-power theory [20] moral circles are called reference groups. These reference groups are always present in the mind of an individual in the form of the 'reference group committee' that helps the individual make decisions.

Why use the concept of a moral circle? To begin with, it is generic. Hofstede et al. [3] use it as a general indication of a human unit of social agency, ranging from a few people to all of humanity, taking inspiration from evolutionary biologist David Sloan Wilson [21], who describes humans as a 'eusocial' species, i.e. one in which the group has supplanted the individual as the main level of evolution.

Now, while in most eusocial species it is rather simple to determine the unit of evolution it would be the colony of bees, for instance this is not so in humans. Yet the assumption is that we have a biological propensity, including moral sentiments, to act as group members. In other words, acting for the survival and prosperity of our moral circles is in our nature. And it is this propensity that is the main justification for our concept of moral circle which we shall often abbreviate 'MC' from this point onwards.

The concept of a moral circle leads to our fourth requirement:

4. Each agent must categorize each individual into moral circles.

... Claudius wonders if he has time to help this stranger. He has an important deadline at work today, and he still has some things left to prepare. Therefore, he is left with a choice: he can either stop for a few seconds and talk to the stranger, or he can choose to ignore the stranger and carry on to work...

Each context shapes its own MC typology, which depends on who is involved and what MCs they perceive to be relevant to the situation. A person can belong to many different MCs at the same time. It is thus that several MCs can affect the actions of any one person at any time, but one MC is usually more salient than others. For instance, in most cultures, leaving work duties to marry or bury a family member would be allowable, or even endorsed. The priority between events is itself symbolic of a prioritisation among MCs.

MCs come in different types. They can range from the default MC of "all people who count as people", to which strangers may or may not belong, to long-lasting organised groups, such as families or ethnic communities or companies, to the relatively informal, such as groups of acquaintances, or even two people meeting in the street by chance.

A more formal MC has both more specific social norms (rules of appropriate behaviour) and a strong inertia in membership; whether you're in or out is usually determined by clear attributes e.g. employment or club membership. Membership changes in more formal MCs are usually mediated by formal rituals, often denoting a change in status.

More informal MCs can be, for example, groups of specific friends (some you might know from your studies, others from your sports club). These more informal MCs still develop guides to appropriate behaviour. Membership of such an informal MC is often not as clearly defined as in more formal MCs. The relevant social norms for an informal MC will not be stated in any text, and can evolve more freely through an emergent consensual process, than is usual in formal MCs.

A particularly difficult social issue is how to behave when more than one MC could be relevant. For example, this would be the case when you fall in love with a colleague from work, or have to operate on a family member. Thus, context codetermines which MC prevails.

One will treat close friends and family differently from strangers. Sometimes you might give them a preferential treatment, while other times you might judge them more harshly than you would others. In other words, each MC has its own centrality; this is defined as Moral Circle Centrality (MCC).

MCC deals with "Those who matter to me" and defines the position of that MC within the entire set of MCs. The most central MCs include groups such as your family or close friends. Less central groups are those groups including strangers and acquaintances. Since each MC only exists in the mind of an individual, perceptions might differ across people. You might consider somebody a part of a 'close friend' MC, but they might not consider you part of theirs.

Based on our examples above, MCC is probably best represented on a sliding scale. As a first step though, we can identify a limited set of categories, e.g. 'in-group' and 'out-group', or 'stranger', 'acquaintance', and 'family member'.

The fifth requirement:

5. Agents must be able to differentiate between types of moral circles; the salience of these moral circles is dependent on their centrality

Relational Primitives. Relational primitives are social variables that exist within the mind of the individual and describe the relational properties of other individuals. In our work, we differentiate between two relational primitives: status and reputation. More can be identified, such as the power dimension identified in Kemper's work [20]; depending on the instantiation in specific applications, additional primitives may need to be defined.

Status
. . . Horatio walks up to Claudius and recognizes that he's dealing with an older man who is wearing a very formal suit. The old man is looking at his watch and Horatio realizes that the older man is probably in a hurry. . .

Many difficulties between individuals arise because there are differences in perceived status ("You're not in charge, I am!"). To avoid such conflicts, formal MCs usually have formal roles with explicit rights and obligations, which can range from that of a managing director of a multinational company to a junior trainee. In our model, we have instantiated this concept as moral circle status (MCS).

In the example above, Horatio is able to make an assumption about the status of Claudius because of two factors: his age, and the suit he is wearing. Note that Horatio might be wrong in his appreciation of these attributes; these symbols might mean something different to Claudius than they do to Horatio.

The sixth requirement:

6. Agents must be able to infer the status of characters, either through public variables, the observation and interpretation of symbols or through information gained from previous interactions.

Reputation
. . . Claudius has also had bad experiences with strangers in the past. Once, while he was helping a stranger, that stranger actually took his wallet. . .

Previous interactions with people will influence the way you treat them at a later stage; you will treat a 'good' friend differently from a 'bad' friend. In our model we have instantiated this as moral circle reputation (MCR).

Reputation can be seen as a social 'standing': an agent could be 'in good standing' versus 'in bad standing' with its fellows [22]. Reputation is essential for agents that interact with each other multiple times; it is likely that they will act differently depending on how previous interactions with that agent have played out.

Each MC has certain rights and obligations conferred on its members, depending on their roles in the MC. MCR can thus be used as a measure of how well a person lives up to their MC derived obligations and their respect for the rights of other MC members; whether a MC member follows or deviates from the norm will have an effect on their MCR.

Each member of the MC has a perception of the MCR of other known members and of their own. So you might think less of yourself if you have done something wrong, and others might also think less of you. This action can then be sanctioned by another member of the MC, and, depending on the level of MCR change, be attenuated by an appropriate atonement. Not wanting to lose reputation can be an important reason for an agent to respect a norm [23].

Two important elements need to be present within our model: actions have to be judged as to whether they deviate or follow the norm, and members of the moral circle need a perceived level of reputation (with unknown people these will be based on cultural meta-norms, see Sect. 3.3).

This leads to the seventh requirement:

7. Appropriate or inappropriate behaviour of other agents should lead to a respective change in Moral Circle Reputation.

Social Norms

...Claudius has no idea where the hotel is that Horatio is looking for. In his eyes, a young person like Horatio was probably not well prepared in planning his trip and it is his own fault. Claudius tells the man that he has no idea where the hotel is, wishes him good luck, says he has to go, and rushes to work...

Social norms help to identify how one should behave in a ritual. These norms reflect underlying value structures, but they are not fully determined by them. They evolve in path-dependent ways, depending on contextual contingencies, to be accepted by a society as a short-term guide to appropriate behaviour. Parts of society may evolve their own social norms, and as such, social norms are present on a group level. Therborn [24] makes the case for the importance of normative questions to the discipline of sociology.

As stated by Hollander and Wu [25] in their review of norms in agent-based simulations "The literature is populated with numerous definitions and uses of the term norm". However, norms are widely understood as rules that specify which behaviours are to be displayed, allowed, or prohibited when in a given context. This is how we conceive of them in this article.

Let us define more precisely how social norms are related to moral circles and the relational primitives (in this case, status MCS and reputation MCR). Operationally, each moral circle can have its own social norms, for example a company, a club or a family. As such, there are often multiple moral circles active at the same time (sometimes without a member even being present; 'what would your mother think of your behaviour'). Knowing the most salient MC in any context indicates to an agent which set of social norms take precedence.

Both the interpretation of the appropriateness of behaviour and the translation of intentions into actions, are mediated by the current social norms. These social norms are the most malleable part of MC rules. A population can come to believe that drunk driving or smoking indoors in the presence of non-smokers is normatively wrong, in a relatively short period of time. People actually use norm-related behaviours (adherence, violation, attempts to change) as a means of maintaining or changing the MC. However, the underlying cultural meta-norm structure and MC dynamics will not have altered significantly, if at all. The detailed functioning of MCs in practice reflects the underlying cultural values.

Let us examine how MCS and MCR within a MC could affect which social norms apply. Some social norms will define how to behave towards those of differing status. Here MCS within a MC determines which norms are applicable. For example, should greater respect be shown to high status family members or colleagues, and if so how? If more than one MC is active, the centrality of these MCs and the status and reputation of the individuals present help to establish the most salient MC (and which social norms take precedence).

In our example, Claudius believes that Horatio should have been more prepared. As a result, Claudius believes that it is more important for him to carry on to work than to help this undeserving youth.

This is the eight requirement:

8. Agents should determine which Social Norms are applicable and when they conflict, which take precedence. This process should be dependent on the salient Moral Circles, and the Relational Primitives of the participants.

3.3 'Society' Level

In their work, Mc Breen et al. [11] defined the notion of 'cultural meta-norm'. A cultural meta-norm has as its pre-conditions (1) the culture of agents in a situation, (2) a relational setting between agents. The culture acts as a perception and interpretation filter on the relational setting. The post-condition of a meta-norm is a tendency to create, strengthen, or weaken a relational goal. This is the reason for the epithet 'meta-', since a norm has specific behaviour as its post-condition. In the case of a cultural meta-norm, the relational goal change might not lead to any behaviour. For instance, depending on the specifics of the situation, the agent might not be empowered to act. Typically, a simulation would take the relational goal change into account alongside specific context factors, such as instrumental goals, to determine the actual behaviour of the agents.

Cultural Meta-Norms
. . . Horatio is left feeling bad and confused: where he is from, you usually help strangers, even if you are in a hurry. He decides to carry on, and continues on his journey. . .

Cultural meta-norms as defined by Mc Breen et al. [11] model agents' propensity to behave in a certain way in certain relational contexts, such as 'meeting a stranger' or 'meeting a person in need' or 'dealing with older people'. In contrast to social norms (middle level of Fig. 1), meta-norms are non-instantiated guides to social behaviour (upper level in Fig. 1). They are about the relational fundamentals of social life, and they are shared within any society that has the same culture. They deal with the basic question of how people should behave with respect to each other depending on who they are. They are close to the values of a culture, in the Hofstede sense of 'cultural programming of the mind', shared tendencies to perceive the social world, and act in it, in certain ways.

In our example, Horatio has a different cultural meta-norm regarding helping a younger stranger in need, than Claudius; Horatio expects Claudius to have a relational goal of providing help, while Claudius has no such goal, as a stranger receives less MCS and MCR in his culture. For Horatio is it unthinkable that you would leave a stranger needing help on the street to go to work. Thus, cultural meta-norms model how culture influences the behaviour of agents.

Within our conceptual model, culture will influence the social structure of MCs, and their social norms. The culturally modifiable parameters are the weight of the relational primitives, the salience of MCs, and the salience of social norms. The most salient MC and the most salient social norms can be established using this operationalization of meta-norms, e.g. "the work MC prevails over others" perhaps qualified by time of the week, or "what a senior person (could be parent, teacher, priest, boss) wants of me is more important than what anybody else wants of me". There should be room to add culture as a weighting and salience mechanism for MCs and social norms.

Every culture, through the different modifications it brings to the content and salience of MCs and social norms, will cause agents to behave differently, and to judge the behaviour of others differently as well.

The final requirement is thus:

9. Cultural Meta-Norms should be used to create weighting and salience mechanisms for moral circles, social norms, and relational primitives.

How can we begin to represent these varying behaviours and judgements in agent architectures? We propose to do this using Hofstede's dimensional model of culture [3].

Operationalizing Culture. We give an example of modifying the behaviour of agents based on their cultural background by linking elements of our conceptual model to Hofstede's dimensions of culture.

Hierarchy: Large Power Distance versus Small Power Distance. The importance given by agents to status depends on the dimension of power distance. This dimension represents the extent to which the less powerful members of a society expect and accept that power and rights are distributed unequally. Large power distance splits up the society into MCs of people with equal status that are not permeable, and depend on position in society. Agents in cultures of large power distance will respond differently to others depending on how they perceive their MCS relative to their own. Status differences will be effective barriers to communication, and particularly to volitional behaviour travelling upwards.

Horatio would feel that the behaviour of Claudius was appropriate if he was from a culture of large power distance. Indeed, if he was from a culture of very large power distance culture he would never have approached Claudius in the first place.

Aggression and Gender: Masculinity versus Femininity. The importance given to reputation depends on the cultural dimension of masculinity. This dimension is about assertive dominance and emotional gender roles. It contrasts a strong-handed, competitive orientation in 'masculine' cultures, in which people in general do not assume others to be trustworthy, men are supposed to be tough and women subservient and tender, versus a consensus-seeking and care-taking orientation for both women and men in 'feminine' cultures. For our relational primitives in masculine cultures, MCR will be very unequally divided across the MC, with a tendency to blame the weak and admire the strong. MCR will be more evenly distributed in feminine cultures, and will not change so radically with poor behaviour.

In our example, if both are from a masculine culture, Horatio would tend to judge Claudius harshly for not helping him, just as Claudius would be likely to judge Horatio harshly for being ill-prepared. In a feminine culture both would be more forgiving of the apparent faults of the other, and would expect this same forgiveness of others for their own mistakes; and Claudius would be more likely to actually help Horatio.

Identity: Individualism versus Collectivism. The importance given to MC centrality depends on the cultural dimension of individualism. An individualistic culture is one in which its members are supposed to be independent, self-motivated individuals. Its opposite, a collectivistic culture, is one in which everyone feels interdependent, and people act based on the social norms that come with their specific role in society.

In our example, Claudius didn't consider helping Horatio because he was a stranger. This is more likely in a collectivist culture, as out-group members are considered less 'my business' than in-group members. In an individualistic culture, helping Horatio would have been more likely, as the divide between in- and out group members is less great than in collectivistic cultures. On the other hand, if a collectivistic Claudius decided to 'adopt' a stranger, he would probably go to greater lengths in helping him.

4   Discussion

4.1   Design Choices

Our design principles were threefold:

1. Re-use simple, broad-range theory from the social sciences;
2. Re-use good properties of existing agent models;
3. Be unconcerned with implementation architecture.

It is our conviction that social sciences have theories on offer that have not yet been used in socio-cultural agents, simply because of a combination of the field's youth, the lack of contact between islands in the 'ivory archipelago' of social science, and the absence of systematic attempts to find such theories.

Theories that could be used are those that are parsimonious, so that they will not tend to create explosive complexity of agent models, and that have proven to be valid across a wide range of circumstances. Theories at different levels of abstraction could be eligible: the individual, the dyad, the group, or the society.

In this model, we have concentrated on three theories. The first is the work of Kemper [20] that models how individuals deal with status and power in their moral circles which he calls reference groups. The second is the work of Rothenbuhler [14] on rituals in groups, in which he generalizes the notion of ritual to include all social interaction in which a group of people have shared attention. There is also a clear conceptual link with Kemper: rituals serve to maintain moral circles, or if they are big rituals, to modify status hierarchies and membership in those moral circles. The third major theory is Hofstede's model of national culture [3], that can explain why similar dynamics, with slightly different parameterizations, lead to such stable differences across national patterns in social reality.

To our knowledge, outside of our work, Kemper and Rothenbuhler have not been used in agent architectures before, although [9] discusses rituals in agent architectures. Hofstede's dimensions have been used in virtual agents before [9,12]. Those attempts showed that culture was not very successful as a direct driver of behaviour; more basic social behaviour was found to be needed for culture to build on. This prompted the search for new theory that led to incorporating Kemper's status-power theory and reference groups.

4.2 Simplified Version

Our design choices imply that we do not believe a simplified version of the model could still plausibly produce equivalent behaviour. In fact we rather expect the opposite: user testing will quickly show model elements that are too simplistic to capture social reality.

Directly instantiating goals for virtual agents based on culture, without what social psychologists would call group dynamics, proved unsatisfactory, as argued above. Excluding culture would preclude making cross-cultural encounters virtual, and is therefore not desirable.

Figure 1 does show a way to simplify our model, though. The bottom layer concepts could largely be left out if the agents were non-embodied. There would still be a simulated process of course, implied by the box 'ritual'. But there would not be any physical context. That also removes the need for model properties that come with embodiment of agents: visible age, gender, status-carrying attributes, non-verbal behaviour, and personality. Actually, simulations have been carried out on this principle. In applications of trade negotiation [26] and consumer behaviour in car choice [27], culture as operationalized by Hofstede dimension scores was used to modify agent behaviour in agent-based models. In the case of trade negotiations, face validity was achieved, and in the case of car selection, the model reproduced cross-national purchase patterns.

Another way to simplify the model, admittedly reducing its allure, would be to limit the number of cultures, or the number of moral circles. For purposes of testing and sensitivity analysis, such steps could certainly be taken.

4.3   Validation Scheme

There are two components to the validation of the model described in this article. The first is the validation of social norms and cultural meta-norms. This can be done using simulations with instantiated agent behaviour based on the model presented here. These rules of behaviour need to be validated by running simulations with a large number of participants from different cultures, to ensure that the behaviour described in these norms is actually representative of realistic differences in behaviour across cultures and groups.

The second is the validation of the model itself. This is a more difficult process. The evaluation of designed scenarios would just test the instantiation of the model, not the model itself. However, through a design-based approach, the model could be tested for its generalizability against a corpus of real-world stories: 'Can you describe every situation in terms of the elements of the model'. This helps to establish the boundaries of the model. There will be obvious boundaries to the model in terms of instantiated virtual worlds available. In future work we aim to instantiate this work for specific application domains and existing agent-based architectures. This will help us to identify if additional elements are needed.

5   Conclusion

The series of requirements that we have presented during the interaction between Horatio and Claudius represent elements that are important to consider when designing socio-cultural virtual agents. Taking these requirements as a starting point, we have discussed elements of our model that will help show realistic social behaviour that can be modified by culture.

Through rituals, in which a set of agents have shared attention in a certain environment, agents are able to act appropriately by applying the relevant moral circles and their social norms. This selection mechanism allows for different interpretations in different contexts.

Culture can then be applied through the use of cultural meta-norms, which, in turn, affect the weighting and salience of the other model components. This allows us to have culture influence social relationships rather than act directly on behaviour. Also, in the absence of familiar moral circles, cultural meta-norms can provide guidance. This is particularly important when meeting with strangers (from different cultures).

We believe that this paper makes some necessary conceptual steps to make virtual agents act more appropriately in any social or cultural context. Agents created with such a model can be used within (existing) agent architectures. Besides their practical use, they can also be used as tools to better understand how people perceive and interact with characters from different cultures.

In future and on-going work, we aim to put the concepts presented in this paper into existing agent architectures to create believable culturally-varying behaviour in agents for educational purposes. The translation of the concepts will allow us to discover flaws and additional modelling requirements for socio-cultural agents.

Acknowledgements. This work was partially supported by European Community (EC) and was funded by the ECUTE (ICT-5-4.2 257666) and SEMIRA projects. This work was also supported by national funds through FCT Fundao para a Cincia e a Tecnologia, under project PEst-OE/EEI/LA0021/2013. The authors are solely responsible for the content of this publication. It does not represent the opinion of the EC, and the EC is not responsible for any use that might be made of data appearing therein.

References

1. Brown, R.: Group Processes: Dynamics Within and Between Groups, 2nd edn. Blackwell, Oxford (2000)
2. Prada, R., Paiva, A.: Believable groups of synthetic characters. In: 4th International Joint Conference on Autonomous Agents and Multiagent Systems, pp. 37–43. ACM, New York (2005)
3. Hofstede, G., Hofstede, G.J., Minkov, M.: Cultures and Organizations: Software of the Mind, 3rd edn. McGraw-Hill, New York (2010)
4. Aylett, R., Paiva, A., Vannini, N., Enz, S., Andre, E., Hall, L.: But that was in another country: agents and intercultural empathy. In: 8th International Conference on Autonomous Agents and Multiagent Systems, pp. 329–336. ACM, New York (2009)
5. Hill, R.W., Belanich, J., Lane, H.C., Core, M.: Pedagogically structured game-based training: Development of the elect bilat simulation. In: 25th Army Science Conference (2006)
6. Johnson, W.L., Vilhjalmsson, H.H., Marsella, S.: Serious games for language learning: How much game, how much A.I. In: Looi, C.-K., McCalla, G.I., Bredeweg, B., Breuker, J. (eds.) AIED 2005, vol. 125, pp. 306–313. IOS Press, Amsterdam (2005)
7. Jan, D., Herrera, D., Martinovski, B., Novick, D., Traum, D.R.: A computational model of culture-specific conversational behavior. In: Pelachaud, C., Martin, J.-C., André, E., Chollet, G., Karpouzis, K., Pelé, D. (eds.) IVA 2007. LNCS (LNAI), vol. 4722, pp. 45–56. Springer, Heidelberg (2007)
8. Endrass, B., Rehm, M., Lipi, A., Nakano, Y., André, E.: Culture-related differences in aspects of behavior for virtual characters across Germany and Japan. In: 10th International Conference on Autonomous Agents and Multiagent Systems, Taipei, pp. 441–448 (2011)
9. Mascarenhas, S., Dias, J., Afonso, N., Enz, S., Paiva, A.: Using rituals to express cultural differences in synthetic characters. In: 8th International Conference on Autonomous Agents and Multiagent Systems, Budapest, pp. 305–312 (2009)

10. Solomon, S., van Lent, M., Core, M., Carpenter, P., Rosenberg, M.: A language for modeling cultural norms, biases and stereotypes for human behavior models. In: 18th International Conference on Behaviour Representation in Modeling and Simulation, Rhode Island (2009)
11. Mc Breen, J., Di Tosto, G., Dignum, F., Hofstede, G.J.: Linking norms and culture. In: 2nd International Conference on Culture and Computing, Kyoto (2011)
12. Mascarenhas, S., Dias, J., Prada, R., Paiva, A.: A dimensional model for cultural behaviour in virtual agents. J. Appl. Artif. Intell. **24**(6), 552–574 (2010)
13. Dias, J., Paiva, A.: Feeling and reasoning: a computational model for emotional characters. In: Bento, C., Cardoso, A., Dias, G. (eds.) EPIA 2005. LNCS (LNAI), vol. 3808, pp. 127–140. Springer, Heidelberg (2005)
14. Rothenbhler, E.W.: Ritual Communication: From Everyday Conversation to Mediated Ceremony. Sage, Thousand Oaks (1998)
15. Bell, C.: Ritual: Perspectives and Dimensions. University Press, Oxford (1997)
16. Hofstede, G.J.: Modelling rituals for Homo biologicus. In: 7th European Conference on Social Simulation Association, Montpellier (2011)
17. Tajfel, H., Turner, J.C.: The social identity theory of intergroup behavior. In: Worchel, S., Austin, L.W. (eds.) Psychology of Intergroup Relations, pp. 7–24. Nelson-Hall, Chicago (1986)
18. Laham, S.: Expanding the moral circle. Inclusion and exclusion mindsets and the circle of moral regard. J. Exp. Soc. Psychol. **45**, 250253 (2009)
19. Singer, P.: The Expanding Circle: Ethics, Evolution and Moral Progress. Princeton University Press, Princeton (2011)
20. Kemper, T.D.: Status, Power and Ritual Interaction: A Relational Reading of Durkheim, Goffman, and Collins. Ashgate, London (2011)
21. Wilson, D.S.: Evolution for Everyone: How Darwin's Theory Can Change the Way We Think About Our Lives. Delacorte, New York (2007)
22. Nowak, M.A., Sigmund, K.: Evolution of indirect reciprocity. Nature **437**, 1291–1298 (2005)
23. Axelrod, R.: An evolutionary approach to norms. Am. Polit. Sci. Rev. **80**, 1095–1111 (1986)
24. Therborn, G.: Back to norms! on the scope and dynamics of norms and normative action. Curr. Sociol. **50**(6), 863–880 (2003)
25. Hollander, C., Wu, A.: The current state of normative agent-based systems. J. Artif. Soc. Soc. Simul. **14**(6), 147 (2011)
26. Hofstede, G.J., Jonker, C., Verwaart, T.: Cultural differentiation of negotiating agents. Group Decis. Negot. **21**(1), 79–98 (2012)
27. Roozmand, O., Ghasem-Aghaee, N., Hofstede, G.J., Nematbakhsh, M.A., Baraani, A., Verwaart, T.: Agent-based modeling of consumer decision making process based on power distance and personality. Knowl.-Based Syst. **24**(7), 1075–1095 (2012)

FAtiMA Modular: Towards an Agent Architecture with a Generic Appraisal Framework

João Dias[(✉)], Samuel Mascarenhas, and Ana Paiva

INESC-ID and Instituto Superior Técnico, University of Lisbon, Tagus Park,
Av. Prof. Cavaco Silva, 2780-990 Porto Salvo, Portugal
{joao.dias,samuel.mascarenhas,ana.paiva}@gaips.inesc-id.pt

Abstract. This paper presents a generic and flexible architecture for emotional agents, with what we consider to be the minimum set of functionalities that allows us to implement and compare different appraisal theories in a given scenario. FAtiMA Modular, the architecture proposed is composed of a core algorithm and by a set of components that add particular functionality (either in terms of appraisal or behaviour) to the architecture, which makes the architecture more flexible and easier to extend.

1 Introduction

FAtiMA (**F**earnot **A**ffec**TI**ve **M**ind **A**rchitecture) is an Agent Architecture with planning capabilities designed to use emotions and personality to influence the agent's behaviour [3]. During the last years, the architecture was used in several scenarios (such as FearNot! [10], ORIENT [14], and a process Model of Empathy [12]) and by different research institutions, which led to the architecture being extended with several new features and functionalities (e.g. Cultural Behaviour [8] and Drives [5]). The resulting architecture has become perhaps difficult to use since the complexity of understanding the architecture escalated with the number of existing features. For this reason, a major effort was put in creating a modular version of the architecture, where functionalities and processes are divided into modular independent components. This enables us to use lighter and simpler versions of FAtiMA with just some of the components (for instance only the reactive and emotional components) for the simpler scenarios. During the refactorization, the most relevant processes were generalized making the architecture easier to extend by allowing us to work independently on different components whose functionality can be easily added to the architecture.

One of the most relevant processes generalized in the architecture was the appraisal process. The rationale followed was that the architecture should be able to later incorporate several distinct appraisal mechanisms and even appraisal theories. There are currently several different appraisal theories that model the process of emotion generation (OCC [9], Roseman's [13], Scherer [15]). Due to the difficulty of implementing them all in a same scenario, there has not been

T. Bosse et al. (Eds.): Emotion Modeling, LNAI 8750, pp. 44–56, 2014.
DOI: 10.1007/978-3-319-12973-0_3

an effort (at least to our knowledge) in directly comparing and evaluating the different theories together. We believe that creating scenarios where the several emotion theories can be integrated and evaluated can help us to learn more about them. For instance, it would be interesting to determine if Scherer's appraisal theory, where facial expressions derive directly from the stimulus evaluation checks instead of the resulting emotions, can indeed generate more natural and believable emotional expressions.

The aim of this paper is thus to present a generic core architecture for emotional agents, and to describe how the generic appraisal mechanism could be used to implement different appraisal theories. This is a first step towards a contribution to the standards in emotion modeling.

2 FAtiMA Core

FAtiMA Modular is composed of a core layer (named FAtiMA Core) on which components are added in order to add functionality. FAtiMA Core is a template that generally defines how the Agent Architecture works. Added components can provide specific implementations for the generic functions defined in the Core. Figure 1 shows a diagram of FAtiMA Core with the basic functionalities for an emotional agent architecture. An agent is able to receive perceptions from the environment (events) which are used to update the agent's memory (or internal state) and to trigger the appraisal process. The result of the appraisal process is stored in the affective state[1], and later used to influence the action selection processes which will make the agent act upon the environment.

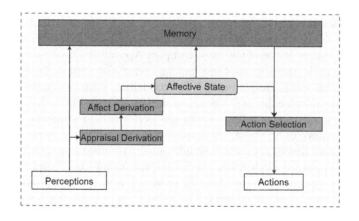

Fig. 1. FAtiMA core architecture

The Core architecture is strongly based in [7] and thus it divides appraisal into two separate processes. The first one, appraisal derivation, is responsible for

---

[1] We call it affective state since it is used to store affective states such as emotions and moods.

evaluating the relevance of the event to the agent and determine a set of appraisal variables (e.g. desirability and desirability for others in the case of OCC). The second process, affect derivation, takes the appraisal variables as input and generates the resulting affective states (emotions or mood) according to an Appraisal Theory. This division into distinct processes is also in accordance with the formal characterization of Structural Appraisal Theories proposed by Reisenzein [11] and with the Set based Formalism proposed by Broekens [2], which identify three main processes in an Appraisal Theory: perception, Appraisal and Mediation (Appraisal Derivation and Affect Derivation in our terminology).

It is important to point out that the Core architecture does not commit itself with the particular methods used. In fact a FAtiMA agent that only has a Core will not do anything. Behaviour is added by adding components that implement the mentioned functionality. However, a component is not required to implement all functionality in the Core, it can implement just one of the processes. In order to differentiate components when adding them to the Core, they are categorized according to the implemented functionality. For instance, an AffectDerivation Component will have to implement an Affect Derivation process, and a Behaviour Component will have to implement the action selection function. All components are designed following two main properties: they must be interchangeable - i.e., being able to be replaced, added or removed with a minimum effort; and they must be loosely coupled - dependencies between components should be avoided unless strictly needed.

2.1 Appraisal Process

We will now look with more detail to the Appraisal Process. One of the main goals when designing the appraisal mechanism was that it would have to be powerful and flexible enough to represent most Appraisal Theories. Given that Scherer's [15] theory is one of the most complex Appraisal Theories, an effort has been made to make the appraisal mechanism compliant with it. Other appraisal theories can be easily implemented by modeling simpler single-component processes of appraisal. Scherer defines appraisal as a process of multilevel sequential checking: a set of evaluation checks are performed in sequence in order to assess the relevance of an event, the implications for self of the same event, coping potential and finally normative significance. Appraisal is sequential because some of the appraisal evaluation checks require others to complete. According to Scherer, appraisal is also done at several levels, a sensory-motor level, a schematic level and conceptual level. The lower levels are usually faster to determine a stimulus evaluation check, but often may offer less than perfect appraisal information. In situations where low-level appraisals cannot properly evaluate a situation, higher level (but more complex and heavier) appraisals take place.

Scherer's notion of evaluation check can easily be aggregated with other theories concept of appraisal variables, so we will use the term appraisal variable henceforth. Furthermore, in order to make the appraisal process as flexible as possible, FAtiMA appraisal is grounded on a set of design principles, which try to generalize Scherer's requirements for its appraisal theory:

1. Appraisal is incremental, i.e. appraisal is not a one-shot process and different appraisal variables and the corresponding emotions may be generated at different points in time. For instance, in the case of OCC, desirability (associated with Joy and Distress) can be determined first while desirability for other could be determined later (associated with Fortune of Others emotions such as Pitty). Consequently, the appraisal process must be continuously executed and is up to each component to decide if and when to return an appraisal variable.

2. An appraisal component may depend on an appraisal variable determined by another component and thus need to access all the appraisal variables generated in the appraisal process. This implies that we need a way to store the result of an appraisal component (a structure akin to SEC registers) and use it as an input to other appraisal components. Furthermore, these first two principles allow us to model sequential evaluation checks (or sequential appraisals). By making a component start the appraisal only after an appraisal variable is defined (or defined with a particular value), we create an implicit dependency and ordering between the components. In order to favor modularity, only the dependent component needs to know the dependency, if we remove it from the architecture the initial component will continue working as normal.

3. Lazarus pointed out that appraisal is often followed by reappraisal, with the purpose to correct the evaluation based on new information or more thorough processing [4]. Therefore, the value of an appraisal variable may change over time, and the affective state must reflect this change. For example, an event may be initially appraised as undesirable by one fast reactive appraisal component, but later considered desirable by a more elaborate cognitive appraisal component. Thus considering an OCC affect derivation component as example, the initial Distress emotion that was triggered by the event should change into a Joy emotion. This means that the Core architecture must enforce that the affect derivation processes are executed whenever there is a new result returned from the appraisal components.

4. Any component can contribute to any appraisal variable. For this reason, we must store the contribution of all components to a given appraisal variable. In order to determine the final value of an appraisal variable, an explicit policy is used. The policy can be choosing the highest value, performing a weighted sum, using the value determined by the latest component to set the variable, or using a priority mechanism. These last two principles enumerated enable us to model Scherer's multi-level appraisal by creating one component for each level. A reactive component can be used to implement Scherer's sensory-motor level (or schematic level) for a given appraisal variable, while a deliberative component can implement the conceptual level for the same variable.

In order to store the intermediate results of the appraisal variables generated, and to allow any appraisal derivation component to access that information, an Appraisal Frame structure is used. An Appraisal Frame is usually associated to an event (internal or external[2]) and stores a list of appraisal variables associated with the event. As mentioned, the Appraisal Frame must store the contribution of all components to an appraisal variable and use a policy to determine its final value. Figure 2 presents a diagram of the appraisal process. An event generated will trigger the start of an appraisal process creating an appraisal frame. The arrow from the appraisal frame to the appraisal components represents that appraisal can take several cycles and depend on the appraisal of other components. In the example provided, one of the components initially defines the appraisal variable with a positive value (4), but another component later defines it as being slightly negative (−1).

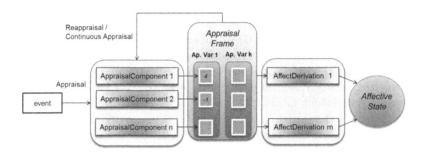

Fig. 2. Appraisal process

Whenever there is a change in an Appraisal Frame, the emotional state of the agent needs to reflect that change. This is handled by the Affect Derivation components, whose sole responsibility is to generate and update the agent's emotions. Emotions are defined as having a type, valence and an intensity which decays with time. Each affect derivation component is informed of changes in the appraisal variables stored in the appraisal frame. This information is then used to decide which emotions to create and their corresponding intensity. Additional modulation factors, such as a personality or cultural bias, might also be used by the component to determine the emotion intensity. Note that affect derivation components are independent from each other and their number is not restricted. As such, several emotions may be added simultaneously to the agent's emotional state, which then results in the agent experiencing mixed emotions. Besides emotions, the agent's affective state also integrates the notion of mood. Mood represents an overall affective state which is influenced by the emotions experienced by the agent (and also decays with time): positive emotions increase mood, while negative emotions decrease it.

---

[2] External events correspond to events that happen in the environment, such as John pushing Luke, while internal events correspond to events that are triggered by architecture's internal processes, for instance the activation, success or failure of a given goal.

One particular affect derivation component that is already implemented in the architecture is the OCC Affect derivation component that, as the name implies, is based on the OCC theory. Whenever this component is informed of a change in any OCC appraisal variables such as desirability, desirabilityForOther, or praiseworthiness, it will generate the corresponding emotion (e.g. given a positive desirability value, a Joy emotion is generated). This component also looks for the agent's predefined emotional thresholds to dampen the final emotion intensity. These emotional thresholds are a mechanism to model the agent's personality by making it harder/easier to experience certain emotions.

One last important mechanism is the way that emotions are stored and organized in the affective state. The third principle requires us to properly update emotions when the value of an appraisal variable changes. This is particularly important because a change in an appraisal variable may even change the type of an emotion generated. To do so, emotions are indexed in the affective state by the set of appraisal variables used to generate them as well as the corresponding event. When a new emotion is added to the emotional state, the emotional state checks if any emotion caused by the same event and triggered by exactly the same appraisal variables already exists. If it does, then it will replace the existing emotion by the new one. If not, it will simply add the new emotion. Imagine an event that is initially appraised with a negative desirability, according to OCC this will generate a distress emotion. However, if the event is later appraised (by another component or by reappraisal) with positive desirability, the distress emotion will be removed and replaced by a new joy emotion. Note that with this mechanism, it is possible to generate several distinct emotions associated with the same event as long as they are triggered by a different set of variables.

Figure 3 presents the resulting pseudocode for FAtiMA Core. The first update function is used to update the components every cycle (used for instance to simulate processes of decay). Then the perceptual process checks if there is a new perception taking place in the environment. If a new event is perceived, it is used to update the agent's memory and all existing components and a new Appraisal Frame will be created associated to the event. The Appraisal Frame will then be used to start the appraisal process.

Once the Appraisal Frame is determined, the function updateEmotions will be used to initiate the AffectDerivation process. According to Fig. 4, whenever there is a change detected in the Appraisal Frame (meaning that one of the components has set at least one appraisal variables), all existing appraisal derivation components are used to generate the corresponding emotions, which are added to the emotional state. Finally, at the end of an agent's cycle, the Core will ask the behaviour components if they want to perform any action. This can be a simple reactive mechanism or a complex deliberative one. As example, FAtiMA reactive component is a behaviour component that will trigger simple action tendencies based on the current emotional state, while the deliberative component uses goals and planning to determine the best course of action to follow. If more than one action is triggered by different components, a priority mechanism

```
while(shutdown != true)
  for each Component c
    c.update();

  e <- perceiveEvent();

  if(a new event is perceived)
    memory.update(e);
    for each Component c
      c.update(e);

    aF <- newAppraisalFrame(e);

    for each AppraisalComponent aC
      aC.startAppraisal(e,aF);
      updateEmotions(aF);

  for each AppraisalComponent aC
    aF <- aC.continuousAppraisal();
    updateEmotions(aF);

  for each BehaviorComponent bC
    bc.actionSelection();

  a <- selectAction();
  executeAction(a);
```

Fig. 3. FAtiMA's core pseudocode

```
updateEmotions(aF)

  if(aF.hasChanged())
    for each AffectDerivationComponent aD
      emotion <- aD.affectDerivation(aF)
      AffectiveState.add(emotion);
```

Fig. 4. Update emotions method

will be used to select the most relevant one. The selected action will then be executed in the environment.

3   FAtiMA Modular

As previously mentioned, a FAtiMA agent that only has a Core will not do anything. FAtiMA Modular architecture is created by adding a set of components to the core. For instance, in the scenario described in [8], the architecture was defined with the following components:

- **Reactive Component -** this component uses predefined emotional reaction rules to determine the value of the following OCC appraisal variables: Desirability, DesirabilityForOthers, Praiseworthiness and Like. When an event is perceived, the reactive appraisal matches the event against a set of emotional rules.

A rule may define a particular value for each of the appraisal variables and can then target a specific event (e.g. the agent finds it desirable whenever it receives a compliment from agent B) or it can be more general (e.g. the agent finds it undesirable whenever the action cry is performed).

- **Deliberative Component** - handles goal-based behavior and adds planning capabilities to the agent. It uses the state of plans in memory to generate appraisal variables for OCC Prospect Based Emotions. These appraisal variables are GoalStatus, GoalConduciveness, and GoalSucessProbability.
- **OCCAffectDerivation Component** - generates emotions from the appraisal variables according to the OCC Theory of Emotions (see Table 1). For instance an event with a positive desirability value for the agent will generate a Joy emotion if it surpasses the agent's predefined threshold for Joy. On the other hand, if the event's desirability is negative, then a Distress emotion is generated instead.
- **Motivational Component** - component that models basic human drives, such as energy and integrity and uses them to help select between competing goals in the deliberative component. The more a certain need is low/high, the more higher/lower the utility of a goal that contributes positively for that need is. Additionally it is also used to determine an event's desirability according to the effects it had on the agent's drives (e.g. an *eat* action lowers the energy need). When an event lowers/raises the agent's needs, it is evaluated as desirable/undesirable for that agent.
- **Theory of Mind Component** - creates a model of the internal states of other agents. This component determines the desirability of an event for others by simulating their own appraisal processes.
- **Cultural Component** - implements cultural-dependent behaviour of agents through the use of rituals, symbols and cultural dimensions. It also used to automatically determine the Praiseworthiness appraisal variable based on cultural values and also on the impact actions have on the motivational states of the agents. For instance, the more collectivistic the agent's culture is, the more praiseworthy is an action that positively affects the need of other agents in detriment of the agent's own needs.

To illustrate how these several components are combined in the scenario to create a complex appraisal process consider the following example. During a dinner party enacted by five different agents, one of the agents informs the others that he is feeling sick. When the agent's culture is defined as highly collectivistic, there is an agent that decides to offer his own medicine. After receiving the medicine, the agent that is sick elicits a Joy and Admiration emotions.

The appraisal process that takes place for the receiving agent occurs in the following manner. First, the motivational state component will quickly determine that receiving the medicine will have a positive effect on the agent's integrity drive (which is low at the moment) generating a strong positive desirability, and store that value in the Appraisal Frame. FAtiMA core will detect a change in the Appraisal Frame and initiate the AffectDerivation process by calling the

Table 1. Association between implemented OCC appraisal variables and OCC emotion types

Appraisal variables	Associated emotion types
Desirability	Joy, Distress
Desirability, DesirabilityForOthers	HappyFor, Gloating, Pitty, Resentment
Praiseworthiness	Pride, Admiration, Shame, Reproach
Praiseworthiness, Desirability	Gratification, Gratitude, Remorse, Anger
Like	Love, Hate
GoalStatus, GoalConduciveness, GoalSucessProbability	Hope, Fear, Relief, Satisfaction, Fears-Confirmed, Disappointment

OCCAffectDerivation Component. This leads to the initial creation of a Joy emotion.

A few cycles later, the Theory of Mind component will also determine that the same event will have a negative effect on the giver agent's integrity drive (since it lost its medicine), determining the same event as undesirable for the giver. AffectDerivation will be called again, but this time no emotion is generated. Since the cultural component requires the two others appraisal variables to generate the appraisal, it will not trigger until both values are determined by the other components. Once this happens, the cultural component determines the praiseworthiness variable according to the formula presented in [8]. In this example, given the collectivistic culture of the appraising agent, he will appraise the event as highly praiseworthy[3]. The OCCAffectDerivation component will then generate an Admiration emotion based on praiseworthiness.

4   Related Work

There is some related work relevant to the generic appraisal model presented here. The FeelME framework proposed by Broekens [1], similarly to the work presented here, addresses the problem of creating a computational emotional system in an modular and extensible way. In the framework, appraisal processes are separated into five main steps: the Decision Support System that corresponds to a perceptual system; the Appraisal System (AS) that evaluates perceived objects and returns a vector of appraisal dimensions; the Appraisal Signal Modulator that can change (for instance amplifying or dampening) the appraisal result vectors; an Emotion Maintenance System responsible for integrating the appraisal-results and maintaining the emotional state, which is also represented as a n-th dimensional vector; and finally the Behaviour Modification System that controls the agent's emotional behaviour. Modularity and scalability is attained by making the AS to be composed of a set of appraisal banks that evaluate specific

---

[3] A collectivistic culture values self-sacrifice for the well being of others.

aspects of the agent's environment. Although the banks are assumed to evaluate independently, an appraisal bank can influence the contribution of another appraisal bank to the EMS through dependencies, thus allowing the framework for instance to model scherer's levels of appraisal and evaluation sequence.

Comparing the FeelME framework with the architecture proposed shows us that there are some similarities. For instance, the way that the appraisal system if composed of independent appraisal banks is similar to our approach of using a set of differentiated appraisal derivation components. However, although computationally flexible, modular and efficient, the framework does not model affect derivation process and uses a continuous representation of emotions directly obtained from the sum of the resulting appraisals. Although a continuous model of emotion per se is not necessarily a disadvantage, the fact that the appraisals of distinct events are combined together may originate a loss of information. As example, if two events e1 and e2 evaluated with opposing appraisal values are perceived close together, the resulting emotional state will be neutral instead of an emotional state with equally strong but opposing emotions.

With the goal of facilitating the comparison and integration of different Cognitive Appraisal Theories and systematically analyzing computational models of emotion, Broekens et al. [2] have put forward a theory-independent formalization that can be used to describe the structure of appraisal. The formalism proposed is based on set theory and models appraisal with the three types of processes identified by Reisenzein [11]: perception processes (P), appraisal processes (A) and mediating processes (M). Perception processes map the external world to mental objects, appraisal processes evaluate perceived mental objects to appraisal dimensions and mediation processes relate appraisal dimensions values to emotion components that can be used to represent emotion categories and intensities. Broekens et al.'s formalization models explicit inhibitory and excitatory dependencies between processes (of perception, appraisal and mediation) through guards and links. It is important to point out that dependencies can be created between processes of the same type (e.g. the appraisal of novelty with high value activates the appraisal of relevance) or processes of different types (the presence of an object returned by a perception process activates an appraisal process).

The formalization proposed by Broekens et al. is more complete than the FeelME framework. It can represent explicit Mediation processes and Emotion Components or categories similarly to our model. As such, there are even more resemblances between this formalization and the model proposed by us. Nonetheless, there are some relevant differences. While in Broekens formalization dependencies are created between processes, in FAtiMA-Core appraisal components depend on appraisal variables and not on other components. Ideally, an appraisal component doesn't need to know what other appraisal components exist. We argue that this is important in order to make the architecture more flexible and modular. Since several components may generate the same appraisal variable, a third component that depends on that variable will still work even if some of the original components are removed. An additional relevant difference is that the proposed semi-formal model was designed with the goal of being easily mapped to a computational model, while the set-based formalization aims at a systematic formal analysis of particular computational models.

The last model analysed, EMA [6], is a very complete computational model of appraisal processes. It focus on explaining both the rapid dynamics of emotional reactions and slower deliberative responses. However, opposingly to multiple-level approaches that use different levels for the reactive and deliberative appraisals, authors argue that a single and automatic appraisal process can be used to generate similar dynamics that result from deliberative and reactive processes operating on a person's relationship with the environment. Moreover, authors argue that appraisal checks occur in parallel and any sequential relation between appraisal is due to the requirements of the cognitive processes involved in the construction of the representation of the appraised event. EMA consists of a set of processes that interpret a representation of the person environment relationship in terms of a set of appraisal variables and a set of coping processes that manipulate this representation in response to the appraisals. To do so, EMA uses a representation built on the causal representations created by decision-theoretic planning, which are capable of easily capturing concepts such as utility and probability that can be directly translated to appraisal variables such as desirability and likelihood. These appraisal variables, which are continuously updated, are stored in a data structure called Appraisal Frame that is created for each proposition inside the causal interpretation. In EMA, emotions correspond to the existing appraisal frames. Although there is mapping between the appraisal variables and emotion labels, it is mainly used to facilitate the facial expression of emotions. The model features a interesting cyclic relationship between appraisal, coping and reappraisal. The initial appraisal of a situation triggers several cognitive and behavioral responses that changes the person's relationship with the environment. These changes will lead to a reappraisal of the initial situation, which may eventually result in additional responses.

While the focus of EMA is on creating a single-level process model of appraisal that can explain the dynamics of emotions, the goal of the structural architecture proposed here is to be able to model several distinct theories of emotions, be it single-level or multi-level sequential theories. In fact, while most of the paper focused on being able to model a multi-level sequential appraisal theory, the presented generic model is currently easily integrated with a single-level appraisal theory. As example, the Deliberative Component, which was not mentioned in detail in this paper has an appraisal mechanism where events are used to update planning structures, which will generate appraisals of goal conduciveness and likelihood, albeit this is done at a much simpler level than EMA. We do not argue which approach is the most correct. Instead we agree with Broekens in that these generic structural models provide an interesting tool to analyse, compare and evaluate distinct appraisal theories.

5   Discussion

This paper proposes a model for an Emotional Agent Architecture that can be easily extended by adding new components that define a set of functionalities used by a core generic algorithm. One of the processes that can be extended is the appraisal process. An effort has been made to make the appraisal mechanism as flexible and dynamic as possible in order to support the implementation of distinct appraisal theories. With this possibility comes the challenge of how to compare and evaluate such distinct appraisal theories. In our view there are two main aspects of appraisal theories that can be analysed. The first one has to do with the internal processes proposed by distinct theories. For instance, it would be interesting to analyse whether the more dynamic appraisal process of Scherer's Theory, which allows an appraisal to change from an initial negative towards a positive one, can in fact generate emotional expressions and behaviour that is perceived as more natural and believable by users.

The second aspect that can be more systematically analysed is the output of appraisal theories, i.e. the resulting emotions generated for a particular situation. To do so, this requires the development of a an agent-based scenario highlighting a particular aspect of emotional appraisal. Then the same situation would be used with two distinct appraisal theories implemented to generate the corresponding emotions. The resulting behaviour would then be observed by human viewers who would rate whether the observed emotional behaviour was or not appropriate (or if they would feel a similar emotion). This methodology can be used to detect certain shortcomings of a specific theory. As an example, Scherer's theory postulates an appraisal variable that is related to how much power one has over a particular situation. This variable helps to determine whether one feels anger or fear when threatened by another person. Comparatively, the OCC theory has no such variable. As such, a situation that is viewed as distressful and blameworthy, such as the one mentioned, will always lead to anger.

In our opinion, the work presented here is a first step towards an important contribution to the creation of standards in emotion modeling. In the future we pretend to implement other appraisal theories (such as Scherer's theory), and create scenarios to analyse and compare some of their features.

Acknowledgments. This work was partially supported by the European Community (EC), through the EU FP7 ICT-215554 project LIREC, and by national funds through Fundação para a Ciência e a Tecnologia (FCT), under project PEst-OE/EEI/LA0021/ 2011 and under two scholarships (SFRH BD/19481/2004 and SFRH BD/62174/2009). The authors are solely responsible for the content of this publication. It does not represent the opinion of the EC or the FCT, which are not responsible for any use that might be made of data appearing therein.

References

1. Broekens, J., DeGroot, D.: Scalable and flexible appraisal models for virtual agents. In: 5th Game-On International Conference: Computer Games: Artificial Intelligence, Design and Education (2004)

2. Broekens, J., DeGroot, D., Kosters, W.: Formal models of appraisal: theory, specification, and computational model. Cogn. Syst. Res. **9**(3), 173–197 (2008)
3. Dias, J., Paiva, A.: Feeling and reasoning: a computational model for emotional characters. In: Bento, C., Cardoso, A., Dias, G. (eds.) EPIA 2005. LNCS (LNAI), vol. 3808, pp. 127–140. Springer, Heidelberg (2005)
4. Lazarus, R.S.: Psychological Stress and the Coping Processes. McGraw Hill, New York (1966)
5. Lim, M., Dias, J., Aylett, R., Paiva, A.: Creating adaptive affective autonomous npcs. Special Issue Journal of Autonomous Agents and Multi-Agent Systems (2011) (to appear)
6. Marsella, S., Gratch, J.: Ema: a process model of appraisal dynamics. Cogn. Syst. Res. **10**(1), 70–90 (2009)
7. Marsella, S., Gratch, J., Petta, P.: Computational models of emotion. In: Scherer, K., Bänziger, T., Roesch, E. (eds.) A Blueprint for an Affectively Competent Agent: Cross-Fertilization Between Emotion Psychology, Affective Neuroscience, and Affective Computing. Oxford University Press, Oxford (2010)
8. Mascarenhas, S., Dias, J., Prada, R., Paiva, A.: A dimensional model for cultural behaviour in virtual agents. Appl. Artif. Intell. **24**(6), 552–574 (2010)
9. Ortony, A., Clore, G., Collins, A.: The Cognitive Structure of Emotions. Cambridge University Press, UK (1998)
10. Paiva, A., Dias, J., Sobral, D., Aylett, R., Woods, S., Hall, L., Zoll, C.: Learning by feeling: evoking empathy with synthetic characters. Appl. Artif. Intell. **19**(3), 235–266 (2005)
11. Reisenzein, R.: Appraisal processes conceptualized from a schema-theoretic perspective: contributions to a process analysis of emotions. In: Scherer, K.R., Schorr, A., Johnstone, T. (eds.) Appraisal Processes in Emotion. Theory, Methods, Research. Oxford University Press, Oxford (2001)
12. Rodrigues, S., Mascarenhas, S., Dias, J., Paiva, A.: I can feel it too! emergent empathic reactions between synthetic characters. In: 3rd International Conference on Affective Computing and Intelligent Interaction and Workshops, ACII 2009, pp. 1–7. IEEE (2009)
13. Roseman, I., Jose, P., Spindel, M.: Appraisals of emotion-eliciting events: testing a theory of discrete emotions. Pers. Soc. Psychol. **59**(5), 899–915 (1990)
14. Ruth, A., Natalie, V., Elisabeth, A., Paiva, A., Enz, S., Hall, L.: But that was in another country: agents and intercultural empathy. In: Proceedings of The 8th International Conference on Autonomous Agents and Multiagent Systems, AAMAS '09, vol. 1, pp. 329–336. International Foundation for Autonomous Agents and Multiagent Systems (2009)
15. Scherer, K., Schoor, A., Johnstone, T.: Appraisal Processes in Emotion. Theory, Methods, Research. Oxford University Press, Oxford (2001)

Programming Agents with Emotions

Mehdi Dastani$^{(\boxtimes)}$, Christiaan Floor, and John-Jules Ch. Meyer

Intelligent Systems, Utrecht University, Utrecht, The Netherlands
m.m.dastani@uu.nl

Abstract. In this paper we show how a cognitive agent programming language can be endowed with ways to program emotions. In particular we show how the programming language 2APL can be augmented so that it can work together with the computational emotion model ALMA to deal with appraisal, emotion/mood generation, and coping.

1 Introduction

A distinguishing feature of an agent is its autonomy, i.e., its ability to decide and to perform actions. This feature requires an agent to have objectives or preferences (desires) regarding the state of its environment (including other agents and itself) and information (beliefs) about the current state of its environment as well as the effect of its actions on the state of the environment. Rational decision theory informs an agent to select those actions that are believed to achieve, or to maximize the chances of attaining, its objectives [3,8,14,25,30]. Although rational decision theory advocates the maximization of goal achievement (i.e. expected utility), the resulting decision behaviour is often not realistic as it does not conform to the practice of actual human behaviour. It is argued that at least part of the discrepancy between the behaviour as prescribed by rational decision theory and that observed in human agents is due to the role of emotions in human decision making [5,9,22,28,29].

That emotions influence the behaviour of humans is immediately clear in the case of distress. When in distress human agents will behave differently and generally take other actions than they would do otherwise. In psychology and cognitive science, a number of emotion theories dealing with several aspects of emotions have been proposed [10,16,19,20,26,27]. These aspects pertain to the appraisal of events, the experience of emotions and to coping with emotions (also called emotion regulation). The goal of emotion regulation is to maintain desirable emotions and to diminish undesirable emotions. Hence emotion regulation has a direct effect on the agent's behaviour.

There are many proposals to model and design artificial agents based on rational decision theory. Examples of such proposals are the Partially Observable Markov Decision Process model (POMDP) [15] and the Belief Desire Intention model (BDI) [21]. POMDP is a quantitative framework that models a sequential decision process in terms of actions, states, transition probabilities, observation probabilities, and a reward function. In contrast, BDI is a qualitative decision

© Springer International Publishing Switzerland 2014
T. Bosse et al. (Eds.): Emotion Modeling, LNAI 8750, pp. 57–75, 2014.
DOI: 10.1007/978-3-319-12973-0_4

model that explains an agent's rational decisions in terms of the agent's information about the current state of the world (Belief), the states the agent wants to achieve (Desire), and its commitments to already-made choices (Intention). The BDI model has proven to be an efficient model for reactive planning and for agents with complex goals interacting with highly dynamic environments (see, e.g., [4]).

In order to build rational software agents, several agent programming languages have been developed [1,2]. These languages, often called BDI-based agent programming languages, provide programming constructs for defining agents in terms of their mental states, actions, events, and plans. The interpreter of those programming languages contains a decision making component that continuously selects and performs actions that best achieve the agent's goals or maximize its preferences. However, we argue that the decision making behaviour of autonomous agents can be made believable by extending their decision making components with an emotion module [7,17,23,31].

This paper proposes to extend the BDI-based agent programming language 2APL [6]. We aim at integrating emotions into the language and its interpreter. This is done by using an existing computational theory of emotions that 1) deals with the above-mentioned aspects of emotions, particularly appraisal and coping, and 2) can be integrated relatively easily in the rule-based architecture of 2APL. Some computational emotion approaches are more suited for this purpose than others. Our aim is to extend 2APL to make it a programming language for agents with emotions, such that we can use it to program, for instance, more believable virtual characters in video games.

2   A Programming Model for Agents with Emotion

In this section we explain BDI-based agent programming languages and computational emotion models in general, and discuss how emotional models can be integrated in BDI-based agent programming languages.

2.1   BDI-Based Agent Programming Languages

To implement autonomous agents a number of dedicated programming languages have been developed [1,2]. The idea is to program (the behaviour of) an agent in terms of cognitive notions such as beliefs, desires, intentions, goals and plans. Typically these are rule-based languages that allow programmers to specify which plans can be followed given a particular mental state of the agent. This is done through the use of Practical Reasoning Rules (PRRs) that associate plans to the agents' states described in terms of beliefs and desires/goals. Programs in these languages are interpreted and executed by means of a so-called deliberation (or sense-reason-act) cycle. Each cycle starts with an agent sensing its environment by processing the incoming events (from the environment) and messages from other agents, and updating the agent's beliefs and goals accordingly. In the reasoning phase, it is determined which practical reasoning rules can be applied by reasoning about the agent's mental state to determine if the preconditions (guards) of the rules are satisfied by the agent's beliefs and goals. Finally, in the last phase of the deliberation process, i.e., the act phase, one or multiple applicable practical reasoning rules are selected and executed.

In the BDI-based programming languages, an agent's beliefs represent what information an agent has about itself, others and the external environment it resides in. In a software model, the beliefs will be stored in a database. This can be implemented in various ways for a specific agent programming model. Note that the beliefs of an agent do not have to be true necessarily; rather, they represent what the agent believes to be true. The desires of an agent represent those states of affairs that the agent wishes to accomplish. In a software model, we use goals to specify the desired state of affairs that the agent wants to pursue. Finally, an agent's intentions consist of desires to which the agent is currently committed i.e., regarding which he has chosen actions to achieve them. In a software model, this means that a plan has been adopted to achieve a goal. It should be noted that BDI-agents can be triggered to act by internal or external events. Internal events can arise when plan failure occurs and the agent has to come up with an alternative plan. External events can be changes in the external environment or messages from other agents.

Basically, the deliberation cycle that constitutes the interpreter of BDI-based agent programming languages consists of the following steps (after initialization).

1. Process (internal and external) events.
2. Update beliefs and goals.
3. Select which plans should be adopted.
4. Update intentions/plans.
5. Execute plans.
6. Drop failed plans and (what the agent believes to be) unachievable goals.

The main idea of BDI-based agent programming languages is that a programmer specifies the initial mental state (i.e., initial beliefs, goals, and intentions) of an agent as well as the actions and plans that the agent can perform. Such a specification constitutes an agent program. The execution of the program is controlled by the deliberation cycle that starts working on the agent's beliefs and goals.

2.2   Emotion Model

It has often been assumed that a human who does not experience emotions would be a purely rational agent, and would therefore make better decisions than actual humans, who experience emotions. However Damasio [5] has shown that humans who cannot experience emotions due to a physical defect of emotion-relevant parts of the brain perform poorly in tests where they have to make decisions. Lacking emotions, they could not decide on which aspect of the test they should focus and make a distinction between what is important and what is not. Emotions thus seem to play an important role in the decision-making process of humans. The quality and effectivity of human decision-making is one reason why we would like to incorporate emotions into virtual agents. Another reason is the desire to make the behavior of agents more human-like and believable.

Various frameworks have been devised to simulate emotion and mood generation. We have reviewed several of these frameworks: EMA [17], Cathexis [31] and ALMA [11]. The way they generate emotions and moods differs, but if we look at these frameworks from a higher point of view we can see several similarities. A first commonality is that a distinction is made in all three models between emotions, moods and personality. Emotions are always caused by (the appraisal of) some event, action or object. They usually only cover a short timespan (seconds to hours). And the evoked emotions can influence the overall emotional state of the individual (mood). Moods are more stable than emotions and they tend to last longer (hours to weeks). Finally a personality is almost unchangeable and influences how emotions and moods are generated e.g., the emotion joy tends to have a greater impact in a person with an extravert personality than in someone with an introvert personality.

Another similarity between the emotion models is the distinction between three sub-processes within the emotion and mood generation process: the appraisal process, the emotion- and mood-generation process, and the coping process. Note however that most emotion models do not cover the last aspect (yet). The appraisal process is concerned with how an agent evaluates and values actions, objects and events. In general, an individual agent can appraise an event as good or bad, an action as right or wrong, and an object as nice or nasty. The valuations/appraisals of the actions, objects or events are internally processed by the agent (and taking into account the agent's mental state) to give rise to an instance of an emotion (e.g. joy, anger, hope). The emotion will then influence the mood of the agent. Finally, based on the generated emotions the agent may stay in, or get into, a desired emotional state by coping in an appropriate way with the current emotions. Hence, coping does not concern just the expression of emotions. Rather, it consists of attempting to come in a desired emotional state through an action that either changes the state of the environment (external action) or the agent's own mental state (mental action).

2.3   Integrating an Emotion Model in Agent Programming Languages

The execution behaviour of BDI-based programs is determined by the deliberation cycle which involves sensing the environment, reasoning to decide on plans, and acting by executing the selected plans. To allow emotions to influence an agent's execution behaviour, emotions need to be integrated into the sense-reason-act phases of the deliberation process. We do this by integrating three emotion processes into the agent's deliberation cycle: appraisal, emotion and mood generation, and coping.

To incorporate the appraisal process, we use emotion rules which specify how an event, object or action will be appraised by an agent. Although emotion rules are usually specific to individual agents, we believe that some emotion rules can be shared by agents. For example, events that inform an agent about the achievement of its desires will be appraised as pleasant/good events.[1] Therefore, we propose to include an additional step in the deliberation cycle that applies emotion rules on the perceived events, objects or actions.

The emotion and mood generation process is incorporated by using an emotion model that can generate emotions and moods based on the appraisal information that is computed by the appraisal process. For this we need a connection between the interpreter of the BDI-based programming language and the used emotion model such that the appraisal information can be passed on to the emotion model. The emotion model in turn generates specific emotions and a mood and passes them on to the interpreter of the agent programming language. This establishes a cyclic connection between the interpreter of the BDI-based agent programming language and the emotion model.

Finally, in order to incorporate a coping process we propose to extend the plans and the plan selection mechanism of the agent programming language. In particular, we propose to enrich the preconditions (guards) of the practical reasoning rules with the current emotions and mood generated by the emotion model such that practical reasoning rules can be applied, not only based on reasoning about the agent's mental state, but also based on the agent's emotion. This allows us to model specific coping strategies for individual agents. In the case of the appraisal process, we believe that certain types of coping strategies can be shared by agents and that such strategies can be provided by means of rule templates. An example would be a rule template that generates escape plans in response to feared events.

3   2APL and ALMA

In this section, we illustrate the integration of an emotion model into BDI agents using the BDI-based agent programming language 2APL (A Practical Agent Programming Language) and the emotion and mood generation model ALMA (A Layered Model of Affect). This can be viewed as a generalization of earlier work [7], in which we expanded the deliberation cycle of a BDI-based programming language with a much more limited emotion model comprising only 4 emotions.

Before explaining 2APL, ALMA and their integration, we would like to stress that we have looked at other frameworks such as EMA and Cathexis. After studying these frameworks we came to the conclusion that ALMA was the best candidate for extending 2APL with emotions. Cathexis is the oldest of the three emotion models and also the most abstract. Cathexis contributes a useful attempt at developing an emotion model, however if one wants to use

---

[1] Of course, events do not carry their desire-fulfilling property in general. An event causes often an update on an agent's beliefs after which it can be evaluated whether the event did in fact contributed to the achievement of the agent's objectives. In this paper, we assume that events do carry their desire-fulfilling property in order to avoid complex belief update and evaluation operations required to program individual agents.

this framework in a language such as 2APL one has to fill in many gaps in the framework; for example one needs to specify which influence different emotions have on each other. EMA is the most advanced emotion model and makes use of different theories and models. It is also the only one of the three models that supports coping with emotions. However, because EMA is so complex it is quite difficult to integrate it with 2APL. ALMA is less advanced than EMA and does not support coping directly, however one can use the emotions generated by ALMA to implement coping strategies. Furthermore, ALMA is based on solid theory and the explanation of the model is clear. We think that ALMA does a fairly good job at simulating emotion and mood generation. A final reason why we have chosen ALMA is the ease of integration with the rule-based approach of 2APL.

3.1 2APL: A Practical Agent Programming Language

2APL was developed (and is still in development) to support programming multi-agent systems which are viewed as consisting of autonomous agents that interact with each other and their environment. An agent is defined in terms of beliefs (represented as a Prolog program), goals (each represented as a conjunction of atoms), intentions (represented as plans consisting of actions), a set of internal actions (belief and goal updates, belief and goal tests) and external actions (e.g., actions to be performed in the surrounding environment, including communication actions), and three sets of practical reasoning rules that generate plans when they are applied. The first type of rules is designed to generate plans for achieving goals (so-called Planning Goal rules, or PG rules), the second to process external events, messages and abstract actions (so-called Procedure Call rules, or PC rules), and the third to repair failed plans (so-called Plan Repair rules, or PR rules). The practical reasoning rules in 2APL have the following general form:

$$\{head\} \leftarrow \{belief\ query\} \mid \{body\}$$

Each practical reasoning rule has a belief query (the expression placed between $\leftarrow$ and |) that specifies the belief state in which the rule can be applied.[2] The exact nature of head and body depends on the type of the rule. PG rules are used to generate plans for achieving specific goals. The following is an example of a PG rule:

$$beHome() \leftarrow hours(X)\ and\ X > 17 \mid \{\pi\}$$

This rule indicates that plan π should be generated and added to the agent's intentions if the agent has the goal $beHome()$ (to be at home) and believes that the current time is later than 17:00 hours.

The second type of practical reasoning rules is the PC rule. The head of a PC rule is an event (either an event received from the environment or a message

---

[2] The sign $\leftarrow$ in the rule should not be read as logical implication. This sign is used in 2APL to separate the head of the rule from its context condition (i.e., belief query), which is in turn separated from the body of the rule by the | sign.

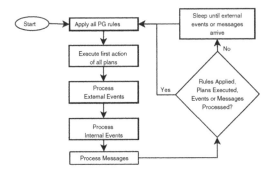

Fig. 1. The 2APL deliberation cycle [6].

received from other agents) and its body consists of a plan. The following is an example of a PC rule.

$$event(rainStarted(), env) \leftarrow noUmbrella \mid \{\pi\}$$

This rule indicates that a plan π should be generated whenever event $rainStarted()$ is received from the environment env and the agent believes it has no umbrella.

The last type of practical reasoning rules is the PR rule. The head and body of this rule type consists of plans. The following rule is an example of PR rule.

$$takeBus; \pi \leftarrow haveMoney \mid \{takeTaxi; \pi\}$$

This rule indicates that whenever a plan starting with the action $takeBus$ (take a bus) fails (the plan fails because the execution of its first action fails) and the agent believes it has enough money, then the agent can repair its plan by replacing the $takeBus$ action with the $takeTaxi$ action (take a taxi).

The execution of 2APL agent programs is performed by the 2APL interpreter which implements the deliberation cycle illustrated in Fig. 1. The deliberation cycle starts by applying applicable PG rules of an agent program to generate plans to achieve the agent's goals. The reasoning cycle continues by executing the generated plans. Then, the received internal and external events and messages are processed by applying PC and PR rules.

3.2 ALMA: A Layered Model of Affect

The ALMA model is based on the EmotionEngine [12,13], which is an implementation of the OCC model of emotion augmented with the Big Five model of personality traits (more about this model later) [12]. According to ALMA, an agent observes the state of its environment (events, actions and objects) and based on its appraisal of these events, actions and objects, and its personality, generates particular emotions. The ALMA model comprises an emotion layer, a mood layer and a personality layer. The corresponding EmotionEngine calculates emotions and moods according to an emotion model proposed by Mehrabian [18].

+P+A+D Exuberant	-P-A-D Bored
+P+A-D Dependent	-P-A+D Disdainful
+P-A+D Relaxed	-P+A-D Anxious
+P-A-D Docile	-P+A+D Hostile

Fig. 2. The eight moods in the PAD-space [11].

In this model, emotions are described by their value in three bipolar dimensions Pleasure/Displeasure (P), Arousal/Sleep (A) and Dominance/Submission (D), each of which has a value that ranges from -1.0 to 1.0. The pleasure dimension determines the level of pleasure of an emotion, the arousal dimension determines the intensity of an emotion, and the dimension of dominance determines the control and dominance aspect of an emotion. Moods are computed by taking the average of multiple emotions over time. As a consequence, moods change less often (and are thus more stable) than emotions. The three dimensions define a three-dimensional space, the PAD-space, that can be divided into 8 octants, each corresponding to a mood with a specific name. This PAD model of moods, which is illustrated in Fig. 2, is closely related to the emotion intensity model as proposed by Reisenzein [24].

For example, when all three dimension values are negative, the mood is called bored. How bored an agent exactly is depends on the specific P, A and D values. Based on the following observations, three levels of intensity of a mood are distinguished. Each axis of the PAD-space has a length of 2 (-1.0 to 1.0). We can thus picture this space as a cube with enveloping planes of size 2 by 2 (see Fig. 3). The distance from the center is maximally $\sqrt{3}$. This distance is divided up into three equal parts. The first part represents a low intensity of the mood, the second part a moderate intensity and the last part a high intensity. Hence the octant in the PAD-space describes the mood the individual is in, and the exact point in PAD-space describes the intensity of the current mood. In the EmotionEngine there exist 24 different emotions. Figure 3 shows a graphical representation of an individual's PAD-space at a given time. The highlighted octant shows the current discrete mood and the big (green) sphere represents the current mood including its intensity. The smaller (red) spheres show the currently active emotions. Note that ALMA does cover appraisal of emotion and mood generation, but it does not cover coping.

It is possible to map all emotions into the PAD-space. According to the mapping, partially devised by Gebhard [11] (fragment of this mapping is shown in Fig. 4), emotions are representing points in a PAD-space.

When an agent is initiated it is assigned an initial (default) mood. We allow that different agents can have different initial (default) moods. To compute the default mood of an agent, we use the agent's personality, which is defined according to the Big Five model [18]. This model assumes that the personality of agents can be described by five factors or dimensions: extraversion, agreeableness, openness, neuroticism and conscientiousness. Personalities can be mapped into PAD-space as shown in Fig. 5. The Big Five factors are mapped to PAD values, which describe the default mood of the agent.

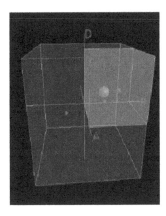

Fig. 3. A graphical representation of the PAD-space [11] (Color figure online).

Emotion	P	A	D	Mood octant
Admiration	0.5	0.3	-0.2	+P+A-D Dependent
Anger	-0.51	0.59	0.25	-P+A+D Hostile
Joy	0.4	0.2	0.1	+P+A+D Exuberant

Fig. 4. A fragment of the mapping from emotions to PAD values devised by Gebhard et al. [13].

$$Pleasure := 0.21 * Extraversion + 0.59 * Agreeableness + 0.19 * Neuroticism$$
$$Arousal := 0.15 * Openness + 0.30 * Agreeableness - 0.57 * Neuroticism$$
$$Dominance := 0.25 * Openness + 0.17 * Conscientiousness + 0.60 * Extraversion -$$
$$32 * Agreeableness$$

Fig. 5. The mapping from a personality in the Big Five model to a PAD-value [11].

In ALMA an AffectML (variation on XML) document must be specified for each agent. This document contains global computational parameters of the agent model, and a personality profile. The personality profile of an agent contains a tag that describes the agent's personality in terms of the five factors of the Big Five model, plus tags that describe so-called "appraisal rules". These rules describe how an agent appraises its environment, i.e., how it appraises actions, objects and events including emotion displays and mood displays. Emotion and mood displays are the visual aspects of emotions and moods respectively; for example, a tear can be part of an emotion display for the emotion sadness. In general, appraisal rules consist of a matching part and an action body. The matching part can describe an action, object or event (including emotion display or mood display). It is compared to input from ALMA scripts (note that ALMA works with scripts, whereas 2APL uses programs). When an event, action, object, emotion or mood display occurs in the script that matches the matching part of an appraisal rule, the action body of that rule is executed. The action body can be one or multiple "appraisal tags", or Emotion Eliciting Conditions (EECs). EECs are entities that cause emotions to be generated according to the OCC model [13] (on which the EmotionEngine is based). Following OCC, the EECs used in ALMA are Praiseworthiness (of actions), Desirability (of events), Appealingness (of objects) and Liking (of a person) (abbreviated PDA(L), not to be confused with the PAD-space). Note that appraisal tags are just abbreviations of EECs. EECs are direct inputs to the EmotionEngine, whereas appraisal tags have to be converted to EECs before they can be used as input for the EmotionEngine, e.g., the appraisal tag goodEvent will be converted to the EEC Desirability: 0.7. In the current implementation of the model, the emotions (intensities) and mood (intensity) (also called the affective profile) are updated every 500 ms. Hence, based on an agent's personality profile (personality description and appraisal rules), events, objects, actions, emotion and mood displays are first assigned to appraisal tags. These appraisal tags are then converted to EECs, which are the input of the EmotionEngine. The EmotionEngine will then generate new emotions (and update the intensities of already existing emotions) and, based on the emotions, it will update the mood of the agent. Emotions are represented by a point in PAD-space. Along with this point also comes an intensity of the emotion that decays over time determined by an emotion decay function.

We conclude our description of ALMA by explaining the phenomenon of mood change. The mood of an agent can change over time. To model such mood-changes we use emotions as the mood changing factor. The agent's mood can change as the result of observing events, actions or objects that elicit emotions which decay over a specified time. Currently active emotions are mapped into a corresponding point in PAD-space, after which the average of all these emotion points is taken. This results in another point in PAD-space that represents a "virtual" center of the agent's current emotions. This point is used to update the current mood using a push and pull mood change function (see Fig. 6). If the current mood is in between the virtual emotion center and the center of the PAD-space, the current mood of the agent is pulled towards the virtual emotion center (pull phase). In contrast, if the current mood is at or beyond the virtual emotion center, the current mood of the agent is pushed further into the current mood-octant (push phase). This push process may at first seem counterintuitive, but it represents the empirical fact that experiences of emotions that are consistent with an individual's current mood increases the intensity of that mood. The higher the intensity of the virtual emotion center, the stronger is its influence on the agent's current mood. Note that although the agent's mood is influenced by its emotions, the mood changes more slowly than the emotions themselves. We would like to emphasize that Fig. 6 visualizes both pull and push phases. This illustration shows that the current mood will be attracted to the virtual emotion center when the current mood is between the PAD-space center and the virtual emotion center. Once the current mood is at the same position as the virtual emotion center, then the current mood will be pushed away from the virtual emotion center further into the PAD-space.

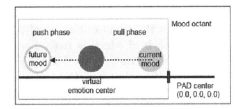

Fig. 6. The push and pull mood change function [11].

Fig. 7. The connection between 2APL and ALMA

3.3   Integration of 2APL and ALMA

As we want to integrate emotions into 2APL we need to add a database in which we can store appraisal data. This is done in a so-called emotion base. The emotion base stores the current mood of the agent (in the form of a PAD value) and the dominant emotion (the emotion with the highest intensity). The emotion base sends the agent ID and a description of the emotion elicitors (events, actions or objects) together with the corresponding appraisal tags to the AffectEngine component. This component is not a part of the ALMA framework; it is just an interface (class/entry-point) we have implemented to connect 2APL to ALMA. The AffectEngine component converts the received appraisal tag to EECs, which are direct inputs to the AffectManager component. In this component, which is an integral part of the ALMA framework [11], the EECs produce specific emotions according to the OCC model which are then converted to PAD values. The PAD values subsequently change the agent's mood by means of the push and pull mood change function (Fig. 6). The output of the AffectManager component is thus a new mood (PAD-value) together with updated emotion intensities. This output is passed back to the AffectEngine component, which determines which emotion is generated by which elicitor. Next, the mood and the elicitor-emotion mapping is passed back to the emotion base of 2APL. The emotion base will then update the current mood, the dominant emotion and so-called coping data (more about the coping data later, for now it is sufficient to know that this is a mapping from elicitor to emotion). We thus get a cycle as shown in Fig. 7. It should be noted that ALMA consists of other components, such as the EmotionEngine, which we have not illustrated in this figure. In the next subsections we focus on appraisal and coping.

Appraisal. In the running applications of ALMA, scripts are used to generate the appraisal input to be fed into the EmotionEngine of ALMA. These scripts contain utterances from agents each of which is tagged with an appraisal tag. The appraisal tags are actually abbreviations for PDA(L) values. That is each appraisal tag is mapped to a PDA(L)-value, e.g., the appraisal tag Good Event is mapped to the PDA(L) values $\langle P = +0.0 , A = +0.0 , D = +0.7 L = +0.0 \rangle$. For the integration of ALMA and 2APL, we do not use scripts to generate appraisal inputs. Instead 2APL programs are used to generate the appraisal input. Below we will explain in detail how and when appraisal data can be generated in a 2APL program.

From the point of view of a 2APL agent, several different emotion-elicitors can arise during its execution. For example, external events can be broadcasted by the environment, external actions can be performed by the agent itself or by other agents, messages can be sent or received, and internal events can be generated in the agents. It is already possible in 2APL to have the agent react to an external events using PC rules as explained before. What we want to achieve now however is not to have the agent execute a plan when the event is perceived, but to generate appraisal input based on the received events. To make this possible, we introduce so-called E-rules into 2APL. Actually, the term 'appraisal rules' would be a better name for this kind of rules, but we do not use this term to avoid confusion with this term as used in ALMA. Let us assume that an agent does not like rain, and hence would appraise events informing it that it is raining as a bad event. To implement this event appraisal in 2APL, we would use the following E-rule:

$$externalEvent : event(rainStarted(), env) => badEvent(1.0)$$

This rule specifies that if the agent receives the event $rainStarted()$ from the environment env, then the appraisal input $badEvent(1.0)$ is generated and passed on to ALMA to be processed further. ALMA then generates an emotion based on the appraisal input, which in turn influences the agent's mood. The number after the appraisal tag (1.0) represents the intensity of the appraisal which can vary from 0.0 to 1.0. The higher (lower) this number, the greater (smaller) the influence of this tag on the mood of the agent will be. In addition to external events, the agent can also appraise other emotion-elicitors. In order to cover all of the possible emotion elicitors, we propose the following types of E-rules.

1. external event E-rules
2. internal event E-rules
3. goal E-rules
4. belief E-rules

External event E-rules can appraise all external events (including messages from other agents). Internal event E-rules can appraise all internal events (plan failures). Goal E-rules can appraise goals and belief E-rules can appraise beliefs. To clarify the E-rules, we will give an example for each type of E-rule.

1. $externalEvent : event(rainStarted(), env) => badEvent(1.0)$
2. $internalEvent : @env(east(), \_); REST => badEvent(0.4)$
3. $goal : reachHome => goodEvent(0.8)$
4. $belief : racesWon(X) \ and \ X > 1 => goodEvent(0.5)$

The first rule appraises the external event rainStarted() as a bad event with intensity 1.0. The second rule appraises the internal event $@env(east(), \_); REST$ as a bad event with intensity 0.4. This event indicates that the action $@env(east(), \_)$ is not successfully executed. It should be noted that the plan expression $@env(east(), \_); REST$ denotes any plan that starts with the external action $@env(east(), \_)$ (i.e., going one step to the east in environment env). In this plan expression, $REST$ is a plan variable that can be instantiated with any (sub)plan. Rule 3 appraises the goal $reachHome$ as a good event with intensity 0.8. If the goal $reachHome$ is added to the goal base, an appraisal tag of $goodEvent(0.8)$ will be passed to the EmotionEngine of ALMA. As long as the goal $reachHome$ stays in the goal base, the appraisal tag $goodEvent(0.8)$ is generated and passed on to ALMA at each deliberation cycle. The fourth rule appraises the belief $racesWon(X) \ and \ X > 1$ as a good event with intensity 0.5. This rule indicates that believing to have won a race is considered as a good event. As long as the agent believes this, at each deliberation cycle an appraisal tag $goodEvent(0.5)$ is produced and passed on to ALMA. These four kinds of E-rules are sufficient to appraise all the possible internal and external events, goals and beliefs. For example, let us assume that an agent does not like rain except when it is hot outside, in which case he likes to cool down a bit. Another assumption we make is that the agent keeps track of the current temperature $Celsius(X)$ in the belief base (where X represents the current temperature in degrees Celsius). The E-rule in question can be modelled as follows: the external event $rainStarted()$ is appraised as $badEvent(1.0)$ if it is colder than 15 degrees Celsius and as a $goodEvent(1.0)$ if it is warmer than 30 degrees Celsius. This situation can be implemented using the following two E-rules.

$externalEvent : (rainStarted(), env) \ | \ B(Celsius(X))\&B(X < 15) => badEvent(1.0)$
$externalEvent : (rainStarted(), env) \ | \ B(Celsius(X))\&B(X > 30) => goodEvent(1.0)$

The first rule applies to the case where it is colder than 15 degrees Celsius, whereas the second rule applies to the case where it is warmer than 30 degrees Celsius.

We can also model cases where a combination of beliefs and goals are relied on to appraise an external event. Let us assume that an agent wants to reach some target at point (X, Y). In 2APL, this can be the case when the goal query $G(reach(X, Y))$ can be performed successfully. When another agent places an obstacle $stone(A, B)$ between the agent's current position (e.g., $pos(C, D)$) and the target position (e.g., $target(X, Y)$) then the agent appraises this as $badActOther(1.0)$. In the situation that is described above, we could use the following E-rule:

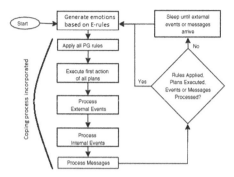

Fig. 8. The extended deliberation cycle of 2APL.

$$externalEvent : (stone(A, B), env) \mid B(pos(C, D)) \ \& \ G(reach(X, Y))$$
$$\& \ B(A >= C)$$
$$\& \ B(A <= X)$$
$$\& \ B(B >= D)$$
$$\& \ B(B <= Y) => badActOther(1.0)$$

All the E-rules for an agent are stored in a so-called E-rule base, which exist inside the agent next to the already existing belief base, goal base, plan base and emotion base.

Coping. Now that we have explained how appraisal, emotion and mood generation are integrated into 2APL we will describe how we have implemented a coping mechanism in 2APL, i.e., how the agent copes with emotions and thus how emotions influence the behavior of the agent. As can be seen in Fig. 8, the coping process is an overarching process over multiple deliberation steps. The coping strategies selected by the agent are determined by the agent's emotions rather than by its mood. Because emotions are triggered by some event, agent or object, the coping strategies are always specified with respect to an emotion and the corresponding eliciting event, agent or object.

The first step of this extended deliberation cycle is "Generate emotions based on E-rules". In this step, all external and internal events, goals and beliefs are appraised according to the agent's E-rules (see the previous subsection for an explanation of E-rules). Based on this appraisal, emotions are generated in the ALMA EmotionEngine. Each emotion will be associated with some event, goal or belief. This mapping between elicitor and emotion is stored and can hence be used in the next deliberation steps. We call this mapping the coping data. Note again that the generated emotions influence the overall mood of the agent, but we do not use the mood for deciding on the coping strategy; we only use the coping data to decide which actions should be decided and performed. To clarify the proposed extended deliberation cycle of 2APL, we give a simple example. Recall the example used in the previous subsection:

$$externalEvent : event(rainStarted(), env) => badEvent(1.0)$$

As mentioned before, this E-rule states that if the external event $rainStarted()$ is received by the agent from environment env, it is appraised as a bad event with intensity 1.0. This appraisal tag is converted to EECs and passed on to the ALMA EmotionEngine, which generates an emotion based on this tag (distress in this case). The emotion is then passed back to 2APL and is stored as the following mapping.

$$< event(rainStarted(), env) \rightarrow distress >$$

We now have a record of the connection between the eliciting event and the emotion it has caused within the agent. This record is the current coping data. When the agent arrives at the deliberation step "Process External Events", it can use this data. In the remainder of this paper, we assume that the agent has an introvert personality (the personality of an agent is specified in an xml-file that has to be supplied for each agent in the multi-agent system). Assume that the agent also has the following PC-rules:

1. $event(rainStarted(), env)::introvert, joy \leftarrow true \mid$
     $print(\text{``rain started, which caused joy''}); \pi$
2. $event(rainStarted(), env)::introvert, distress \leftarrow true \mid$
     $print(\text{``rain started, which caused distress''}); \pi'$
3. $event(rainStarted(), env) \leftarrow true \mid$
     $print(\text{``rain started, no emotion generated for this event''}); \pi''$

In 2APL we need to make five checks to decide if a rule is applicable. The first step is to check if the head unifies with the event. After that, it is checked whether the personality specified in the rule matches the personality of the agent. In addition, the emotion specified in the rule (which is optional) is checked against the stored coping data. This requires searching the head of the rule in the coping data. When the rule head is found, the corresponding emotion is retrieved. If this emotion matches the emotion specified in the PC-rule, the preconditions of the rule have to be evaluated (against the belief base) and if this evaluates to true, the rule is applied.

It is possible that multiple PC-rules are applicable to an event. In this case, only the first applicable rule is applied in each deliberation cycle (Programmers should keep in mind that the rules are checked from top to bottom in 2APL). As readers may have noticed, we have not discussed explicit coping strategies yet. We have described a mechanism that adjusts the behavior of the agent according to its personality and emotions with respect to events, goals and beliefs. The next step is to construct templates ($*.2apl$ files) in which coping strategies are described. In these templates one can specify for example, that if an agent is sad about a certain internal event (e.g., a plan failure), then a particular repair action should be performed before the agent tries to execute the failed plan anew. The 2APL programmer can use the existing templates as guidance, however one can also decide to devise templates describing other coping strategies.

4 A Simple Demo

To demonstrate the new functionalities of "emotion-enhanced" 2APL, we have developed a demo application. In this application two agents operate in a grid world: agent 1 and agent 2 (Fig. 9). Each agent represents a robot. In the grid one can place a target which will initiate a race between the two agents towards the target position. Using E-rules we specified that agents appraise losing a race as a bad event and winning a race as a good event. In the grid one can also place red and blue oil barrels. Again using E-rules, we specified that agent 1 thinks red barrels are nice and blue barrels are nasty, and for agent 2 vice versa. Coping behavior can be modelled by specifying that if an agent comes across an oil barrel that he appraises as nice (which will lead to an emotion of liking) it will consume it and when it appraises a barrel as nasty (leads to disliking), it will leave the barrel where it stands. In this demo application the agents can also become angry and take revenge on the opponent by trying to delay it by placing objects between the opponent and the target.

During the run of the demo, when certain events happen (winning/losing a race), objects are spotted (red or blue oil barrels) and actions are executed (opponent trying to obstruct the agent) these elicitors are appraised in certain ways by E-rules. Based on these appraisals, emotions are generated. On the right side of the graphical user interface (Fig. 9) one can see the five emotions that have the highest intensity and the dominant emotion (the emotion with the highest intensity) is also represented by an emoticon. This way one can verify that the various events elicit the correct emotions. One can also see which influence the emotions will have on the mood in the long term. Because the emotion and mood generation process is executed by ALMA we only need to verify that the emotion and mood data is correctly passed on from ALMA to 2APL.

As explained earlier (Sect. 3), the coping mechanism is an extra check on the current personality and dominant emotion of an agent during the application of PG, PC and PR-rules. To verify that this works correctly, we have to examine the currently dominant emotion and personality of the agents and check whether

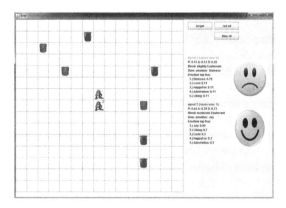

Fig. 9. The graphical user interface of the demo application.

they display the expected (coping) behavior. For example, if the agent has a dominant emotion of disliking with respect to an oil barrel then he leaves it where it is. Another example is one where an agent is obstructed by its opponent. This generates an emotion of reproach, which inclines the agent to take revenge and try to obstruct his opponent too. In contrast, if the agent reacted with admiration to the same action of its opponent (blocking him), then he would not take revenge.

5 Conclusion

In this paper we have described how we can enrich a cognitive agent programming language with emotions. In particular, we showed how 2APL agents can be endowed with emotions by incorporating the ALMA emotion system into 2APL. In order to do this we have modified 2APL slightly. In particular, the practical reasoning rules of 2APL are modified in order to allow the incorporation of emotions as mental states in the preconditions of the rules. Although we have done this for the language 2APL, we would like to stress that this work can easily be generalized to other agent programming languages, as long as they are rule-based. For future work we plan to use the described version of 2APL for applications such as programming virtual characters in video games, and evaluate this use. In summary, we have augmented the BDI-based programming language 2APL with E-rules (for appraisal), which are fed to ALMA, returning emotions that next can be used by (augmented) PG/PC/PR rules to implement certain coping strategies.

We stress that we did not devise a new computational model for emotions; rather we provided a programming language in which the programmer may devise agents with capabilities to make appraisals, generate emotions and moods, and perform coping. To this end we have equipped the language 2APL with general tools such as E-rules and (augmented) PG/PC/PR rules. The augmented rules can be used to predispose an agent to particular classes of strategies when certain emotions are generated. It is up to the programmer to use these tools to program particular appraisal and coping strategies by configuring/instantiate the abstract affect model provided by the language. Of course, it may be useful for certain applications (such as programming virtual characters in video games) to have certain preset strategies available. This gives rise to the idea of a library of templates, which we will investigate in the future.

Acknowledgment. We thank Rainer Reisenzein (University of Greifswald) for his extensive comments on the draft version of this paper.

References

1. Bordini, R.H., Dastani, M.M., Dix, J., El Fallah Seghrouchni, A. (eds.) Multi-Agent Programming: Languages, Platforms and Applications. International book series on Multiagent Systems, Artificial Societies, and Simulated Organizations, edited by Weiss, G. Springer, New York (2005)

2. Bordini, R.H., Dastani, M.M., Dix, J., El Fallah Seghrouchni, A.: Multi-Agent Programming: Languages, Tools and Applications. Springer, New York (2009)
3. Boutilier, C.: Towards a logic for qualitative decision theory. In: Proceedings of the Fourth International Conference on Knowledge Representation and Reasoning (KR'94), pp. 75–86. Morgan Kaufmann (1994)
4. Bratman, M.E., Israel, D.J., Pollack, M.E.: Plans and resource-bounded practical reasoning. Comput. Intell. **4**, 349–355 (1988)
5. Damasio, A.R.: Descartes' Error: Emotion, Reason and the Human Brain. Grosset/Putnam Press, New York (1994)
6. Dastani, M.M.: 2APL: a practical agent programming language. Int. J. Auton. Agents Multi-Agent Syst. (JAAMAS) **16**(3), 214–248 (2008). (Special Issue on Computational Logic-based Agents, (eds.) Francesca Toni and Jamal Bentahar, 2008)
7. Dastani, M.M., Meyer, J.-J.C.: Programming emotional agents. Int. J. Intell. Syst. **25**(7), 636–654 (2010)
8. Dastani, M.M., Hulstijn, J., van der Torre, L.: How to decide what to do? Eur. J. Oper. Res. **160**(3), 762–784 (2005)
9. Elster, J.: Rationality and the emotions. Econ. J. **106**(438), 1386–1397 (2004)
10. Frijda, N.H.: The Emotions. Cambridge University Press, Studies in Emotion and Social Interaction (1987)
11. Gebhard, P.: ALMA - A layered model of affect. In: Proceedings of the Fourth International Joint Conference on Autonomous Agents and Multiagent Systems 2005, pp. 29–36 (2005)
12. Gebhard, P., Kipp, M., Klesen, M., Rist, T.: Adding the emotional dimension to scripting character dialogues. In: Proceedings of the 4th International Working Conference on Intelligent Virtual Agents, pp. 48–56 (2003)
13. Gebhard, P., Klesen, M., Rist, T.: Coloring multi-character conversations through the expression of emotions. In: Proceedings of the Tutorial and Research Workshop on Affective Dialogue Systems (2004)
14. Jeffrey, R.C.: The Logic of Decision. McGraw-Hill, New York (1965)
15. Kaelbling, L.P., Littman, M.L., Cassandra, A.R.: Planning and acting in partially observable stochastic domains. Artif. Intell. J. **101**, 99–134 (1998)
16. Lazarus, R.S.: Emotion and Adaptation. Oxford University Press, New York (1994)
17. Marsella, S., Gratch, J.: EMA: A computational model of appraisal dynamics. J. Cogn. Syst. Res. **10**(1), 7090 (2009)
18. Mehrabian, A.: Analysis of the big-five personality factors in terms of the PAD temperament model. Aust. J. Psychol. **48**, 86–92 (1996)
19. Oatley, K., Jenkins, J.M.: Understanding Emotions. Blackwell Publishing, Oxford (1996)
20. Ortony, A., Clore, G.L., Collins, A.: The Cognitive Structure of Emotions. Cambridge University Press, Cambridge (1988)
21. Rao, A.S., Georgeff, M.P.: Decision procedures for BDI logics. J. Logic Comput. **8**(3), 293–342 (1998)
22. Reisenzein, R., Hudlicka, E., Dastani, M., Gratch, J., Hindriks, K.V., Lorini, E., Meyer, J.-J.C.: Computational modeling of emotion: Toward improving the inter- and intradisciplinary exchange. T. Affect. Comput. **4**(3), 246–266 (2013)
23. Reisenzein, R., Junge, M.: Language and emotion from the perspective of the computational belief-desire theory of emotion. In: Wilson, P.A. (ed.) Dynamicity in Emotion Concepts, vol. 27, pp. 37–59. Peter Lang, Frankfurt am Main (2012)
24. Reisenzein, R.: Pleasure-arousal theory and the intensity of emotions. J. Pers. Soc. Psychol. **67**(3), 525–539 (1994)

25. Savage, L.J.: The Foundations of Statistics. Wiley, New York (1954)
26. Klaus, R.: Scherer Facets of Emotion: Recent Research. Erlbaum, Hillsdale (1988)
27. Scherer, K.R., Schorr, A., Johnstone, T.: Appraisal Processes in Emotion: Theory, Methods, Research. Series in Affective Science. Oxford University Press, New York (2001)
28. Johns, M., Silverman, B.G.: How emotion and personality effect the utility of alternative decisions: A terrorist target selection case study. In: 10th Conference On Computer Generated Forces and Behavioral Representation, SISO (2001)
29. de Sousa, R.: The Rationality of Emotion. MIT Press, Cambridge (1987)
30. Tan, S.-W., Pearl, J.: Qualitative decision theory. In: Proceedings of the Thirteenth National Conference on Artificial Intelligence (AAAI'94), pp. 928–933. AAAI Press, Seattle (1994)
31. Velásquez, J.D.: Cathexis: A computational model for the generation of emotions and their influence in the behavior of autonomous agents. In: Proceedings of the First International Conference on Autonomous Agents (AGENTS'97), pp. 518–519 (1997)

Utilizing Emotions in Autonomous Robots: An Enactive Approach

Robert Lowe$^{(\boxtimes)}$ and Kiril Kiryazov

Interaction Lab, University of Skövde, Skövde, Sweden
robert.lowe@his.se

Abstract. In this chapter, we present a minimalist approach to utilizing the computational principles of affective processes and emotions for autonomous robotics applications. The focus of this paper is on the presentation of this framework in reference to *preservation* of agent autonomy across levels of cognitive-affective competences. This approach views autonomy in reference to (i) embodied (e.g. homeostatic), and (ii) dynamic (e.g. neural-dynamic) processes, required to render *adaptive* such cognitive-affective competences. We hereby focus on bridging bottom-up (standard autonomous robotics) and top-down (psychology-based dimensional theoretic) modelling approaches. Our *enactive* approach we characterize according to *bi-directional grounding* (interdependent bottom-up and top-down regulation). As such, from an emotions theory perspective, 'enaction' is best understood as an embodied and dynamic appraisal perspective. We attempt to clarify our approach with relevant case studies and comparison to other existing approaches in the modelling literature.

Keywords: Homeostasis · Autonomy preservation · Allostasis · Neural-dynamics

1 Introduction

Much research in affective computing, and its application to physical systems, has centred on the cognitive aspects. So-called 'appraisal theory' has been in evidence since the 1960s whereby emotions, from appraisal pioneer [1] onwards, have typically been considered hot action responses triggered by, and independent from, cold cognitive judgments of the significance of stimuli to the well-being of the organism. Insofar as biological affective mechanisms are engendered by appraisal processes, however, they are so in the context of being imbedded within autonomous and physically embodied agents operating in a dynamic world.

This chapter centres on a modeling approach that enables robotic agents to utilize emotions adaptively independent of, or in interaction with, others (robots and humans), and de-emphasizes the role of (strong) cognitive appraisal. The central argument of this chapter is that adaptive robotic agents with human-like cognitive-affective capacities, must per force be imbued with autonomous capabilities. There are at least three areas in which implementations of adaptive cognitive-affective processes can enhance robotic performance in human environments [2]: (i) improved human-interactor experience, (ii) facilitated competence, e.g. in joint human-robot tasks, (iii) safety - in relation to

© Springer International Publishing Switzerland 2014
T. Bosse et al. (Eds.): Emotion Modeling, LNAI 8750, pp. 76–98, 2014.
DOI: 10.1007/978-3-319-12973-0_5

robot-environment 'awareness'. For such emotions to be adaptive, however, robots need to be imbued with some measure of autonomy.

Autonomous capabilities entail agents acting in the world (real or simulated) in ways that have not been explicitly pre-designed. Such capabilities, in order for agents to be adaptive in the world, require 'grounding' – having hierarchically 'higher' levels of sensorimotor organization built on (nested within) 'lower' levels and having the higher levels simultaneously modulate (parameterize) the lower levels on which they are built, in such a way that sustainable patterns of sensorimotor activity ensue. This 'bi-directional' grounding for imbuing robots with autonomy occurs with respect to the embodied and dynamic aspects of the agent's environmental interaction.

Whether they are considered discrete or dimensional, emotions are 'embodied' phenomena. In recent years, emotion theory has evolved to acknowledge the role of the body in appraisal as a form of affective computing. The embodied agent does not play a merely passive role in affective computing – its bodily activity is not simply the output triggered by a 'feed-forward' cognitive appraisal. Rather, the body itself, in interaction with its external environment, influences how real, or imagined, environmental stimuli are perceived and acted upon. The body *behaviourally* orients and acts, and *internally* physiologically 'prepares' in relation to its external environment. Affective processing and 'computation' is, from this perspective, a phenomenon for which brain, body and physical environment are inextricably entangled. The view of the role of the body being central to emotion underlies embodied appraisal theory [3]: neural patterns reflective of changes in the internal milieu and skeletomusculature of biological organisms serve as embodied appraisals (perceptions and feelings). These appraisals track the relevance of an external stimulus to the well-being of the organism thereby establishing organism-environment relations.

Emotions are also dynamic phenomena – they manifest over time windows integrating 'internal' and 'behavioural' information in relation to external events. Scherer's [4] component process model de-emphasizes pre-bodily cognitive appraisal and rather highlights mental and bodily inseparability the *interactive dynamic* from which constitutes the emotion as it unfolds over time. Lewis [5] reduces the primary cognitive status of appraisal further by dividing appraisal and emotion into cognitive and physiological elements whose dynamic inter-dependencies give rise to neurophysiologically stable states that provide the condition on which phenomena such as attention and learning can be achieved. Affective phenomena, in this view, are emergent and distributed and have dynamic properties upon which higher order cognitive capabilities can be constructed.

In the remainder of this chapter, we discuss our own embodied and dynamic appraisal perspective. Our motivation is imbuing cognitive-affective processes in autonomous robots. We view the preservation of autonomy as fundamental to agent adaptivity and that this in turn requires *bidirectional grounding* – a dynamic process which entails the integration of internal (physiological activity preparatory to action) and behavioural (including proprioceptive) activity with respect to competences fundamental to autonomous, but also from the human perspective 'useful', robots.

In Sect. 2, we describe more precisely our perspective on bidirectional grounding and present a schema from which adaptive affective activity can be realized. We consider our approach to fit within the scope of enactive cognition [6, 7] – that cognitive-affective (constitutive) and internal-behavioural processes are inextricably linked. We also compare our approach to existing views. In Sect. 3, we summarize the findings of investigations concerning simulated and actual robots that are compatible with the perspective provided. Finally, Sect. 4 provides concluding comments.

2   Autonomous Affective Robots: Embodied, Dynamic Appraisal

If virtual or robotic agents, in expressing and utilizing emotional and affective processes, are to interact in an adaptable, believable and safe way with their physical and social environment, a degree of autonomous control is fundamental. While biological agents are constrained genetically and artificial agents are constrained by design (to achieve some end that suits the designer's aims), biological and artificial agents alike must have some freedom of control to act and adapt in an ever-changing and unpredictable world. They must not be 'over-designed'.

McFarland and Spier [8] suggested autonomous embodied dynamics, in the form of homeostatic cycles of activity, enables agents to persist in the world. Homeostasis as a biological phenomenon is typically conceived as a regulatory process that ensures that bodily variables essential to the constitution of the agent (e.g. blood glucose, blood water levels) are neither too high nor too low. McFarland and Spier, in the context of robotic agents, consider homeostasis not just *constitutively*, but *behaviourally*, the activity of both being fundamental to adaptive behaviour. Adaptive agents are required to homeostatically cycle among multiple behaviours in order to satisfy constitutive (e.g. essential variables) and designer-based (e.g. multiple goal requirements) needs. In this sense *embodied activity* is an inextricably constitutive and behavioural phenomenon linked to the very survival of the agent. Enduring cycles of behavioural activity demonstrate that agents are in equilibrium with their environment (behaviourally stable – [9]) and in this sense adapted to it. A conceptual and practical difficulty for designers of autonomous agents in how to preserve autonomy when incorporating multiple designer-specified competences. McFarland [10] has suggested the need to account for multiple levels of robot autonomy:

> "Autonomy implies freedom from outside control. There are three main types of freedom relevant to robots. One is freedom from outside the control of energy supply. Most current robots run on batteries that must be replaced or recharged by people. Self-fuelling robots would have *energy autonomy* [our italics]. Another is freedom of choice of activity. An automaton lacks such freedom, because either it follows a strict routine or it is entirely reactive. A robot that has alternative possible activities, and the freedom to decide which to do, has *motivational autonomy* [our italics]. Thirdly, there is freedom of thought. A robot that has the freedom to think up better ways of doing things may be said to have *mental autonomy* [our italics]" [10, p. 15].

These three levels of autonomy correspond to three respective competences in 'useful' robotic agents: (i) managing energy levels, (ii) managing multiple goal requirements, (iii) planning and constructing behaviour sequences according to context.

Damasio [11–13] in his embodied perspective of emotion, also emphasizes the role of homeostasis but in this case as a grounding principle for a hierarchy of affective (constitutive) processes. At the highest level, for Damasio, emotional feelings simulate bodily (internal milieu) changes in relation to expression of skeletomuscular systems and external stimuli. Figure 1, provides an illustration of his nesting principle as it spans four levels of homeostatically regulated neurophysiological activity ranging from basal metabolic activity to drives, motivations and emotions ('proper').

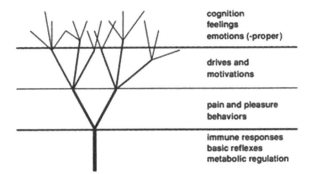

cognition
feelings
emotions (-proper)

drives and
motivations

pain and pleasure
behaviors

immune responses
basic reflexes
metabolic regulation

Fig. 1. Illustration of Damasio's homeostatic grounding principle (adapted from [12]).

Both McFarland and Damasio, thus view levels of cognitive-affective competences as being tied to a form of embodiment that emphasizes homeostatic regulation.

2.1 An Enactive Approach

To summarize our objectives, we posit that in order for affective (robotic) agents to interact in the physical and social environment in an adaptive, believable and safe manner, they need autonomous capabilities. In order for this autonomy to be preserved in relation to levels of cognitive-affective processing such agents are required to have these levels: (i) *bottom-up* built upon and nested within lower constitutive levels, (ii) *top-down* modulate (parameterize) lower levels across a temporal goal-directed (emotion) episode. This *bi-directional grounding* approach is characteristic of the enactive approach that will be further discussed in this section.

A critical aspect of the enactive approach we hold to is the notion of constitutive and behavioural homeostasis as referred to at the start of Sect. 2. Following the two above-mentioned homeostasis-centred perspectives on autonomy and affect, respectively, we have developed a schema that illustrates a conceptual link between McFarland's view of behavioural and constitutive homeostasis in relation to autonomy, and Damasio's view of homeostasis in relation to grounding emotions and emotional feelings. Figure 2 depicts the *enactive cognitive-affective schema* which provides a template for producing a multiply-competent autonomous robotic agent. This provides an adaptation of an approach put forward in [14–16]. It is important to emphasize that this schema is *not* a particular instantiation of an architecture. It is, in fact, absolutely essential to the approach that the schema is not over-interpreted or over-detailed as this is counter to the grounding process. This process emphasizes using minimal constraints to enable the emergence, e.g. using evolutionary algorithmic, or neural-dynamic, approaches, of embodied activity suited to the particular environmental dynamics and task demands of the agent.

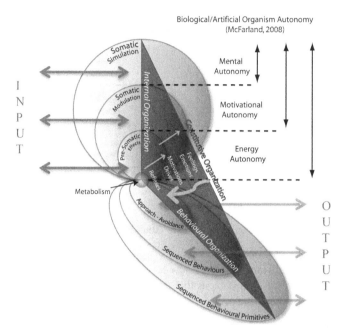

Fig. 2. The enactive cognitive-affective schema (see [14–16]). The constitutive organization dimension implements the nested homeostatic hierarchy identified by Damasio as grounding progressively complex cognitive-affective processes. This perspective has been amplified by a further two dimensions – *internal* and *behavioural* organization – that enable/constrain constitutive organization and are simultaneously inter-dependent with it. Like McFarland we consider constitutive and behavioural homeostatic regulation to be inextricably linked. Each dimension at every level (three of each here) can affect any other but the lower levels ground (provide the building blocks for) the higher levels while the highest level exerts top down control (i.e. transient parameterization) of lower levels across a goal-directed behavioural episode. McFarland's [10] autonomy levels flank the diagram and broadly correlate with the constitutive levels.

The schema is parsimoniously summarized thus:

"[the schematic shows] a single spectrum of constitutive organization brought about by the recruitment of a progression of [affect], from reflexes, through drives and motivations, to emotions-proper and feelings. Each level in the constitutive organization is associated on the Internal Organization axis with an increasing level of homeostatic autonomy-preserving self-maintenance … each level in the constitutive organization is associated on the Behavioural Organization axis with an increasing level of complexity in behaviour …" [17, p. 183].

As referred to by Vernon et al. [17] above in their description, the schema centres around a *Constitutive Organization* dimension. It is this dimension which, compressed into three levels, describes Damasio's homeostatic grounding principle (Fig. 1). In the *enactive cognitive-affective schema*, however, activity within this dimension is enabled/constrained by the interaction of internal and behavioural organization.

The focus of the cognitive-affective schema is to provide a core template for preserving robot autonomy given the (designer) requirement of multiple competences and that can potentially be incorporated into different architectures with different morphological details. Sensory perceptual *inputs*, therefore, are viewed as external to the schema but nevertheless interface with the internal organization dimension. Behavioural *outputs* interface with the behavioural organization dimension and may utilize more elaborate cognitive-behavioural components, e.g. involving language. Internal and behavioural organization permit *embodied appraisals* where stimuli, objects and events external to the agent are perceived as a function of internal state preparatory to action and behaviour itself (e.g. orientation).

We now describe the three schema dimensions in turn and their relation to each other:

Constitutive Organization. This dimension implements a type of *value function* across three levels of complexity of use in relation to goal-directed behaviour.

1. *Reflexes*: automated (unlearned) corrective responses regulated by internal and behavioural organization (see next section for an example).
2. *Drives and Motivations*: Drives reflect intensity of deviation from the 'ideal' range of metabolic variables (internal); Motivations emerge from the strength of drives and perceived opportunities, i.e. cues linked to behavioural affordances.
3. *Emotions and (emotional) Feelings*: Emotions (proper) reflect behavioural tendencies and embodied appraisals over the goal-directed behavioural episode; Emotional Feelings are founded on neural-dynamic maps of lower level constitutive states, e.g. motivation-gated inputs (reward/punishment signals) and intensity levels, as they interact with anticipated action preparation (somatic simulation) and behavioural 'planning' (sequencing of behavioural primitives).

Constitutive organization also implements the bi-directional grounding that we suggest is characteristic of our enactive approach. This entails:

- *Bottom-up nesting*: Level 1. is nested within or constrains 2. and both levels are nested within 3. (e.g. variables are mapped into 3.). This is not equivalent to a subsumption architecture (cf. [18]) since the lower levels are constitutive of the higher levels and are not independent building blocks.
- *Top-down parameterization*: Level 3 provides a neural-dynamic mapping of lower constitutive levels. Across internal dimensions of this mapping attractor states hold stable a constitutive state that describes embodied need with respect to a goal-directed episode (e.g. regarding a plan juncture, cf. [19], see next section). This top-down modulation *transiently parameterizes* lower level parameter values in the service of the adaptivity of the whole organism. This is a type of allostatic regulation and a manifestation of complex *internal* and *behavioural* cycles of activity as the highest constitutive level is also regulated by internal-bodily (e.g. physiological preparatory 'coping' potential), and sociobehavioural constraints, respectively. Its regulative (top-down) function is also of a predictive nature (see next section). While top-down regulation may encourage persistence of internal, constitutive and

behavioural activation patterns over the goal-directed behaviour, it is still open to strong bottom-up inputs that can perturb the higher level state and lead it into a new neural dynamic pattern.

Internal Organization. This is a neurophysiological dimension pertinent to Damasio's [11] somatic marker hypothesis. This dimension serves *action preparation*. We list three levels of somatic states whose activations are intimately related to behavioural/sensorimotor activity:

1. *Pre-Somatic Effects*: changes in bodily state as a result of internal deficits lead to automatic internal corrective mechanisms (e.g. via monitoring processes, see more in next section).
2. *Somatic Modulation*: bodily state changes leading to diffusive changes that endure across an emotion episode, e.g. hormonal. Such diffusive, enduring changes allow for populations of neurons in three-dimensional bodily space to synchronize activity in the service of a goal-directed episode.
3. *Somatic Simulation*: Neurally registered/mapped anticipated bodily changes that concern behavioural preparation provide an estimation of the agent's coping potential (cf. [20]) in relation to the goal-directed episode.

These levels of internal organization pertain to embodied perceptual processes associated with external sensory perturbations, e.g. from stimulus features, objects, events.

Behavioural Organization. This manifests in more or less tractable behavioural activity cycles (cf. [8]).

1. *Approach-Avoidance*: automated orientation tendencies in relation to internal homeostatic change.
2. *Sequenced Behaviours*: goal-directed chains of action tendencies regulated in relation to persistent drives that may be overridden by opportunistic affordances.
3. *Sequenced Behavioural Primitives*: goal-directed chains of adaptive behaviour sequences overtly or covertly expressed across the goal-directed episode.

The term 'enactive' is here meant in the broad sense of viewing cognition-affect as grounded in self-maintenance processes (cf. e.g., Vernon et al. [7]: "The only condition that is required of an enactive system is *effective action* [our italics]: that it permit the continued integrity of the system involved."), not in the narrower sense involving a specific commitment to autopoietic organization [21]. Another important perspective on enaction is that the parameters of the system should be 'operationally closed' [6], i.e. both influencing and influenced by other parameters within the system. This means that parameters should not be fixed by a designer a priori (though they may be initialized). The enactive approach as described here, is consistent with McFarland's homeostatic-centred view on adaptive behaviour in that 'effective action' entails persistent cycles of behavioural activity that do not fall into irrecoverable deficits [9]. The three levels of autonomy identified by McFarland necessarily entangle constitutive and behavioural organization in accordance with the principle of homeostasis. However, inconsistent with the second perspective on enaction we allude to, McFarland did not discuss his three levels in terms of ('constitutive' organizational) grounding – for an autonomous agent to also be adaptive in using human-like cognitive-affective processes requires grounding the mechanisms requisite to one level of autonomy into another. An agent endowed with the three levels of autonomy that are not so grounded is impoverished in its ability to produce 'effective action'.

Are All Dimensions Critical to a Minimalist Approach?

Might the *enactive cognitive-affective schema* be simplified by dimensional reduction? To what extent is internal organization a type of constitutive organization? To what extent is internal organization a type of behavioural organization? Damasio [11] distinguishes between somatic/bodily changes preparatory to action, and overt behaviour. Emotion-relevant bodily change (somatic markers) are used not just in preparing the body for action but as effective embodied appraisals (feelings) that guide cognition and action in conditions of uncertainty. Similarly, in our schema, internal organization is considered a type of *action preparation* in response to stimuli (external or imagined). Action preparation has two functions: (i) primes and synchronizes motor programs for quick responding, (ii) provides information about action tendencies (contributing to an embodied appraisal). In a previous paper [22], based on a review of emotion theory, we have proposed that the *feeling* of action tendencies regulates contextually inappropriate or insufficient pre-action activity. In the absence of such regulation, expressions of anger in the presence of dominant persons, or expressions of anxiety when presenting ideas to colleagues, might go unchecked. Adaptive emotion regulation implies anticipating bodily state so as to avoid not just inappropriate overt action but inappropriate action tendencies that manifest in perceptible expressions.

We similarly distinguish between internal organization and constitutive organization where the latter we view as computing the normative significance of an embodied and dynamic appraisal. Internal organization, rather, offers more a measure of invigoration (potential to act), which may or may not be suppressed. However, in combination with the normative component (value function) that constitutive organization provides, internal organization provides an appraisal of action tendencies – what type of behaviour the agent is likely to produce. It is an indispensable dimension of an embodied and dynamic appraisal made whole by a behavioural organization dimension which orients and positions the agent in relation to external and internally perceptible perturbations. Emotional feelings are thus viewed as a form of multi-dimensional top-down regulation over the goal-directed episode.

In summary, the *enactive cognitive-affective schema* provides a template for designing robotic architectures centred on preserving autonomy in the face of increasingly complex cognitive-affective processes. We suggest this is critical to adaptive function. The levels in the schematized hierarchy must be integrated using a bidirectional grounding approach so as to preserve autonomy. Not all levels within each dimension are required to be implemented in order for the approach to be at least bottom-up grounded. Furthermore, some dimensions at some levels may be implemented with more or less detail. However, an *enactive* approach requires all constitutive levels to be implemented in order that bidirectional grounding (with top-down transient parameterization over the goal-directed episode) is achieved – to fulfill the operational closure requirement. In Sect. 3, we will elucidate further how this can be achieved with respect to McFarland's levels of autonomy.

2.2 Comparison with Other Affective Modelling Approaches

While space precludes an in-depth comparison to a large number of models in the affective computing literature, this sub-section makes an attempt to pit our enactive approach against comparable existing affective and emotion modelling approaches.

Firstly, we should provide our definitions of affect and emotion as they are terms often open to interpretation and the subject of confusion. We consider emotion to be a type of affect – an umbrella term that includes other normative processes, e.g. motivation, drives, arousal. This contrasts with some perspectives on affect (e.g. [2]) where affect concerns generation, expression and perception of emotion. Emotion, in our view, includes emotional feeling states as well as embodied appraisals ('triggers') and bodily state changes that prepare for action (cf. [16, 22]). These three aspects are indispensable to the emotional state and modulate one another across the emotion episode. Emotions, per se, while dimensionally distributed, are only fully realized at the top level of our three-dimensional enactive schema as they require feeling states – as top down regulatory phenomena – for their 'proper' actualization.

Our approach has something in common with Scherer's [23] *component process model* (CPM) as we similarly advocate a dynamic systems perspective for modeling affective and emotion processes. Figure 3 shows Scherer's model as one consisting of multiple appraisal processes whose cognitive activity is dynamically modulated by affective components (vertical) and also by other cognitive processes.

In common with the CPM, our enactive approach views affective processes emerging from the interaction of parts and elicited by the perception of a triggering event (e.g. an interrupt in a goal-directed behaviour or plan, cf. [19]). It agrees with the notion that the execution of emotional behaviours are "multiply determined" [23, p. 48]. The CPM, like our enactive approach, entails recurrent cognitive-affective processes whose distributed activities over time constitute the emotion episode.

A main difference between our enactive approach and the CPM is our de-emphasizing of 'strong' (i.e. human-specific) cognitive aspects, e.g. appraisals of external stimuli with respect to normative significance (in relation to the agent's moral code), or language and verbalization in relation to feeling states. The aim of the *enactive cognitive-affective schema* is to provide a minimalist starting point for building robotic architectures that preserve autonomy in relation to increasing cognitive-affective complexity. Secondly, we emphasize bottom-up constitutive grounding, e.g. (artificial) metabolic or energy constrained, and top-down regulation where emotional feeling states are considered to have the function of neural dynamic predictive regulation of whole-organism mechanisms. Thirdly, in contrast with the CPM, while precedence in the CPM is set with the appraisal process – a cognitive process that precedes the activations of subsequent processes, in line with our focus on preservation of autonomy at multiple cognitive-affective levels, we rather view appraisal as being an embodied phenomenon. This 'embodied appraisal' is influenced by ongoing goal-directed activity and is not purely externally driven – the agent *looks for* and does not passively process (cf. [24]). In this respect, our enactive approach might be classed as a closed-loop perspective (cf. [25]).

From a dynamic systems perspective, our approach also shares something of an affinity with Lewis' [5] view of an *inseparability* between emotion and cognition

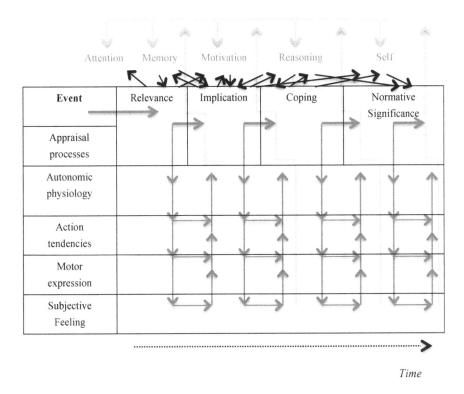

Fig. 3. The Component Process Model of emotion (adapted from [23]).

(appraisal) whereby components of each domain interact and give rise to a stable neurophysiological state that persists across the emotion episode. We view embodied appraisals as ongoing processes that trigger or perturb behavioural, e.g. orientation, and internal changes (e.g. metabolic) over time which in turn impact on the appraisal.

Another particularly relevant comparison is with respect to existing three-layered architectures or schemas. One of the most famous is the *CogAff* schema of Sloman (cf. [26]) – see Fig. 4. Similar to the *enactive cognitive-affective schema* the *CogAff* schema consists of three dimensions – in this case perception, central processing and action dimensions – and three layers – in this case corresponding to phylogenetic ancestry (the lowest levels being the 'oldest').

We can say that the 'perception' dimension roughly corresponds to the 'Internal Organization' dimension in our schema insofar as it is linked to embodied appraisal. The 'perception' dimension, however, concerns "discretization" or categorization of the environment enabling different levels of central processing, whereas our enactive approach is non-committal on sensory cognitive processing of this complexity. The action dimension may also be linked to our 'Behavioural Organization' dimension where in the case of *CogAff* quality and complexity of action is linked to the central processing level activated. The activation of levels within the *CogAff* schema depends on the triggering of alarm signals said, in biological organisms, to emanate from the

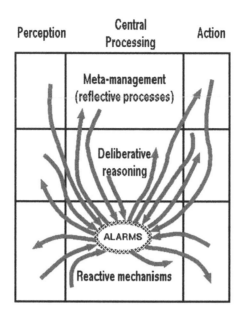

Fig. 4. The *CogAff* schema of Sloman et al. [28] (reprinted with permission).

limbic system and entail a "redirection of global processing" [26]. The bidirectional links from the alarm systems (stored within a reactive layer of the central processing dimension) and the other components of the schema can be likened to the bidirectional regulation that is requisite to the *enactive cognitive-affective schema* – resource redirection in our case concerns transient parameterization, i.e. overriding of 'basal' homeostatic processes in the service of the whole organism so that it may meet the predicted demands of the present goal-directed emotion event. This is the essence of the predictive regulation, or 'allostasis', perspective. Our schema, however, differs from *CogAff* in a number of ways:

- *Homeostatic organization* – our focus concerns the (predictive) regulation of bottom up and top-down activity across dimensions and layers. In *CogAff* components may be 'fixed' [26, p. 223] and yet conform to this schema.
- *Grounding* – our focus concerns higher levels in the schema being constructed from, or constrained by, variables of the lower levels. A dimensional feeling model, e.g. 'PAD' [27], a candidate implementation of the *feeling and emotions* layer is required to receive inputs in relation to its specific dimensions from lower levels.
- *Deliberative reasoning and reflection* – our schema does not focus on the implementation of particular ('strong') cognitive capacities. Sloman et al. [26] might consider the highest level of our schema to permit only proto-deliberative activity, e.g. where emotional feelings are instantiated using a neural-dynamic approach and a winner-take-all attractor dynamics (see next section). Our schema is meant to provide only a core for cognitive-affective processing that can be elaborated with particular cognitive capacities, e.g. planning and social expressive capacities.

- *Autonomy* – we suggest that embodiment as imbued in homeostatic organization, and a grounding principle, provides a means of preserving levels of autonomy (in the sense of McFarland [10]). Autonomy requires non-fixity of components in relation to sustainable behaviour, which we argue requires bi-directional grounding.

Another cognitive-affective architecture that bears interesting comparison to our approach is that of [28]. The focus of the architecture is on preservation of autonomy and energy ('power') management where higher level cognitive processes, e.g. planning, concern taking into account current resource availability, i.e. battery level. Theirs is a three-layer architecture, the lowest layer accounts for physical interfacing the robot with the real world, e.g. basic sensing and actuating. The middle layer is concerned with basic energy management and is responsible for the robot utilizing sequences of actuation and sensing in the service of refueling. The top-most layer consists of FAtiMA (*Fearnot AffecTIve Mind Architecture*; cf. [29]) – an architecture that considers the dynamic and incremental nature of appraisal. This level is responsible for 'socially constrained' energy management and exploits higher cognitive functions (memory, reasoning, goal management, action selection). This approach is motivated by a need to carry out social interaction tasks while simultaneously accounting for energy/power management requirements. It has a focus on energy autonomy whilst incorporating high level cognitive-affective competences but it does not, however, show how such higher level capabilities are 'grounded' in 'lower' level capabilities, an approach that we suggest is critical for maintaining autonomy and for mediating between top-down versus bottom-up dominance over behaviour.

3 Bidirectional Grounding of Levels of Autonomy and Cognitive-Affective Capacities in Robotic Agents

In this section we present example work and implementation ideas that for grounding emotional and affective processes in robotic agents while preserving the levels of autonomy put forward by McFarland [10]. These levels we consider broadly map to the constitutive levels of Damasio's nesting principle that concerns the 'Constitutive Organization' dimension of our *enactive cognitive-affective schema* described in Sect. 2. We have suggested that for autonomy to be preserved at the different levels of Damasio's 'hierarchy' we must use an enactive approach that homeostatically nests embodied mechanisms and top-down parameterizes constitutive organization.

3.1 Energy Autonomy and Physiological Drives

Energy autonomy concerns the homeostatic regulation of basic drives, e.g. in relation to energy or water depletion, that signal potentially irrecoverable energy deficits. The energy autonomous agent is able to refuel itself as a function of its own internal and behavioural dynamics. At this point, it is helpful to consider drives with respect to 'essential variables' [30]. Ashby [30] described a highly robust control system (the *ultrastable system* consisting of the agent in its environment) inspired by understanding of bioregulation and homeostasis. Control variables are considered as 'essential variables' (e.g. glucose and water levels in the blood) and error signals induce random parameter alterations affecting interactions between organism and environment in a trial and error manner until such a point at which a stable equilibrium is (re)established. Essential variable (EV) activity entails reflexive, in the pavlovian sense of being activity automatically generated by stimuli, corrective responses. EV activity is, however, contingent upon sensorimotor activity that serves to deplete or replenish the values of these variables. In this conditional manner, Ashby promoted an abstract link between (non-neural) metabolic variables and sensorimotor activity (pre-somatic, in the Damasio sense, and approach-avoidance related - see Fig. 2).

An aspect of the ultrastability concept that is fundamental to our bottom-up grounding approach is the inextricable link between internal organization (given by the dynamics of the essential variables) and the behavioural (e.g. randomly parameterized sensorimotor activity). Adapted sensorimotor activity will be that which has resulted from parameter changes following a homeostatic imbalance registered by essential variable monitors.

Possible robotics applications have been posited for the cybernetics and control theoretic principles of the above in light of modern understanding of bioregulation. Fricke et al. [31], for example, applied cybernetics ideas to feeding regulation as identified in a hypothalamus-centred control system. They were able to describe the various hormonal and neuromodulatory processes involved in terms of controller mechanisms, e.g. hypothalamic neurons can act as sensors to controlled variables such as leptin and insulin. Ecobot, developed at the Bristol Robotics Laboratory (cf. [32]), produces *energy autonomous behaviour* in accordance with satisfying its drives to 'eat' and 'drink' fuelled by electric energy generating microbial fuel cells (MFCs). The MFCs' essential variables, in the case of Ecobot, are level of raw substrate ('fuel') in the anode compartment and level of water in the cathode compartment. Maintenance of levels within appropriate limits is essential for energy to be generated at the cell capacitor to then be dispatched to the motors.

3.2 Motivation Autonomy

McFarland and Spier [8, 33] suggested a minimal, ethological, model of motivation that captures motivation autonomous processes. Motivated behaviour, in their view, satisfies basic drives and is a function of processing 'cues' (intensity of external stimuli) and 'deficits' (values of 'essential' variables that fall outside the ideal range/ homeostatic regime). McFarland and Spier [8] referred to the two-resource robotic problem of adaptively and viably trading off a need to carry out some kind of useful work (which in a biological agent might instead concern reproduction) and refueling. Essential variables in this case concern fuel and work 'levels', respectively. The specific implementation of the cue-deficit model in the case of [8] used a simple product of bounded drive values (deficits of essential variables) but in principle could be adapted to more complex functions of cues and deficits. Avila-Garcìa and Cañamero [34, 35], for example, who explicitly used Ashby's notion of essential variables, implemented a variation on McFarland and Spier's [8] original cue-deficit model. In their work 'deficits' in essential variables, e.g. energy or heat, provide drives to produce error correcting behaviours, e.g. search for food. Viable behaviour was measured in relation to the production of sustainable behavioural cycles that enabled maintenance of internal (essential) variables within the homeostatic regime. In principle, more elaborate motivation mechanisms could be incorporated within the banner of cue-deficit models, for example, value functions (e.g. reinforcement learning models [36, 37]) as constrained by homeostatic drives (cf. [38]) that enable associative learning and learning of goal-directed (sequential) behaviour and not just reactive processes.

3.3 Motivation Autonomy Grounded in Energy Autonomous Processes

Case Study 1: A Static Two-Resource Problem.
The investigations carried out here concern the use of a form of artificial metabolism to provide essential variables with biologically realistic dynamics whilst, at the same time, implementing an energy autonomy provisioning process. For this pur- pose we used a model of the Microbial Fuel Cell (MFC) stacks deployed in Ecobot [32] in order to generate energy autonomous behaviour. The MFC model is introduced in depth in [39] and designed at a level of abstraction purpose-made for autonomous robotics investigations. Critical to energy-motivation autonomous level integration is the charge-discharge electric output dynamics that gate motor wheel activation. At a threshold of electricity storage at the MFC capacitor bank energy is utilized by motors that indirectly contribute to the maintenance of the charge-discharge dynamic, i.e. through feeding/drinking. After a period without substrate, the charge is not arrived at in spite of periodic rehydration at the cathode. Re-establishment of an efficient output dynamic owes to simulated fuel source provision at the anode. Both water and substrate (EVs) are, therefore, needed to be replenished for efficient system level energy to be produced. Reduced charge rate ensures less energy for the motors.

In the investigation of [39] and [40] the MFC model was utilized in the context of two-resource problems whereby robots were required to make adaptive selections between the two resources that served to replenish the MFC essential variables.

As space limitations dictate, in this subsection we focus only on the work of [40]. The MFC model was interfaced with an ANN with evolvable topology. This type of ANN represents an adaptation of the GasNet [41], where the only nodes in the network that emit the characteristic diffusive neuromodulator are EV monitor nodes (e-nodes) – see Fig. 5. As an expression of the preserving of motivation autonomy through bottom-up grounding energy autonomy enabling processes, the lower limit thresholds delineating comfort from critical ('deficit') zones of EV activity were determined by a genetic algorithm (GA). The connectivity schema and number of nodes of the network were similarly evolved so that the sensory input (channeled via a type of active vision) could combine with the essential variable output as a function of a cue-deficit ANN providing a sort of 'proto-appraisal' state. The e-nodes emit diffusive gas when the critical zone of activity is arrived at reflective of GA determined metabolically grounded drives. The gas slowly and transiently modulates the activation function gain parameter of neighbouring nodes as a function of radial distance from the e-node – a simple form of somatic modulation of approach-avoidance tendencies. The network implemented a distributed cue-deficit model grounded in the essential variable dynamics given by an artificial metabolism (MFC).[1] In this sense it provides an example of a robot with motivational capacities that preserves autonomy across McFarland's energy and motivation levels.

Following the evolutionary grounding of the motivation level corresponding to motivation autonomy preservation (cue-deficit ANN), the e-nodes provided a distributed interface to MFC dynamics sensitive to the spatial-temporal task features.

Viable robots were able to survive 20 cycles (the maximum evaluated) according to timely switching between selections. The e-nodes mediated this selection behaviour. Two interesting findings emerged. Firstly, the pulsed behavior constraint, inherent in all evolved robots, was exploited via 'retinal' actuation. This entailed e-nodes' gaseous outputs slowly impacting on the activity of motor and also pan and tilt nodes projecting to a low resolution retinal image. The non energy-constrained panning and tilting exploited the MFC capacitance inter-pulse waiting interval by directing the fast-moving retina to the 'selected' resource. Robots could then produce efficient motor trajectories

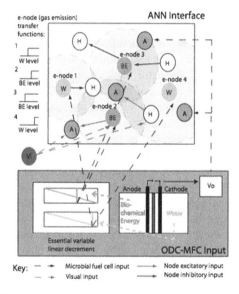

Fig. 5. The MFC-E-GasNet. Left: MFC-sensorimotor architecture using GA-determined ANN interface. Nodes: H = hidden, A = actuator, Vi = Visual input, W = water monitoring node, BE = biochemical energy monitoring node, V0 = MFC voltage input which gates motor activity. E-nodes are essential variable monitor nodes that have separate, GA-determined gas emission transfer functions delineating effective 'comfort' and 'critical' zones of activity. Grey shaded circles depict potential e-node gas emissions. Both water (in the cathode) and bio-chemical energy (in the anode) decrement linearly – water decrements approximately 6x faster.

---

[1] The artificial metabolism is not autopoietic and to the extent that incorporation of such a constitutive system into an architecture is in line with our enactive approach that requires operational closure, top-down parameterization of the system is prerequisite.

that minimize the Euclidean distance between the robot and the 'selected' resource. In a control condition where no retinal movement was permissible, no such 'anticipatory' behavior could occur. This result provides an example of how metabolic constraints can be cognitively exploited.

The EVs of the MFCs inform about energy availability. According to the Ashbyan approach, embraced by McFarland, EV monitor mechanisms can detect EV state error signals via the use of non-linear transfer functions interfacing EVs with the control architecture. As for classical control systems, error signals instigate correction procedures via internal change or use of a particular behavior, e.g. in the robot, feeding to correct biochemical energy deficit. Using an artificial metabolism, such as MFCs, to provide EVs to a robotic system means that the EVs are not just viability indicators but also predict future energy output. This means that consideration for *how* EV monitor mechanisms that link (reflexive) metabolic processes to drives are integrated adaptively into the decision process of the robot is of critical importance. The use of arbitrarily set thresholds (or gains, sensitivity ranges etc. in semi-linear functions) to delineate EV states and instigate error correcting change will not be optimal if the energy required to carry out the error correction is not accounted for. In this sense there is a need to ground motivation in energy constraints. The E-GasNet implements a type of ultrastable system but falls under the banner of a *non-random self-configurable approach* [42] where parameter updates are non-random (unlike for Ashby's ultrastable system) but GA-determined. The approach here is in the spirit of enactivism but the E-GasNet is not operationally closed – as thresholds that denote essential variable deficits are GA-determined and fixed within the lifetime of the agents, thereby not open to modulation from any other parameters in the network.

Case Study 2: A Dynamic Two-Resource Problem.
In case study 1 we described an investigation concerning a simulated wheeled robot in an environment where the task for the robot was to cycle behavioural activities critical to refueling (self-maintaining in relation to internal organization). The resources – 'water' and 'food' – were static, insofar as the robot had useful 'work' to do it might be abstractly related to passive environmental monitoring, i.e. we can imagine the robot transmitting information about the temperature of the environment or concentration of chemicals in the environment similar to that of Ecobot [32]. In many cases, however, robots are required to carry out tasks that are more challenging, possibly involving a dynamic component. This is particularly relevant in human-robot interaction scenarios where the task may involve dealing with potential environmental hazards or otherwise moving objects.

We extended our work of [43] that used an arousal mechanism in relation to a two-resource problem for a simulated Nao robot with the work of [44, 45] testing both a simulated and physical iCub robot on a two resource problem that required tracking of a moving object – this constituted a 'dynamic' form of 'work'. The robot was evaluated for its ability to produce viable activity cycles for recharging (the iCub would put its arms by its sides) and for working – the robot would track a moving ball (held by the human experimenter) and be rewarded for having its hand within a certain distance of the ball. The iCub was able to cycle activities effectively when using an arousal function – a component of emotion [27]. The central motivation of this work has been to ground a higher level feeling substrate of emotion – the PAD dimensional model ([27], see also [46] for a simulated model used in the WASABI architecture) where P = 'pleasantness', A = 'arousal', D = 'dominance'. In our work, the arousal function was grounded in energy-motivation autonomous processes, i.e. a basic cue-deficit model constrained by the energy consumption of the robot and captured in (1).

$$Arousal = Energy \cdot (Cwork \cdot Dwork + Cenergy \cdot Denergy) \qquad (1)$$

where $Cwork$ = the cue intensity for work: distance from the ball of the robot hand, $Dwork$ = the deficit of the work essential variable, $Cenergy$ = cue for energy: distance from the charging position of the robot hand, $Denergy$ = deficit of energy relative to a threshold for battery level consumption. Energy consisted of the current level of the battery degraded according to the sum of electrical current and motor voltage for all joints (in arms, head and torso) in the physical robot and approximated in the simulator. Behaviour selection was also calculated using the basic cue-deficit model of [8]. The arousal impulse directly impacts on the speed of movement of the robot thus permitting 'catch up' reaching to the ball when lagging behind and is effectively sensed through a decrementing 'work' essential variable value. For further implementation details see [44, 45]. Figure 6 examines the functional role of arousal in relation to permitting motivated autonomous behaviour to be adaptive. It can be seen (bottom left) that arousal increases when work level drops (top right). The arousal impulse (at approximately 1500 and 2500 timesteps) serves to increase the speed of the robot ball tracking enabling it to re-establish behavioural stability (bottom right, via improved work performance after a short time lag).

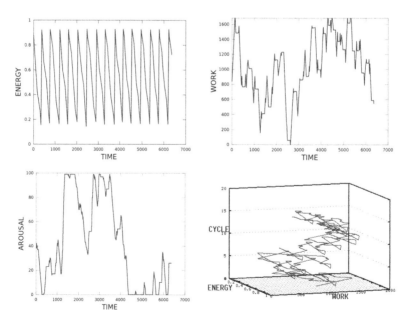

Fig. 6. Top-left: Battery level (*internal cycles*); Top-right: Work Utility; Bottom-left: Arousal level, Bottom-right; Work-refuel *behavioural cycles*. Time is measured in program cycles.

The robots in these studies should not be considered energy-motivation autono-mous in the same sense as those discussed in case study 1. The cue-deficit functions are not specifically grounded in the essential variables of an artificial metabolism. How-ever, the arousal mechanism does constrain the manner by which behaviours are car-ried out according to present energy levels as well as overall motivation state. The simple arousal mechanism when considered as a motivation mechanism that, in itself, partially grounds a three-dimensional feeling space (PAD) can be seen as grounded in a *drive* (*Denergy,* and also *Dwork*) that monitors energy deficits. Energy here is provided by a battery level proffering, in this case, the single essential variable for refueling the linear drive to reduce *Denergy*. The logic behind the design choice is that arousal depends somewhat on agents having energy as well as being motivated in respect to their various needs. The arousal mechanism is shown as being essential to escape potentially irrecoverable deficits (see Fig. 6).

3.4 Mental Autonomy: The Role of Feelings and Prediction

Robotics work concerning McFarland's notion of mental autonomy is of interest here insofar as it pertains to emotion states. Emotions promote creative and flexible means of producing behaviour ('freedom of thought'). We consider that in order to relate this level of autonomy to Damasio's nested hierarchy we must imbue robots with emotional feeling states. Such states exert a top-down influence on the lower levels of robotic activity and exert a predictive regulatory control.

The notion of allostasis [47, 48] is of use here. It encourages a rethink of the classical control theoretic perspective on homeostasis revolving around feedback loops respecting set points that demarcate "ideal" states. According to [47], allostasis can be conceived in terms of prediction where brain areas implicated in planning and decision making are viewed as supplying inputs that may override other inputs that signal errors from ideal homeostatic balance. Such overriding of "basal" homeostasis operates in the service of supplying the organism with the resources previously learned to be necessary to meet predicted environmental pressures. Sterling considers allostasis as a means of permitting adaptive bodily regulation according to "stability through change" which accounts for both internal needs and external pressures (or opportunities) and compares to the Bernard notion of "stability through constancy."

Sterling's [47] perspective on allostasis has a strong link with emotion regulation involved as it is with prefrontal cortex and amygdala activity (two oft-implicated emotion brain areas). Damasio's 'as-if body loop' hypothesis posits that parts of the brain including prefrontal cortex, amygdala and somatosensory cortex activated during appraisal events that elicit bodily (constitutive) changes may be reactivated even in the absence of those bodily changes.

Damasio himself has suggested that emotional feelings are perceptions of the body in preparation for, or during, action:

> "[f]eelings of emotion [...] are composite perceptions of what happens in our body and mind when we are emoting. As far as the body is concerned, feelings are images of actions rather than actions themselves; the world of feelings is one of perceptions executed in brain maps" [13, p. 110].

We have suggested that the as-if body loop can be reinterpreted in terms of predictive regulation (allostasis; cf. [22]). The faster neural activity of the as-if body loop (compared to the standard appraisal-body loop) necessarily anticipates bodily change (when such change occurs at all) which may have an important function in regulating contextually (in)appropriate action tendencies. Both [49] and [50] have discussed emotions in terms of multiple stages of regulation depending on context. Berkowitz [51] has also suggested that emotional feeling states play a control theoretic regulatory role in relation to action. Such regulation may require stable neural activation states (cf. [5]) across the emotion episode transiently parameterizing the agent in relation to the immediate exigency. Emotional feeling states thereby exert top down influence on more fundamental constitutive neurophysiological levels during the emotion episode [22].

A promising way to capture emotional feeling states, in relation to the function of predictive regulation, might be to ground psychological dimensional models of emotion. Typically, such dimensional models, e.g. *core affect model* [52], PAD [27], are derived from verbal or written reports by human participants and as such provide insights into the dimensions of emotional feelings as they concern affective-constitutive phenomena, e.g. arousal/activation, pain-pleasure. Such dimensional models could be instantiated as neural maps whose constitutive inputs could lead to stable activation patterns across the emotion episode exerting top-down control. Of what might the neurocomputational properties of stabilization dynamics be comprised? Stabilization dynamics have been mathematically and computationally formalized through the differential equations of [53] initially deployed to model the topographic spatial representations in the visual cortex according to neural fields. Dynamic field theory (DFT) has since been particularly noteworthy in capturing infant cognitive–behavioral phenomena (cf. [54]). However, it has also been posited to be of relevance to modeling emotional phenomena in the context of Bechara et al.'s [55] Iowa gambling task [56, 57]. The DFT approach has spawned a perspective on representations in the brain that map cognitive phenomena to continuous dimensions.

At present we are not aware of the existence of a grounded emotional feeling network/map – implemented as a model that utilizes constitutive inputs, e.g. from value functions. We have previously [58] used a reinforcement learning approach to adapt meta-parameter[2] [59] values according to a (non-neural dynamic) mapping function that determines how planning extent varies with exploration tendency. The meta-parameters involved may also be linked to the role of particular neuromodulators, e.g. noradrenaline (exploration) – see also [60] – whose activations might implement dimensions on a neural-dynamic feeling map. A neural-dynamic feeling map might permit a transient adaptation of (meta-)parameters at lower levels of the homeostatic hierarchy (e.g. regarding EV thresholds/gains) thereby implementing something of a closed loop in relation to top-down and bottom-up activation modulation.

---

[2] Meta-parameters are the parameters used in reinforcement learning algorithms whose values are typically fixed. Allowing for these parameters to vary as a function of regulatory feedback provides a way to reduce the design and potentially increase the adaptivity of the agent.

4 Concluding Comments

In this chapter we have described an approach for grounding emotions and allowing for autonomous behaviour in robots so that they may (i) increase viability and adaptive behaviour, (ii) interact more naturally in physical and social environments. We considered that typical computational models of affect, specifically appraisal theoretic models, do not sufficiently take into account the role of the body. We have suggested that both bottom-up (e.g. evolutionary) and top-down (e.g. neural-dynamic implementations of minimalist psychology models) approaches, and the bidirectional regulation of applicable components offers a promising minimalist approach for developing computational processes that can be embedded in the above-mentioned types of robots. We discussed example implementations of bottom-up grounded architectures deployed by wheeled and humanoid robots and other potential approaches that would fit within our template/schema for building enactive cognitive-affective agents.

References

1. Arnold, M.B.: Emotion and Personality. Columbia University Press, New York (1960)
2. Hudlicka, E.: Computational Affective Modeling and Affective User Modeling, T13: Tutorial Notes. HCI International, Crete (2014)
3. Prinz, J.J.: Gut Reactions: A Perceptual Theory of Emotion. Oxford University Press, New York (2004)
4. Scherer, K.R.: Emotions are emergent processes: they require a dynamic computational architecture. Philos. Trans. R. Soc. Lond. B Biol. Sci. **364**, 3459–3474 (2009)
5. Lewis, M.D.: Bridging emotion theory and neurobiology through dynamic systems modeling. Behav. Brain Sci. **28**, 169–245 (2005)
6. Thompson, E.: Mind in Life: Biology, Phenomenology, and the Sciences of Mind. Harvard University Press, Cambridge (2007)
7. Vernon, D., Metta, G., Sandini, G.: A survey of artificial cognitive systems: implications for the autonomous development of mental capabilities in computational agents. IEEE Trans. Evol. Comput. **11**(2), 151–180 (2007)
8. McFarland, D., Spier, E.: Basic cycles, utility and opportunism in self-sufficient robots. Rob. Auton. Syst. **20**, 179–190 (1997)
9. McFarland, D., Bösser, T.: Intelligent Behavior in Animals and Robots. The MIT Press, Cambridge (1993)
10. McFarland, D.: Guilty Robots, Happy Dogs. Oxford University Press, New York (2008)
11. Damasio, A.R.: The Feeling of What Happens: Body, Emotion and he Making of Consciousness. Vintage, London (1999)
12. Damasio, A.R.: Looking for Spinoza: Joy, Sorrow and the Feeling Brain. Harcourt, Orlando (2003)
13. Damasio, A.R.: Self Comes to Mind: Constructing the Conscious Brain. Pantheon Books, New York (2010)
14. Morse, A., Lowe, R., Ziemke, T.: Towards an enactive cognitive architecture. In: Cognitive Systems, 1st International Conference on Cognitive Systems (2008)
15. Ziemke, T., Lowe, R.: On the role of emotion in embodied cognitive architectures: from organisms to robots. Cognit. Comput. **1**, 104–117 (2009)

16. Lowe, R., Ziemke, T.: The role of reinforcement in affective computation. In: Computational Intelligence for Creativity and Affective Computing (CICAC), 2013 IEEE Symposium, pp. 17–24 (2013)
17. Vernon, D., von Hofsten, C., Fadiga, L.: A Roadmap for Cognitive Development in Humanoid Robots, COSMOS 11. Springer, Berlin (2010)
18. Brooks, R.A.: Cambrian Intelligence. MIT Press, Cambridge (1999)
19. Oatley, K., Johnson-Laird, P.N.: Towards a cognitive theory of emotions. Cogn. Emot. **1**, 29–50 (1987)
20. Scherer, K.: Emotion and emotional competence: conceptual and theoretical issues for modelling agents. In: Scherer, K., Bänziger, T., Roesch, E.B. (eds.) Blueprint for Affective Computing: A Sourcebook, pp. 3–21. Oxford University Press, New York (2010)
21. Froese, T., Ziemke, T.: Enactive artificial intelligence. Artif. Int. **173**, 466–500 (2009)
22. Lowe, R., Ziemke, T.: The feeling of action tendencies: on the emotional regulation of goal-directed behavior. Front. Psychol. **2**, 1–24 (2011)
23. Scherer, K.: The component process model: architecture for a comprehensive computational model of emergent emotion. In: Scherer, K., Bänziger, T., Roesch, E.B. (eds.) Blueprint for Affective Computing: A Sourcebook, pp. 47–71. Oxford University Press, New York (2010)
24. Noë, A.: Action in Perception. MIT Press, Cambridge (2004)
25. Marsella, S., Gratch, J., Petta, P.: Computational models of emotion. In: Scherer, K., Bänziger, T., Roesch, E.B. (eds.) Blueprint for Affective Computing: A Sourcebook, pp. 21–41. Oxford University Press, New York (2010)
26. Sloman, A., Chrisley, R., Scheutz, M.: The architectural basis of affective states and processes. In: Fellous, J.-M., Arbib, M.A. (eds.) Who Needs Emotions? The Brain Meets the Robot, pp. 203–245. Oxford University Press, New York (2005)
27. Mehrabian, A.: Pleasure-arousal-dominance: a general framework for describing and measuring individual differences in temperament. Curr. Psychol. **14**, 261–292 (1996)
28. Deshmukh, A., Vargas, P.A., Aylett, R., Brown, K.: Towards socially constrained power management for long-term operation of mobile robots. In: Towards Autonomous Robotic Systems (2010)
29. Dias, J., Mascarenhas, S., Paiva, A.: Fatima modular: towards an agent architecture with a generic appraisal framework. In: International Workshop on Standards for Emotion Modeling (2011)
30. Ashby, W.R.: Design for a Brain: The Origin of Adaptive Behaviour. Chapman and Hall, London (1960)
31. Fricke, O., Lehmkuhl, G., Pfaff, D.W.: Cybernetic principles in the systematic concept of hypothalamic feeding control. Eur. J. Endocrinol. **154**, 167–173 (2006)
32. Melhuish, C., Ieropoulos, I., Greenman, J., Horsfield, I.: Energetically autonomous robots: food for thought. Auton. Robots **21**, 187–198 (2006)
33. Spier, E.: From reactive behaviour to adaptive behaviour. Ph.D. thesis, University of Sussex (1997)
34. Avila-Garcìa, O.: Towards emotional modulation of action selection in motivated autonomous robots. Ph.D. thesis, Department of Computer Science, University of Hertfordshire, Hatfield (2004)
35. Avila-Garcìa, O., Cañamero, L.: Hormonal modulation of perception in motivation-based action selection architectures. In: Proceedings of Agents that Want and Like: Motivational and Emotional Roots of Cognition and Action, Symposium of the AISB05 Convention, pp. 9–17. University of Hertfordshire, Hatfield (2005)
36. Sutton, R.S., Barto, A.G.: Time-derivative models of Pavlovian reinforcement. In: Gabriel, M., Moore, J. (eds.) Learning and Computational Neuroscience: Foundation of Adaptive Networks, pp. 497–537. MIT Press, Cambridge (1990)

37. Jacobs, E., Broekens, J., Jonker, C.: Emergent dynamics of joy, distress, hope and fear in reinforcement learning agents. In: AAMAS (2014, in press)
38. Gadanho, S.G.: Learning behavior-selection by emotions and cognition in a multi-goal robot task. J. Mach. Learn. Res. **4**, 385–412 (2003)
39. Montebelli, A., Lowe, R., Ieropoulos, I., Greenman, J., Melhuish, C., Ziemke, T.: Microbial fuel cell driven behavioral dynamics in robot simulations. In: Fellermann, H., Drr, M., Hanczyc, M., Laursen, L., Maurer, S., Merkle, D., Monnard, P.-A., Sty, K., Rasmussen, S. (eds.) Artificial Life XII, pp. 749–756. The MIT Press, Odense (2010)
40. Lowe, R., Montebelli, A., Ieropoulos, I., Greenman, J., Melhuish, C., Ziemke, T.: Grounding motivation in energy autonomy: a study of artificial metabolism constrained robot dynamics. In: Fellermann, H., Drr, M., Hanczyc, M., Laursen, L., Maurer, S., Merkle, D., Monnard, P.-A., Sty, K., Rasmussen, S. (eds.) Artificial Life XII, pp. 725–732. The MIT Press, Odense (2010)
41. Husbands, P., Smith, T., Jakobi, N., O'Shea, M.: Better living through chemistry: evolving GasNets for robot control. Connect. Sci. **10**(3/4), 185–210 (1998)
42. Lowe, R.: Designing for emergent ultrastable behaviour in complex artificial systems – the quest for minimizing heteronomous constraints. Constr. Found. (special issue on 'computational approaches to constructivism', open peer commentary on the target article "Homeostats for the 21st Century? Simulating Ashby Simulating the Brain") **9**(1), 105–107 (2013)
43. Kiryazov, K., Lowe, R., Montebelli, A., Ziemke, T., Becker-Asano, C.: From the virtual to the robotic: bringing emoting and appraising agents into reality. In: FET Conference (2011)
44. Kiryazov, K., Lowe, R., Becker-Asano, C., Randazzo, M.: The role of arousal in two resource problem tasks for humanoid service robots. In: 22nd IEEE International Symposium on Robot and Human Interactive Communication (Ro-Man) (2013, in press)
45. Kiryazov, K, Lowe, R.: The role of arousal in embodying the cue-deficit model in multi-resource human-robot interaction. In: European Conference of Artificial Life (ECAL) (2013, accepted)
46. Becker-Asano, C., Wachsmuth, I.: Affective computing with primary and secondary emotions in a virtual human. Auton. Agents Multi-Agent Syst. **20**, 32–49 (2010)
47. Sterling, P.: Principles of allostasis: optimal design, predictive regulation, pathophysiology and rational therapeutics. In: Schulkin, J. (ed.) Allostasis, Homeostasis, and the Costs of Adaptation. Cambridge University Press, Cambridge (2004)
48. Schulkin, J.: Social allostasis: anticipatory regulation of the internal milieu. Front. Evol. Neurosci. **2**(111), 1–15 (2011)
49. Koole, S.L.: The psychology of emotion regulation: an integrative review. Cogn. Emot. **23**, 4–41 (2009)
50. Frijda, N.H.: Emotions and action. In: Manstead, A.S.R., Frijda, N., Fischer, A. (eds.) Feelings and Emotions, pp. 158–173. Cambridge University Press, Cambridge (2004)
51. Berkowitz, L.: The Causes and Consequences of Feelings. Cambridge University Press, Cambridge (2000)
52. Russell, J.A.: Core affect and the psychological construction of emotion. Psychol. Rev. **110**, 145–172 (2003)
53. Amari, S.: Dynamics of pattern formation in lateral-inhibition type neural fields. Biol. Cybern. **27**, 77–87 (1977)
54. Thelen, E., Schöner, G., Scheier, C., Smith, L.: The dynamics of embodiment: a dynamic field theory of infant perseverative reaching. Behav. Brain Sci. **24**, 1–86 (2001)
55. Bechara, A., Damasio, A.R., Damasio, H., Anderson, S.W.: Insensitivity to future consequences following damage to human pre-frontal cortex. Cognition **50**, 7–15 (1994)

56. Lowe, R., Ziemke, T.: Towards a cognitive robotics methodology for reward-based decision-making: dynamical systems modelling of the Iowa Gambling Task. Connect. Sci. **22**, 247–289 (2010)
57. Lowe, R., Duran, B., Ziemke, T.: A dynamic field theoretic model of Iowa gambling task performance. In: IEEE 9th International Conference on Development and Learning (ICDL), Michigan, pp. 297–304 (2010)
58. Lowe, R., Ziemke, T.: Exploring the relationship of reward and punishment in reinforcement learning. In: Adaptive Dynamic Programming And Reinforcement Learning (ADPRL), 2013 IEEE Symposium, pp. 140–147 (2013)
59. Doya, K.: Metalearning and neuromodulation. Neur. Net. **15**, 495–506 (2002)
60. Broekens, J.: Affect and Learning: A Computational Analysis. Ph.D. thesis, University of Leiden (2007)

Evaluations of Specific Models

The Effect of Dominance Manipulation on the Perception and Believability of an Emotional Expression

Wim F.J. van der Ham[1](✉), Joost Broekens[2], and Peter H.M.P. Roelofsma[1]

[1] AAL-VU, VU Amsterdam, De Boelelaan 1105,
1081 HV Amsterdam, The Netherlands
wfjvdham@gmail.com
[2] II, TU Delft, Mekelweg 4, 2628 CD Delft, The Netherlands

Abstract. Models of affect are used in virtual characters to predict the emotions that can be shown by the character and thus to increase the believability of the character. In some specific situations it may not be clear which appraisals are the most important and thus which emotion should be generated. For example, both anger and sadness can be shown if another person does something blameworthy that is negative for one's own goals. Based on experimental and theoretical findings in emotion psychology, we propose a model using social dominance as a way to choose between anger and sadness. We hypothesize that anger should be generated (and expressed) in the dominant virtual character and sadness in the non-dominant character. We test this hypothesis with a virtual reality scenario in which a user and an agent negotiate about job options. The negotiation always fails as a result of actions of the user. We have a 2×2 experimental setup with agent role (dominant/submissive) and expressed emotion at the end of the scenario (angry/sad) as factors. No significant effect on the believability measure between the different conditions was found so the hypotheses cannot be confirmed. A significant influence of agent role was found on the perception of the emotional expressions, showing that social context influences perception of expressed emotions.

1 Introduction

One of the reasons to use a model of affect in a virtual agent is to enhance human-computer interaction with an agent [25]. A popular way to model affect in a virtual agent is by making use of appraisal based theory [19]. Some well-known examples of such models include EMA [9] and FLAME [7]. In appraisal theory, emotion is argued to arise from patterns of individual judgment concerning the relationship between events and an individual's beliefs, desires and intentions, sometimes referred to as the person-environment relationship [13]. In some situations it is not clear which type of person-environment relationship is most important for emotions at a specific time. In such situations the question

© Springer International Publishing Switzerland 2014
T. Bosse et al. (Eds.): Emotion Modeling, LNAI 8750, pp. 101–114, 2014.
DOI: 10.1007/978-3-319-12973-0_6

remains which of the possible emotions is perceived as more believable and what the factors are that determine believability.

According to all the previously mentioned models of emotion, both sadness and anger can be elicited if another person does something that has negative consequences for your own goals. Anger can be elicited as a result of the blameworthiness of the other person for an event and sadness can be elicited as a result of negative consequences of the event. Which appraisal the most important is, is not clear from the theories mentioned. According to recent research [14], the affective states sadness and anger have contradicting effects on the cognition and behavior of the agent and it is thus important to know which of those states is elicited in the specific situation described earlier. In this paper we use dominance as the appraisal factor that determines which of the two emotions should be expressed in that situation, with the aim to measure if this will increase the believability of the agent.

In other research about models of affect [1,8,16,22] sadness is related to low dominance or control and anger is related to high dominance or control. Also in research on the perception of emotional expressions the relation is found between anger and high dominance and sadness and low dominance [11]. In this paper we try to validate a simple model that uses dominance to make a distinction between the expressions of sadness versus anger. We hypothesize that a high dominant character is more believable if it expresses anger instead of sadness, while for a submissive character this is reversed.

We test our model with a scenario in which the user acts in a way that is negative for the goals of the agent, a situation that would predict both anger and sadness. The scenario used in this experiment is a negotiation between a boss and a candidate. The boss is the high dominant character and the candidate is the low dominant character. Depending on the experimental condition the subject is either the boss or the candidate and the agent expresses itself with either anger or sadness. Subjects received a role description before playing the scenario. We test a 2×2 setup with role (boss/candidate) and expression (anger/sadness) as factors. The hypothesis is supported when we observe that a boss who expresses anger and a candidate who expresses sadness both have higher believability than a sad boss and an angry candidate.

The negotiation is done with a virtual character that is able to show different emotions. The perception of these emotions has been evaluated in previous research [3]. We choose for this virtual character instead of a human character, because a virtual character offers much greater flexibility in the virtual training domain, as is also shown in [21]. The character can be manipulated to have different styles end preferences. The user can learn about the different situations that can occur during a negotiation.

In this experiment we evaluate the influence of the dominance variable on the perception of an emotional expression. Perceptions of emotional expressions have been studied before [3,11,12] but not much research has examined this within a social context [24]. Recent psychological studies [23] show that the processing of a facial expression depends on the observer's information processing and on social-relational factors, for example dominance. In other research [18] it is argued that for the perception of an emotion it can be important to show the emotion in a sequence of expressions. But since we are interested in the emotional reaction to a very specific action we use only a static response after the action.

The structure of this paper is as follows: first we discuss background research on the difference between sadness and anger. Then we explain our model and the experimental setup in more detail, after which we present the results. Finally, we discuss our findings in a broader context.

2   Anger and Sadness Background

Anger and sadness both result from an appraisal of an individual that an event has negatively impacted the individual's goals (see e.g. [19]). Anger is the emotion attributed to the acting agent that has responsibility for the event, while sadness is the emotion attributed to the event itself. In other words, anger is the result from the perception of a blameworthy agent while sadness is the result of a loss or anticipated loss. More specific differences between anger and sadness have been studied in the past. According to [14] a general negative emotion (sadness) and the specific negative emotion anger differ from each other because angry people believe that they have control over the situation. This 'control' variable can be found in more literature as a difference between anger and sadness. Probably the most important work that uses control to divide between the two emotions is the PAD scale described in [17]. The D in the PAD scale stands for dominance and is defined as:

> Dominance was defined as a feeling of control and influence over one's surroundings and others ... (e.g. anger ...)

The control from [14] and the dominance from [17] have essentially the same meaning. The way humans process an emotional expression of another human depends on the motivation to process the information from that expression [23]. This motivation depends on the dominance of the perceiver of the expression. A dominant character does not care much about the information of the expression of the submissive character and responds to this expression using its gut feelings. The submissive character on the contrary is interested in the information from the expression of the dominant character and changes its behavior accordingly. In this research we manipulate the dominance of the perceiver of the emotion and see if this influences perception. Obviously both emotions make sense to express; however it can very well be that depending on the context one should be expressed, while the other should not. A pilot study is conducted to examine this in a structured way.

3   Method

We test our hypothesis with a scenario in which the users action is negative for the goals of the agent (he/she cuts of a negotiation), a situation that would predict both anger, as a result of the blameworthiness for the quitting of the negotiation, and sadness, as a result of not achieving an agreement at all. The scenario used in this experiment is a negotiation between a boss and a candidate. The boss is the high dominant character and the candidate is the low dominant character. Depending on the experimental condition the subject is either the boss or the candidate and the agent expresses itself with either anger or sadness.

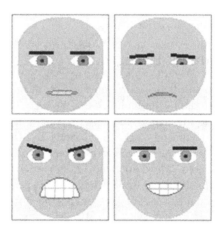

Fig. 1. Different expression of the AffectButton [2]

The experiment is conducted using an online questionnaire and a download-able virtual reality scenario. A subject is semi-randomly allocated to one of four experimental conditions. The user can be the boss or the candidate and the reaction of the virtual agent can be either sad or angry (2×2 between subject design). The experiment starts with some general questions and explanation of the procedure of the experiment in general. After that, the subject reads a short story explaining the role of the subject in the negotiation. The subject is asked to read this thoroughly and to immerse him/herself as much as possible. Immediately after the story we checked our initial dominance manipulation by asking subjects to rate perceived dominance of both the user and the agent with the AffectButton [2]. The AffectButton is a button with a face that changes depending on the position of the cursor on the button. An example of a few different expression of the button is given in Fig. 1. If the button is pressed the face remains fixed and a value for each of the PAD dimensions [17] is selected. The subject has to use the AffectButton to evaluate his/her own feeling at that moment and to evaluate how he/she thinks the agent is feeling. Next the subject plays the virtual reality scenario. Then the subject again rates his/her feeling and that of the virtual character using the AffectButton. Further, after playing the scenario, we asked subjects to rate (a) the expression of the agent, (b) the user's typical feeling as well as (c) expression in the presented situation. Rat-ing was done by selecting on a 1 to 5 point scale the emotional intensity for 6 basic emotions [6], where 1 stands for not present and 5 stands for very present. Finally we asked the subjects about the believability of the virtual character's reaction using the following 5-item questionnaire (Cronbach's alfa = 0.73):

- The reaction of the agent was normal for this situation.
- I would have reacted in the same way as the agent.
- The reaction of the agent was believable.
- The reaction of the agent was human like. [4, 12]
- The reaction of the agent was predictable. [12]

The answers on these question are given on a 1 to 5 Likert scale [15], where 1 means totally disagree and 5 means totally agree.

In total we have as output measures (a) an AffectButton rating after the scenario, (b) three basic emotion intensity ratings, and (c) a believability rating.

3.1 Scenario Material

During the scenario the user has to negotiate with an agent in a virtual environment about a new job, or more specifically, about the amount of working hours for the candidate. The boss wants the candidate to work for five days in a week so he can pay enough attention to the customers, while the candidate wants to work for four days in a week to spend relatively more time with his daughter. The scenario is scripted in such a way that the interview always fails and the user is the cause of the failure, in other words the user can be blamed for the failure. This situation has negative consequences for the goals of the agent and produces sadness or anger in the agent according to the models of affect. To avoid potential biases in the scenario itself, other than our experimental ones, the scenario has been created by a professional scenario developer without knowledge of the experiment's goal and the voice of the virtual character has been recorded by a colleague without knowledge of the experiment. The character's expression used in this experiment has been validated in previous research [3].

The scenario is a turn based negotiation in which the human participant has two different options to choose from at every turn. For the scenario it does not matter which option the user chooses, the two options contain the same information but different text. They are only there to give the user the idea that he actually has some influence on the scenario and to immerse the user more in the scenario. The agent selects one of the two options randomly. At the end of the scenario the user can only choose to reject the offer and to quit the negotiation. The agent expresses either sadness or anger in reaction to the action of the user as shown in Fig. 2. During the rest of the scenario the expression of the agent is neutral.

4 Results

The experiment was conducted with in total 36 primarily Dutch participants, 8 (22 %) women and 28 (78 %) men not distributed equally between the groups,

Fig. 2. The expressions of the virtual agent from left to right: neutral, angry and sad

with an education level equal to high school or university. The average age was 25,8 with a range between 18 and 60 years. The average experience with virtual environments of the participants was 3.4 on a scale from 1 to 5 where 1 means no experience and 5 means a lot of experience.

4.1   Affect Measured with the AffectButton

A MANOVA was run to test the statistical significance of the results. The result of the multivariate ANOVA, with the role of the agent as independent variable and the PAD-values rated with the AffectButton about the expected feelings of the virtual agent before the negotiation scenario as dependent variables, was significant ($p = 0,028$). From the univariate analysis it appeared that the dominance dimension differed significantly ($p = 0,011$) between the two roles. The effect of role on the pleasure dimension is nearly significant ($p = 0,054$). Mean dominance and pleasure are higher if the agent is the boss (mean $= 0,275$ STD $= 0,103$ and mean $= 0,360$ STD $= 0,106$), than if the agent is the candidate (mean $= -0,109$ STD $= 0,103$ and mean $= 0,063$ STD $= 0,106$). The multivariate ANOVA with the role of the agent as the independent variable and the PAD-values for the feeling of the self before the scenario as dependent variables did not result in a significant difference ($p = 0,216$). This means that dominance manipulation was successful with respect to the perceived dominance of the virtual character before the scenario, but not with respect to the subject's own feeling of dominance before the scenario.

After the scenario was completed, the subject rated their own feeling and that of the agent again using the AffectButton. The multivariate ANOVA on the PAD-values as dependent values and the role as the independent variables was significant ($p = 0,007$) if the question is about the feelings of the other and not significance ($p = 0,582$) if the question was about the feeling of the user himself. According to the between subjects test this significance was caused by the pleasure dimension ($p < 0,001$). Although the pleasure was below zero in both cases, it is higher if the agent was the boss (mean $= -0,144$ STD $= 0,084$) and lower if the agent was the candidate (mean $= -0,560$ STD $= 0,082$). The difference in the dominance dimensions was not different anymore as was the case with the measurement before the negotiation.

We also did a univariate analysis with the perceived dominance of the agent obtained through the AffectButton after the negotiation as independent variable and the expression of the agent as dependent variable. This produces a significant result $(p = 0,039)$ where the perceived dominance is higher when the agent expresses anger and lower when the agent expresses sadness (mean $= 0,155$ STD $= 0,580$ and mean $= -0,255$ STD $= 0,552$).

4.2   Evaluation of the Reaction

The matrix containing the intensity values of the six basic emotions was used to measure the perception of the reaction (expression) of the agent. We did a multivariate ANOVA with the expression as the independent variable and the intensity values for the six emotions as the dependent variables. This test resulted in significant difference $(p = 0,026)$. The results are shown in Table 1 and confirm that the subjects perceived the expressions as intended.

Table 1. Intensities of the perceived sadness and anger depending on the expression of the agent

Expression of the agent	Perceived anger		Perceived sadness	
	Mean	STD	Mean	STD
Expressed anger	3,389	0,288	2,389	0,278
Expressed sadness	2,056	0,288	3,444	0,278

The ANOVA with the role as the independent variable and the intensity values for the six emotions as the dependent variables showed a significant effect between the roles $(p = 0,013)$. The univariate analysis showed that role significantly influences the perceived intensity of expressed surprise $(p = 0,003)$ and expressed anxiety $(p = 0,022)$. Other emotions did not produce a significant difference. Expressed anxiety was perceived stronger if the agent was the candidate (mean $= 1,889$ STD $= 0,195$) as compared to when the agent was the boss (mean $= 1,222$ STD $= 0,195$). Expressed surprise was perceived to be of higher intensity if the agent was the boss (mean $= 2,556$ STD $= 0,193$) as compared to if the agent was the candidate (mean $= 1,667$ STD $= 0,193$). As this is a role effect, this means subjects interpreted the basic expressions differently depending on social context. The effect of role on the perceived intensity of expressed happiness approached significance $(p = 0,082)$. The agent's reaction is perceived to be happier if he plays the role of the boss (mean $= 1,333$ STD $= 0,109$) than if he plays the role of the candidate (mean $= 1,056$ STD $= 0,109$). This observation is in accordance with the results from the AffectButton on the pleasure dimension.

4.3 Believability

A multivariate ANOVA (2×2) with role and expression as independent factors and the questions about the believability as dependent values did not produce any significant differences between the groups. The believability was not significantly different for the four conditions, not on the total combined scale, nor for any of the individual items.

4.4 Normal Feelings and Expressions

We did a multivariate ANOVA with role and expression as independent variables and the intensity on the six basic emotions of the normal feelings a subject reported in such a situation as the dependent variables. A significant effect of role $(p < 0,001)$ was observed. The result of the univariate analysis can be found in Table 2. If the agent is the boss the normal feeling attributed to the agent is more happy and surprised and less sad and anxious than if the agent is the candidate.

A multivariate ANOVA with role and expression as independent variables and the intensities on the six basic emotions of the normal reaction in such a situation as the dependent variables did not show a significant main effect. However, univariate analysis showed an effect of role of the agent on the emotion anxiety $(p = 0,025)$. The value for the intensity of the normal expression for the agent is higher if the agent is the candidate (mean $= 1,833$ STD $= 0,183$) than if the agent is the boss (mean $= 1,222$ STD $= 0,183$).

Table 2. Intensities for the emotions the agent should feel normally in a specific condition according to the subjects

Role of the agent	Happiness		Anger		Surprise		Sadness		Anxiety	
	Mean	STD	Mean	STD	Mean	STD	Mean	STD	Mean	STD
Boss	1,558[a]	0,126	2,611[b]	0,274	2,833[a]	0,213	2,777[a]	0,261	1,111[a]	0,190
Candidate	1,056[a]	0,126	2,778[b]	0,274	2,166[a]	0,213	3,888[a]	0,261	2,222[a]	0,190

[a] Significant difference, $p < .05$
[b] No significant difference, $p > .05$

5 Discussion

From these results several conclusions can be drawn. Manipulating the dominance dimensions did not result in an increase of the believability according to the participants. No significant difference between the four groups was found. There was however a difference in perception measured between the four groups. More surprise was perceived if the agent was the boss and more anxiety if the agent was the candidate. This result was true after seeing an expression of anger and after seeing an expression of sadness. It is interesting that the virtual agent's role in a negotiation, the social context, has an impact on the perception of the virtual agent's emotional expression.

Anxiety and surprise are perceived in the same way as how people think the agent should normally feel after the negotiation scenario. Subjects project their own expectations on the expression of the agent. The dominance of the agent was perceived differently during the two measurements, using the AffectButton, conducted during the experiment. Before the negotiation scenario the boss agent was perceived as dominant but after the scenario the agent that expressed anger was perceived as dominant, regardless if that agent played the role of the boss or the candidate. These two findings result in the notion that emotional expressions as well as social context influence the internal model a person has about someone, and that this model in turn influences the perception of the emotional expression.

We will now discuss our findings in greater detail and give suggestions for future research as well as improvements to the current experimental set-up.

5.1   Perceived and Felt Dominance

Our analysis showed that subjects interpreted the boss agent to be more dominant than the candidate before the scenario, which was exactly the purpose of the manipulation. However, when the subjects rated the dominance of themselves, this was not significantly different between the two roles. It is probably harder to change the way you feel than to imagine how somebody else is feeling. The feeling of the self can also be influenced by experiences before the experiment. Since the agent is only introduced during the experiment, previous feelings do not have any influence on the dominance of the agent. After the negotiation scenario the perceived dominance of the agent was measured again using the AffectButton. Now there was a significant difference in this dominance based on the expressed emotion of the agent and not based on the role of the agent in the scenario. When anger is expressed, the perceived dominance of the agent is high and when sadness is expressed, the perceived dominance is low. This is in line with the reverse appraisal work as presented in [5]. The expression of the agent is interpreted as showing information about the mental state of the agent, in this case specifically the dominance.

The gender ratio was different between the conditions, but as shown in other research about the perception of emotional expressions [11] gender does not seem to influence the perception of emotional expressions.

5.2   Evaluation of the Reaction

The expression of the agent in the virtual scenario was perceived by the subjects. If the agent expresses anger the intensity of perceived anger is higher while if the agent expresses sadness the intensity of the sadness is higher. Interestingly, part of the effect on the interpretation of the expression of the agent is not dependent on the actual expression, but can only be explained due to the agent's role. If the agent is the boss, the expression is perceived to contain more surprise and happiness and less anxiety than if the agent is the candidate. The difference in happiness is also found using the AffectButton directly after the scenario; the pleasure dimension is higher if the agent plays the boss than if the agent plays the candidate. Because of this difference it can be concluded that the perception of an emotional expression is dependent on the context of the expression. Even very strong basic emotions (anger and sadness) are perceived differently if the context of the expression is different. This effect was also shown in [24] where the same facial expression is judged differently depending on the clip that was shown before the expression.

The character's expressions used in this experiment have been validated in previous research [3]. However, these expressions have not been validated when used in a social context. As such, the result of this experiment also helps us understand the influence of social context on the perception of basic emotions. The expression is perceived in the direction of the reported normal feeling of the subject. The normally expected feeling is predicted to contain higher happiness and surprise for the agent if he plays the role of the boss and a high sadness and anxiety if the agent plays the role of the candidate. The intensity values for the emotions that are not expressed by the agent - happiness, anxiety and surprise - are rated by the subjects in agreement with what they think is normal to feel in such a situation.

5.3 Believability

An important potential explanation for the absence of a difference in believability between the groups is the changed perception of dominance. Before the scenario the boss agent is perceived as the most dominant one, but after the scenario the agent who expresses anger is perceived as the most dominant one, independent of the role of the agent in the scenario. This can be explained using the theory of mind [20]. People construct an internal model about the goals and the feelings of the agent. For this model they use all the information that is available to them; the introductory story (or context of the negotiation), the behavior during the negotiation and the final emotional reaction of the agent. The internal model of the agent is constantly updated to match the reality as closely as possible. This 'reverse engineering' of the internal model of the agent [10] or reverse appraisal [5] is in line with findings in other research. The fact that the pleasure and dominance values as derived from the AffectButton are significantly different before and after the negotiation, implies that the user changes his internal model of the agent depending on the negotiation and the final emotional expression.

Interesting future research that could confirm this theory could be to ask why people think the agent expressed a certain emotion. This way the internal model the user has about the agent can be retrieved and it can also be determined if the users interpret the situation in a broader context or in a narrow *negotiation goals not achieved* context. In the broader context it might be that subjects thought that surprise would have been an emotion to expect for the boss, when the user rejected the offer (which equally makes sense from an appraisal theoretic principle, as it would not be expected from a candidate in need to reject a job offer). This points towards another important notion for future research: a very detailed, well validated scenario is required to test hypotheses about computational models of appraisal theory. A small change of perspective can change the interpretation of the situation by subjects.

5.4   Normal Feeling of the Agent

Now we look at what subjects think is normal for the agent to feel. It interesting to see that for the intensity of anger the agent is expected to feel, it does not matter if the agent plays the role of the boss or the candidate. Since in both situations the agent is expected to feel anger in equal amounts, this probably means that the blameworthiness of the user is more or less the same in both situations and thus independent of the role of the agent. However, the intensity of the expected anger felt by the agent is low relative to the intensity of the expected felt sadness. An explanation for this can be that it is not clear who is to blame for the failure of the negotiation. The negotiation is always ended by the user, but it can be argued that this is not sufficient for the user to be deemed blameworthy. If one of the sides is not giving in at all and leaves no option to the other side than to quit the negotiation, this side can be deemed blameworthy as well. To simulate the situation in which anger is elicited, in a future scenario it must be made very clear that one of the sides is responsible for the failure of the negotiation. This manipulation should also be checked by asking the user who he thinks is responsible for the failure of the negotiation.

The expected intensity of the sadness felt by the agent is dependent on the role of the agent. If the agent is the boss he is expected to feel less sadness than if the agent is the candidate. So the perception of loss is dependent on the context of the negotiation, where the loss is bigger for the candidate than for the boss. This makes sense if one takes into account the position of the candidate and of the boss before the negotiation, not achieving agreement is much worse for the candidate than for the boss. The intensity of the anxiety felt by the agent is also dependent on the role of the agent. In the candidate role the felt anxiety is much higher than in the role of the boss. This is probably because the perceived future loss for the candidate is higher than for the boss. Anxiety is the result of a negatively valenced event in the future [9,19].

5.5   Normal Expression of the Agent

Although subjects clearly indicate different felt emotions for the dominant and submissive roles, they do not show a clear preference for how an agent should express himself. The subjects only agree that the agent should express more anxiety if he plays the role of the candidate than if he plays the role of the boss. This lack of a clear effect on how one should express oneself can possible be explained by the presumption that subjects had different norms on which emotions to express in a situation, or by the presumption that in this situation one typically does not express a clear emotion. In future research it will be required to ask the participants why they think it is normal to express a certain emotion. This way it can be identified how the scenario is interpreted by different users and a step forward can be made towards an unambiguous and validated scenario.

Beside the absence of a benchmark scenario, methodological issues could also explain for the absence of an effect. The study contained a large number of variables which from a methodological and statistical perspective ideally should have a larger number of subjects. One interesting idea for follow up is to do a conceptual replication with a larger number of subjects.

6   Conclusion

We have conducted an experiment to investigate the effect of social dominance on perceived emotion expression of a virtual character that expresses anger or sadness. We hypothesized that the believability of the character depended on the correct selection of anger versus sadness depending on social dominance. When a character is in a high dominant role, anger was hypothesized to be more believable; while in a submissive role sadness would be the preferred reaction.

The believability measure did not produce a significant difference in the four conditions. The hypothesis that dominant character are more believable when expressing anger and submissive characters are more believable when expressing sadness cannot be confirmed for this scenario. However, the intensity of the felt anger by the agent in the described scenario was not different depending on the role the agent plays according to the subjects. In future research a scenario should be used where there is a difference in intensity of felt anger between the roles, to see if the believability is not dependent on the dominance in all situations. Subjects do not agree with each other on what they think is normal to express in a specific situation. This difference could also explain why the believability is not different for the conditions.

Further, we showed that social role influences how the agent's perception is interpreted. A dominant agent's expression is perceived to be more surprised while a submissive character's expression is perceived to be more anxious. It is an important finding that perception of a facial expression is not fixed for a specific graphical representation, but is influenced by the scenario and social context in which the expression is shown.

The expression of anger by a dominant character is not perceived as in indication of negative affect, while the expression of a submissive character is. This effect does not exist for the expression of sadness which is always interpreted as an indication of negative affect.

Finally, to validate this model one should ask the subject to explain the expression of the agent. This explanation can then be compared to the explanations offered by appraisal theories. From this it can be concluded if dominance is a factor in the perception of the emotional expressions.

Our research shows the importance of a tight relation between emotion psychology and virtual character evaluation, as well as the need for well-validated test scenarios to evaluated virtual characters and appraisal theories. Further, we showed that even basic emotions like sadness and anger are perceived differently when in different social contexts. People perceive an expression in agreement with what they think is normal to feel in such a situation.

References

1. Becker-Asano, C., Wachsmuth, I.: Affect simulation with primary and secondary emotions. In: Prendinger, H., Lester, J.C., Ishizuka, M. (eds.) IVA 2008. LNCS (LNAI), vol. 5208, pp. 15–28. Springer, Heidelberg (2008)
2. Broekens, J., Brinkman, W.-P.: Affectbutton: towards a standard for dynamic affective user feedback. In: 3rd International Conference on Affective Computing and Intelligent Interaction and Workshops 2009, ACII 2009, pp. 1–8, September 2009
3. Broekens, J., Qu, C., Brinkman, W.-P.: Dynamic facial expression of emotion made easy. CoRR abs/1211.4500 (2012)
4. de Melo, C.M., Carnevale, P., Gratch, J.: The influence of emotions in embodied agents on human decision-making. In: Safonova, A. (ed.) IVA 2010. LNCS, vol. 6356, pp. 357–370. Springer, Heidelberg (2010)
5. de Melo, C.M., Carnevale, P.J., Read, S.J., Gratch, J.: Reading peoples minds from emotion expressions in interdependent decision making. J. Pers. Soc. Psychol. **106**(1), 73 (2014)
6. Ekman, P.: Basic Emotions, pp. 45–60. Wiley, New York (2005)
7. El-Nasr, M.S., Yen, J., Ioerger, T.R.: Flame-fuzzy logic adaptive model of emotions. Auton. Agent. Multi-Agent Syst. **3**, 219–257 (2000)
8. Gebhard, P.: Alma: a layered model of affect. In: Proceedings of the Fourth International Joint Conference on Autonomous Agents and Multiagent Systems, AAMAS '05, pp. 29–36. ACM, New York (2005)
9. Gratch, J., Marsella, S.: A domain-independent framework for modeling emotion. J. Cogn. Syst. Res. **5**, 269–306 (2004)
10. Hareli, S., Hess, U.: What emotional reactions can tell us about the nature of others: an appraisal perspective on person perception. Cogn. Emot. **24**(1), 128–140 (2010)
11. Hareli, S., Shomrat, N., Hess, U.: Emotional versus neutral expressions and perceptions of social dominance and submissiveness. Emotion **9**(3), 378 (2009)
12. Höök, K., Persson, P., Sjölinder, M.: Evaluating users' experience of a character-enhanced information space. AI Commun. **13**, 195–212 (2000)
13. Lazarus, R.: Emotion and Adaptation. Oxford University Press, New York (1991)
14. Lerner, J.S., Tiedens, L.Z.: Portrait of the angry decision maker: how appraisal tendencies shape anger's influence on cognition. J. Behav. Decis. Making **19**(2), 115–137 (2006)
15. Likert, R.: A technique for the measurement of attitudes. Arch. Psychol. **22**(140), 1–55 (1932)
16. Marinier, R.P., Laird, J.E., Lewis, R.L.: A computational unification of cognitive behavior and emotion. Cogn. Syst. Res. **10**(1), 48–69 (2009). (Modeling the Cognitive Antecedents and Consequences of Emotion)
17. Mehrabian, A.: Pleasure-arousal-dominance: a general framework for describing and measuring individual differences in temperament. Curr. Psychol. **14**, 261–292 (1996). doi:10.1007/BF02686918

18. Niewiadomski, R., Hyniewska, S., Pelachaud, C.: Evaluation of multimodal sequential expressions of emotions in ECA. In: 3rd International Conference on Affective Computing and Intelligent Interaction and Workshops 2009, ACII 2009, pp. 1–7. IEEE (2009)
19. Ortony, A., Clore, G.L., Collins, A.: The Cognitive Structure of Emotions. Cambridge University Press, Cambridge (1984)
20. Premack, D., Woodruff, G.: Does the chimpanzee have a theory of mind? Behav. Brain sci. **1**(04), 515–526 (1978)
21. Prendinger, H., Ishizuka, M.: The empathic companion: a character-based interface that addresses users' affective states. Appl. Artif. Intell. **19**(3–4), 267–285 (2005)
22. Sander, D., Grandjean, D., Scherer, K.R.: A systems approach to appraisal mechanisms in emotion. Neural Netw. **18**(4), 317–352 (2005). (Emotion and Brain)
23. van Kleef, G.A.: Emotion in conflict and negotiation: introducing the emotions as social information (EASI) model. In: Ashkanasy, N.M., Cooper, C.L. (eds.) Research Companion to Emotion Inorganizations, pp. 392–404. Edward Elgar, London (2008)
24. Wallbott, H.G.: In and out of context: influences of facial expression and context information on emotion attributions. Br. J. Soc. Psychol. **27**(4), 357–369 (1988)
25. Wehrle, T.: Motivations behind modeling emotional agents: whose emotion does your robot have? (1998)

Modelling Two Emotion Regulation Strategies as Key Features of Therapeutic Empathy

Juan Martínez-Miranda$^{(\boxtimes)}$, Adrián Bresó, and Juan Miguel García-Gómez

ITACA Institute, Biomedical Informatics Group, Universitat Politècnica de València,
Camino de Vera s/n, Valencia, Spain
{juama25,adbregua,juanmig}@upv.es

Abstract. Computational models of affective processes have allowed the construction of synthetic characters able to produce empathic behaviours. The use of empathy, as a strategy to enhance engagement and cooperation with human pairs has proved good results in different application domains. Mental care is a particular area where the use of empathic virtual characters would offer several advantages facilitating the self-treatment management. Empathic responses in counselling and psychotherapy differ from "natural" empathy produced in everyday situations. Therapeutic empathy requires an emotional involvement of the therapist with the patient and an emotional detachment for a more objective appraisal of the situation. This paper introduces a model of emotion regulation as the first steps to get therapeutic empathy responses in a virtual agent constructed to support the treatment of major depression. The modelling of two specific strategies of emotion regulation based on Gross theory (cognitive change and response modulation) is described.

Keywords: Affective process modelling · Emotion regulation · Reappraisal · Response modulation · Virtual agents

1 Introduction

The interest in the development of Embodied Conversational Agents (ECAs) as advanced human-computer interaction interfaces has generated a good number of initiatives aimed to construct the underlying mechanisms able to produce more human-like behaviours in those agents. The modelling of the emotional phenomenon, as a basic component of human behaviour, has produced different computational models of emotion that are used to analyse and simulate different aspects of this complex process. Most of these computational architectures of emotion are based on different cognitive and psychological theories influenced by the particular components and phases of the emotional phenomenon that the model tries to represent. Examples of these architectures include FLAME [16] and EMA [27] based on appraisal theories of emotion; WASABI [2] based on dimensional theories of emotion; or the model proposed in [1] which is based on the anatomic approach of emotions (for a deeper discussion refer to [29]).

© Springer International Publishing Switzerland 2014
T. Bosse et al. (Eds.): Emotion Modeling, LNAI 8750, pp. 115–133, 2014.
DOI: 10.1007/978-3-319-12973-0_7

A common expected benefit from these tools is the construction of more believable ECAs that better engage their human pairs during interaction.

One emotion-related element well studied and commonly used to create better interactive scenarios with ECAs is empathy. Empathic agents have been constructed to achieve a better cooperation and complete longer interaction sessions in different domains, including learning [8], training [34] and clinical applications [3]. Within the clinical domain, a particular area where the use of empathic virtual agents can be particularly beneficial is in the treatment of mental health disorders [24]. Empathy is considered a fundamental aspect in promoting therapeutic change when providing counseling and psychotherapeutic interventions [36] and some studies concluded that empathy accounts for between 7–10 % of the variance in therapy outcome [4].

The modelling of empathic responses in ECAs as virtual assistants to support the treatment of mental health disorders faces some challenges that need to be carefully addressed. For example, in the treatment of major depression, an interactive virtual agent must not display a "pure emotional" empathic behaviours by adopting the same—typically negative—mood of the patient. The disadvantage is that these behaviours can be interpreted as sympathetic expressions of condolence that may imply a sense of unintended agreement with the patient's (negative) views [11]. What is most beneficial from a clinical perspective is not to produce "only" natural empathic reactions as response to the patient's input, but to generate *therapeutic-empathy* responses in the agent.

As mentioned in [38], it is important to distinguish *natural empathy* (experienced by people in everyday situations) from *therapeutic empathy* in order to provide the patients with useful feedback for their particular condition. One of the key differences between natural and therapeutic empathy is the "addition of the cognitive perspective-taking component to the emotional one; the cognitive component helps the therapist to conceptualize the client's distress in cognitive terms" ([38], pp. 594). In other words, a therapist should "assume both the role of an emotional involvement in an interview with a patient and an emotional detachment that allows for a more objective appraisal" ([11], pp. 102); a wrong empathic attitude is generated when the therapist does not to some degree maintain an emotional distance from the patient [39].

In this paper, we describe the modelling of this *perspective-taking component* aimed to produce in a virtual agent the required emotional detachment or emotional distance at specific stages of the interaction with patients with major depression. The theoretical basis of the proposed model lies in J. J. Gross' process model of emotion regulation [18]. In particular, we are modelling two strategies of emotion regulation: *(i) cognitive change* and *(ii) response modulation*. The **cognitive change strategy** is triggered when the patient is reporting a *bad situation* (e.g. low mood level) which in a first step would also produce (empathically) a negative emotion in the virtual agent. Once triggered, the cognitive change strategy seeks for additional information that can change (positively) the significance of the detected situation (e.g. finding a positive tendency in the mood level regarding the reported values in past days) allowing *a more objective* *appraisal.* Complementarily, the **response modulation strategy** is used to regulate those negative emotion-expressive behaviours in the agent produced when the cognitive change strategy has not succeed (i.e. there is no information that changes the -*negative*- situation meaning). The suppression of negative expressive behaviour helps the virtual agent in not to convey a sense of condolence that would be counterproductive due to the patient's condition. The implementation of the model have been developed as an extension of the FAtiMA (appraisal-based) computational architecture of emotions [14].

The rest of the paper is organised as follows: in Sect. 2 we put in context our research by introducing the Help4Mood project, which aims to remotely support the treatment of major depression. Then, in Sect. 3 we present in more detail the relevant parts of Gross' emotion regulation theory used in our model, complemented by some related work in the ECAs community. Section 4 presents in detail our model of emotion regulation as the core component able to produce better therapeutic empathy reactions in a virtual agent. Section 5 describes the first steps towards the evaluation of the model and finally, Sect. 6 presents the conclusions and further directions of the presented work.

2   A Virtual Agent to Support the Remote Treatment of Major Depression

The model reported here is part of the work developed in an EC-FP7 research project called Help4Mood (www.help4mood.info). The main aim of the project is the development of an interactive system designed to support the treatment of people who are recovering from major depressive disorder in the community, with the focus being on promoting adherence to the therapy through engaging the patients. The complete Help4Mood system is composed of three main components: a virtual agent (VA), which acts as the main interface with the user; a Decision Support System (DSS) which manages, analyses and summarises the user's daily sessions; and the Personal Monitoring System (PMS) in the form of sensor devices used to collect objective measures from the user, including physical activity and sleep patterns.

The virtual agent has been designed to facilitate the collection of relevant data including subjective measures (by applying standardised questionnaires and guided interviews), and neuropsychomotor measures (by offering tasks for speech input and/or selected games) which are designed to complement the objective measures obtained from the PMS. The collection of the patient data is carried out through daily sessions between the patient and the system; the content of each session varies, with some tasks being carried out every day (such as the Daily Mood Check consisting of a single item measuring overall mood plus four items of the CES-D VAS-VA questionnaire [30]), and some others executed weekly (e.g. the standardised PHQ-9 questionnaire [26], for example). Moreover, the virtual agent also helps users to identify negative thinking (a key characteristic of depressive disorder) and challenge it by adapting a protocol

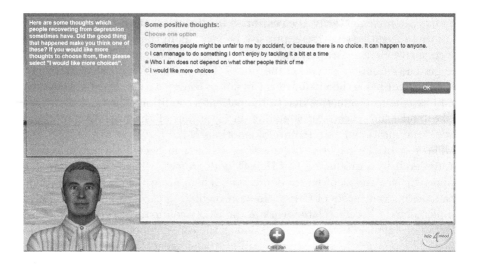

Fig. 1. The Help4Mood GUI

in concordance with the principles of Cognitive Behaviour Therapy (CBT), the main non-pharmacological treatment method for major depressive disorder.

The VA agent is composed by different but inter-related components which process and generate different aspects in the agent's behaviour. The components include the cognitive-emotional module which receives the events inferred in the DSS (using the PMS and user inputs) during a session with the patient. These events are used by the cognitive-emotional module to produce the specific task and the corresponding—if any—emotion to be disclosed during the inter-action with the patient. A second component is the Dialogue Manager System (DM) which transforms the task received from the cognitive-emotion module as dialogue acts. The dialogue acts are passed to The Natural Language Generator (NLG), which produces the content of the agent's verbal response in an appropri-ate style. The generated text string is sent to the Text-To-Speech (TTS) engine which realises the audio with the appropriate tone of voice. The audio and time-aligned phonemes used for lip-syncing are passed to the graphical representation of the virtual agent which takes the form of a talking head immersed in the GUI of the application (see Fig. 1). The current active emotion is also passed to the GUI for the rendering of the corresponding non-verbal communication (i.e. head movements and a set of facial expressions to convey the triggered emotion).

The cognitive-emotional module, which is the focus of this paper, has been developed as a Java-based application which makes use of the FAtiMA architec-ture [14]. For the Help4Mood scenario, we authored all the goals, actions and action tendencies to cope and react towards the events produced during the interaction with the patient. All these events are directly related with the user's responses and are the basis to produce the next more adequate action and emo-tion in the VA. As all the actions in the VA are directed to provide the different standardised questionnaires or CBT-based activities defined by the clinicians, the range of user's responses is delimited to provide the input and follow up of the offered activities. When new questionnaires and/or exercises are necessary to be added -which in turn extend the content of the daily sessions- new goals, actions and action tendencies are authored in the VA to correctly cope with the user's inputs to the new events.

With the aim to promote the usability and acceptability of the Help4Mood solution in the potential users (i.e. patients, clinicians and caregivers), the development of the integrated system has followed the user-centered design methodology [33]. The functionalities of each component are cyclically developed following the feedback and suggestions of the involved users. In the initial usability study of the integrated system[1] (PMS + DSS + VA), we followed the recommendations from the clinical experts of the project. One of them was related with the emotional behaviour in the VA: **it must not convey any negative emotion** during the interaction with the patient. The main reason behind this requirement was to avoid any interpretation of negative emotions as expressions of condolence in the side of the patient that would be clinically counter-productive. Thus, three positive emotions from the OCC model [31] (implemented as the appraisal and affect derivation mechanism in FAtiMA) were used during the interaction:

1. **Joy**: activated when an event is appraised as *desirable* for the VA (e.g. when the user accepts the activities offered by the VA during a session).
2. **Happy-For**: elicited when an event is appraised as *desirable for the patient* (e.g. good self-reported moods, thoughts or scores in the proposed activities).
3. **Admiration**: activated when an event is appraised as a *desirable consequence of a patient's action* (e.g. the correct completion of the proposed activities during the session or the completion of the whole session).

When something *goes wrong* in the clinical condition of the patient (inferred in the DSS from the PMS data or from patient's self-reports), a neutral attitude (i.e. no emotion) is adopted by the VA. The three positive emotions, when elicited, are conveyed to the patient through the combination of open and close mouth smiles plus some head movements such as nodding (identified as a key element to reinforce the sense of attention and understanding during clinician-patient communication [35]). As stated in [15], most of the positive (*enjoyable*) emotions share the smiling expression and it is not straightforward to differentiate them just through the face but other signals, such as the voice, are required. The strategy followed in our scenario was to use the intensity of the triggered emotion to display a mouth open (greater intensity) or mouth closed (lesser intensity) smile. Moreover, the positive emotions are also used by the Dialogue Manager to select and add specific utterances to the verbal feedback provided by the VA (e.g. *"That's great!"* or *"Well done!"*).

---

[1] Five people, two males and three females, who recovered from depression were recruited to use the system during a week in daily sessions with a length between 5 to 8 min.

An interview was applied to all the patients at the end of the system's usage to collect their impressions in the utilisation of the hardware (sensors) and software of Help4Mood. The feedback obtained from this initial acceptability study regarding the virtual agent was divided. Two female participants, P2 and P3, liked the virtual agent and found it "cute". P2 also noticed that the virtual agent reacted to her responses on the Daily Mood Check. While P2 thought that the virtual agent's voice was nice and calm, P3 characterised her as sounding upbeat. In contrast, P5, the third female participant, found the voice depressing; she did not pay any attention to the virtual agent and would have preferred the ability to talk to a human via teleconferencing. In terms of the emotional behaviour only 1 of the 5 users noted the emotional reactions in the VA. This result was not much unexpected since the emotional reactions in the VA were displayed only when the participants responded with *good mood*-related values in the Daily Mood Check questionnaire. In all other cases the VA simply asks the next question adopting a neutral stance.

The noted lack of responsiveness in the VA's behaviour is likely to have more than one cause, including the very short interaction time, not much variability in the response dialogues, a not enough adequate emotional intonation in the VA's speech and the aforementioned neutral attitude adopted by the VA in front of negative situations. As more content (i.e. new activities) is added to the daily sessions, longer interactions between the patient and the VA are produced offering a good opportunity to produce more variability in the different aspects of the VA's behaviour.

In terms of the cognitive-emotional component, the production of richer emotional responses became necessary to better engage the users. The inclusion of negative emotions which produce affective reactions to adverse situations would contribute to perceive a more empathic agent. The challenge here is to generate an optimal intensity in these negative emotions that allows an adequate response (in terms of action-selection and feedback provided) during the interaction with the user. To face this challenge, we have incorporated a model of emotion regulation aimed to modulate the negative emotions elicited in the VA. The emotional regulation is achieved following two strategies: changing the perspective of the current situation (producing an emotional detachment), and suppressing the expressive (negative emotion-based) behaviour to convey the appropriate reactions.

3   Emotion Regulation

3.1   Theoretical Foundations

The study and understanding of the emotion regulation process has attracted the interest of an important number of researchers in the last three decades [10,20]. Although some works consider the emotion regulation process as part of the emotion generation process [9,17], some others show the neural differences between them [12] and the benefits of studying emotion and emotion regulation separately [21,25]. In line with the second view, J. J. Gross [18,21] proposed a theoretical model of emotion regulation which refers to *the heterogeneous set of processes by which emotions are themselves regulated*. In detail, the process model of emotion regulation covers the conscious and unconscious strategies used to increase, maintain, or decrease one or more components of an emotional response. The main characteristic of this model is the identification and definition of five families of emotion regulation processes: *situation selection, situation modification, attentional deployment, cognitive change* and *response modulation*.

Situation selection is described as when an individual takes the necessary actions to be in a situation the individual expects will raise a certain desirable emotion. *Situation modification* refers to the efforts employed by the individual to directly modify the actual situation to alter its emotional impact. The third family, *attentional deployment*, refers to how individuals direct their attention within the current situation in order to influence their emotions. *Cognitive change* is described as when the individual changes how the actual situation is appraised to alter its emotional significance, either by changing how the individual thinks about the situation or the capacity to manage it. Finally, the *response modulation* family refers when the individual influences the physiological, experiential, or behavioural responses to the situation.

Each family of emotion regulation processes occurs at different points in the emotion generation process and there are substantial differences between them (see details in [21]). An important aspect to consider is that the first four emotion regulation families occur before any appraisal produces the full emotional response (antecedent-focused), while the last family (response modulation) occurs after response tendencies have been initiated (response-focused). Two particular strategies of emotion regulation have been studied in [18]: one is *reappraisal* as a type of cognitive change (antecedent-focused) and the other is *suppression* as a type of response modulation (response-focused). According to the authors, reappraisal occurs early in the emotion generation process and it involves cognitively neutralizing a potentially emotion-eliciting situation. In consequence, reappraisal should decrease experiential, behavioural, and physiological responses. On the other hand, suppression occurs later in the emotion generation process and requires an active inhibition of the emotion-expressive behaviour that is generated when the emotion is triggered.

3.2   Computational Models of Emotion Regulation

The Gross process model of emotion regulation has inspired the development of some computational models of emotion regulation. The group of Bosse and colleagues have formally modelled the four antecedent-focused emotion regulation strategies and incorporate it in synthetic characters as participants in a virtual storytelling [6]. In a subsequent work, Bosse and colleagues constructed virtual agents not only with the capacity of regulate their emotions, but also with the ability of *reasoning* about the emotion regulation processes of other agents [5]. This model has been called CoMERG (the Cognitive Model for Emotion Regulation based on Gross) and it formalizes Gross model through a set of difference equations and rules to simulate the dynamics of Gross' emotion-regulation strategies [7].

CoMERG identifies a set of variables and their dependencies to represent both quantitative aspects (such as levels of emotional response) and qualitative aspects (such as decisions to regulate one's emotion) of the model. These variables include e.g. the level of -the actual- emotion, the optimal -desired- level of emotion, the personal tendency to adjust the emotional value, or the costs of adjusting the emotional value, among others which are used to simulate and evaluate the results in the use of the four antecedent-focus strategies of emotion regulation. The modelling and simulation of the different emotion regulation strategies is the main aim of CoMERG, but the underlying appraisal and affect derivation mechanisms required to generate specific emotions according to the observed world-state are not explicitly addressed. In a more recent work [23] the integration of CoMERG with other two computational models of emotions EMA [27] and I-PEFIC^{ADM} [22] is proposed to cover the complete process of emotion generation, regulation and action responses in virtual agents.

Similarly, the work presented in [37] proposes an extension of CoMERG by adding an emotion-dependent regulation process based on the mood and personality of individuals. Moreover, the occurrence of new (positive and negative) events during the simulation time was included to analyse the influence of these events on the emotion regulation process. However, as an extension of CoMERG, this approach does not have an appraisal and affect derivation mechanism for monitoring events in the world nor have been reported its integration in virtual characters.

It is important to mention that FAtiMA also applies its own strategy (which is based on [28]) for changing world interpretation and lowering strong negative emotions. This mechanism is part of the FAtiMA deliberative layer which implements two types of coping to deal with changes in the environment. The problem-focused coping acts on the agent's world to deal with the situation and consists of a set of actions to be executed to achieve the desired state of the world. The emotional focused coping is used to change the agent's interpretation of circumstances. When a specific plan or action fails in the intention to achieve or maintain a desired goal, a mental disengagement is applied. Mental disengagement works by reducing the importance of the goal, which in turn reduces the intensity of the negative emotions triggered when a goal fails [14].

For the Help4Mood scenario, what is still needed is the mechanism to re-interpret (i.e. reappraise) a situation that is detected as adverse to the patient's condition and that could lead to the triggering of a negative emotion. While the current emotion-focused coping of FAtiMA is concentrated in the achievement/maintenance, or not, of the agent's internal goals and the reduction of the intensity of the negative OCC prospect based emotions (i.e. *disappointment* and *fears_confirmed*), we need an emotional regulation module that down-regulates the intensity of the negative affective state produced by a situation derived from those negative events in the patient's status. Thus, the verbal and non-verbal feedback provided to the patient based on the VA's affective state would contribute to a better therapeutic empathy communication during the session. The design and implementation of this module is detailed in the following section.

4 Adapting a Model of Two Emotion Regulation Strategies

The initial version of the cognitive-emotional module in the Help4Mood's virtual agent has been extended by allowing the elicitation of two OCC-based negative emotions. *Pity* is activated as a result of appraising some events as *not desirable for the patient* (e.g. when reporting a low mood, negative thoughts or decreased physical activity). *Distress* is triggered when an event is appraised as *not desirable for the agent itself* (e.g. when a not daily use of the system is detected). The challenge is how to communicate these emotions not as a sense of condolence due to the adverse events, but as a sense of understanding and provide useful feedback that motivates the patient towards the daily use of Help4Mood. As with the positive emotions, the negative emotions are reflected through a particular facial expressions and some dialogues constructed in the Dialogue Manager. The main objective is to produce the optimal intensity in the negative emotion to display an adequate facial expression, and at the same time, take the necessary actions to cope with the situation.

The proposed solution is to implement a mechanism of emotion regulation that can be used to modulate the negative emotions and produce an emotional detachment from the situation which helps to provide useful responses during the interaction. Based on Gross theory of emotion regulation, we have implemented two of the strategies defined in Gross's model of emotion regulation: cognitive change (through the reappraisal of events) and response modulation (through suppression of the emotion-expressive behaviour). At the moment, we are not considering the inclusion of the other three antecedent-focused emotion regulation strategies.

The main reason behind this decision is the particular context of the VA's environment in the Help4Mood scenario: the main events received and appraised by the VA are all closely related with the actual detected or reported condition of the patient. During the interaction cycle, there are no other alternative situations to select, i.e. there are no other possible values in the patient's condition (situation selection) that the VA can concentrate on. Also, the VA cannot modify by itself the detected or reported patient condition (situation modification) and it is desirable that the VA should appear focused on what the patient is actually reporting (attentional deployment). Nevertheless, it is still possible to positively *reappraise* the current situation by analysing how the patient's condition has evolved during past sessions. If after the reappraisal process the current situation cannot be assessed in positive terms, some *suppression* in the intensity of the activated negative emotion is still possible to modulate the displayed facial expression and/or head movements related with the current negative affective state of the VA.

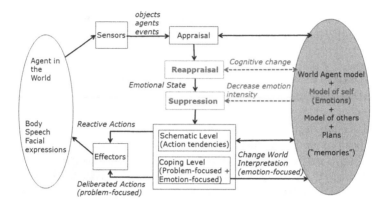

Fig. 2. The FAtiMA architecture [14] with an added emotion regulation component

We have incorporated an initial model of these two emotion regulation strategies as an extension of the FAtiMA architecture. A key advantage of FAtiMA is its modular implementation which is composed of a core functionality plus a set of components that add or remove particular functionalities (in terms of appraisal or behaviour) making it more flexible and easier to extend [13]. Thus, the proposed model of emotion regulation has been added as an extended component of the FAtiMA core functionality as presented in Fig. 2 (the new component is displayed using dotted red lines).

4.1   Modelling Cognitive Change - Reappraisal

Based on Gross theory of emotion regulation, we have implemented a mechanism to reappraise those events susceptible to triggering a negative emotion in the VA. Following the concepts of Gross theory, we represent a situation composed by the event or events produced in the VA's environment. The actual situation meaning can be changed using a pre-defined set of situation meanings which in turn are formed by the different events that are used during the reappraisal process. The reappraisal process is triggered only when the target (negative) emotion exceeds a configured threshold which represents the maximum intensity allowed in the target emotion. The reappraisal process can produce a different -positive-emotion or the same negative emotion with a decreased -*down-regulated*- intensity. In the case where the resultant emotion is still negative with an intensity greater than the desired maximum threshold, the suppression emotion strategy is applied (see next section). The diagram in Fig. 3 graphically represents the different concepts and the flow of the cognitive change process.

According to Gross's theory, the cognitive change is an antecedent-focused strategy of emotion regulation, which means that it occurs before appraisals give rise to full-blown emotional response tendencies [21]. Thus, our model of cognitive change is activated when a new event is received from the environment. A prospective appraisal is executed to assess if the event derives from

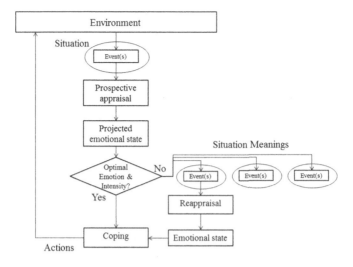

Fig. 3. Cognitive change model diagram

a desirable or undesirable (in terms of the agent's goals) situation related to the patient's condition. The result of this prospective appraisal is the projection of the potential emotional state produced by the event. In other words, our model "simulates" the appraisal and affect derivation processes to analyse the emotional consequences of the current situation, but without producing the full-blown emotional responses.

If the projected emotional state involves the activation of a positive emotion— no emotion regulation is required—then the same event is used to execute the *real* appraisal and generates the corresponding responses in the VA. On the other hand, if the projected emotional state includes the activation of a negative emotion with intensity greater than the pre-defined maximum threshold, the corresponding pre-defined alternative event(s) is selected for reappraisal which would construct a more positive meaning of the original situation. If the emotional state produced by the reappraisal is better (i.e. produces a positive emotion or the same negative emotion with a reduced intensity) than the simulated situation, all the (reactive and deliberative) responses are executed continuing with the next interaction cycle.

To exemplify this process consider the following: during the current Help4Mood session one of the activities to perform is the assessment of the patient's depression level in the last 7 days through the PHQ-9 questionnaire. If the score obtained indicates that the depression level is quite high, the VA can appraise this result as highly undesirable for the patient's condition, generating a strong *pity* emotion. Using the cognitive change strategy of emotion regulation, the VA can change the meaning of this situation using an alternative view. In the example, the VA can consult the results obtained in the PHQ-9 questionnaire during previous sessions (stored in the model of the patient maintained in the DSS module) and check whether the current result shows a positive tendency in the patient's condition taking into account the previous results. If this positive tendency is found, the original event would be reappraised as "not much undesirable" to the patient (thought the current PHQ-9 score is still not the optimal). This reappraisal can change the emotional state or the emotion's intensity in the VA which is reflected in the feedback provided to the patient, something like "Ok, it seems that your current condition is not very good, but in general terms you are making good progresses in the last days". This is different from the feedback that the VA would provide if the response is based only on the negative meaning of the current situation (e.g. "Ok, it seems that you have had some difficult days, but please continue with the treatment"). In both cases, the verbal feedback is accompanied by the appropriate facial expression according to the activated emotion and its intensity.

Similar events to change the meaning of the current situation can be predefined to cope with the result of other session activities (e.g. the Daily Mood Check questionnaire, the negative thoughts challenge, or the behaviour activation modules). All the targeted emotions to be regulated, the maximum intensity threshold and the different situation meanings with the events used during the reappraisal can be authored in an XML file in a similar fashion as the emotional thresholds and decay rates; the emotional reaction rules; the set of action tendencies; and the goals and actions that form the whole VA's behaviour are currently authored in FAtiMA. A simple example of this XML-based file is as follows:

```
<EmotionRegulation>
  <!--Targeted emotions for regulation-->
  <EmotionalDesiredIntensities>
    <EmotionalDesiredIntensity emotion="Distress" desiredIntensity="3"
                               suppressionRate="3">
    <EmotionalDesiredIntensity emotion="Pity" desiredIntensity="3"
                               suppressionRate="4">
  ...
  </EmotionalDesiredIntensities>

  <!--Situation meanings used for reappraisal-->
  <SituationMeanings>
    <Situation name="High_Depression_Score">
      <ElicitingEmotion type="Distress" minIntensity="6">
        <CauseEvent subject="User" action="High_Score_PHQ-9">
      </ElicitingEmotion>
      </EventForReappraisal subject="[SELF]" action="getPreviousDepressionScore"
                            target="User" parameters="2">
    <Situation>

    <Situation name="Low_Mood">
      <ElicitingEmotion type="Distress" minIntensity="6">
        <CauseEvent subject="User" action="Low_Score_DailyMoodCheck">
      </ElicitingEmotion>
      </EventForReappraisal subject="[SELF]" action="getPreviousMood" target="User"
                            parameters="5">
    <Situation>
  </SituationMeanings>
</EmotionRegulation>
```

The content of the file is divided into two main parts: the first part under the `<EmotionalDesiredIntensities>` tag defines the targeted emotions that will be regulated (in our case, we concentrate only on negative emotions). It contains the values for the maximum desired intensity of the emotion and the suppression rate value used in the response modulation strategy (see next section). The second part of the content under the `<SituationMeanings>` tag defines the set of situations that are candidates to be reappraised with a more *positive* perspective. Each situation contains the event (`<CauseEvent>`) that would elicit the *negative* emotion (`<ElicitingEmotion>`) and the definition of the event used for the reappraisal (`<EventForReappraisal>`). The event that is used during the reappraisal process is composed by four fields following the same definition of an event used in FAtiMA [14]:

- The *subject* who performs the action
- The *action* to perform
- The *target* of the action
- A list of parameters that specify additional information about the action

The mechanism to select the specific situation in the emotion regulation component is based on the activation of action tendencies process provided in FAtiMA. When executing the prospective appraisal using the event defined in the `<CauseEvent>` tag, if the projected emotional state activates the emotion type with an intensity equal or greater than the *minIntensity* value, then the event defined in `<EventForReappraisal>` is selected for the reappraisal. This event contains the action that will be executed to get an alternative meaning of the current situation (e.g. in the *Low_Mood* situation of the XML example, the virtual agent gets the scores of the mood reported by the patient in the past 5 days to detect if the mean of the previous values is high or if there is a positive tendency in the mood of the patient).

The result of the reappraisal does not necessarily change a negative situation. Continuing with our example, the result of the previous depression scores could indicate a negative tendency in the evolution of the patient. In these cases, the resultant emotional state could even increase the intensity of the negative emotion. As a requirement of the VA in the Help4Mood scenario is not to convey strong negative emotional responses during the interaction, the response modulation strategy is activated in these cases.

4.2 Modelling Response Modulation - Suppression

Response modulation is an emotional regulation strategy that occurs late in the emotion-generative process, once the response tendencies have been initiated [21]. According to [19], a common form of response modulation involves regulating emotion-expressive behaviour. In this sense, suppression as a form of response modulation can be used to model the regulation of the activated ongoing expressive behaviour in the VA during the interaction with the patient. The activation of negative emotions in the VA could be useful in selecting the appropriate action to cope with specific situations. An example that can occur during the daily sessions is when the VA detects cues that indicate thoughts of self-harming (i.e. a high score in question number 9 of the PHQ-9 questionnaire).

In this case, an action tendency triggered by the activated -negative- emotional state is the execution of the Help4Mood crisis plan: display contact information for crisis services and trusted family/friends plus discontinuing the use of Help4Mood. The expressive behaviour (i.e. the displayed facial expression and the verbalised utterances) during the execution of the crisis plan should avoid an unnecessary sense of alarmism, but promote calming and understanding of the situation.

The way to regulate the expressive behaviour in the VA produced by the on-going emotional state is through decrementing the intensity of the emotion. As the intensity is used to generate the corresponding facial expression (stronger intensity means more marked expressivity in the face of the VA), what we need is a mechanism to down-regulate the intensity of the activated negative emotion. In FAtiMA, the intensity of an emotion is a variable which depends on the elapsed time and it is influenced by a pre-defined decay rate parameter. The decay function for each emotion is implemented in FAtiMA using the following formula, as proposed in [32]:

$$Intensity(em, t) = Intensity(em, t0) \cdot e^{-bt} \tag{1}$$

Where the *Intensity* of an emotion *(em)* at any time t depends on the intensity of the emotion when it was generated *Intensity(em, t0)* and the value of the decay rate b determines how quickly the intensity of the emotion decays over time. A slight modification of this formula by introducing an additional value called suppression rate sR is used to introduce a high decrement in the emotion intensity aiming to reach the optimal intensity value in the regulated emotion:

$$Intensity(em, t) = Intensity(em, t0) \cdot e - bt \cdot \frac{1}{sR} \quad \text{where } sR >= 1 \tag{2}$$

The two values, the optimal intensity and the suppression rate, are pre-configured for each emotion in the emotion regulation XML-based file presented in the previous section. Different values for these parameters will generate different behaviour in the VA: higher values in the *desiredIntensity* parameter will allow stronger intensities in the negative emotions triggering the corresponding coping behaviour. In contrast, low values for this parameter will force the application of the implemented emotion regulation strategies to achieve the desired intensity in the negative emotions. On the other hand, higher values in the *suppressionRate* parameter will produce a faster decrement of the emotion intensity and the suppression of the emotion expressive behaviour.

5   Evaluation

The evaluation of the proposed model is currently ongoing within the evaluation of the whole Help4Mood system through the running of the final pilot involving patients recruited by the clinicians of the consortium. The inclusion criteria for the participants include those patients with major depressive disorder as a

Table 1. Questions for the assessment of the agent interaction

Number	Question	Anchor 1	Anchor 5
Q1	The virtual agent behaves cold and aloof	Strongly disagree	Strongly agree
Q2	The virtual agent looks emotionally stable	Strongly disagree	Strongly agree
Q3	I am comfortable with the emotional responses of the VA	Strongly disagree	Strongly agree
Q4	The virtual agent is trustworthy	Strongly disagree	Strongly agree
Q5	I would like to continue interacting with the virtual agent	Strongly disagree	Strongly agree
Q6	The virtual agent motivates me to use the Help4Mood system on daily basis	Strongly disagree	Strongly agree

primary diagnosis with a mild to moderate range[2]; aged between 18 and 64 inclusive; and living at home. Excluded participants are those with a recent major adverse life event such as bereavement; a history at any time of other disorders such psychotic depression, bipolar disorder or substance misuse; difficulties in comprehension, communication or dexterity; requirement of personal assistance for activities of daily living; or people whose antidepressant medication had been changed within three months prior to enrolment.

The participants will use the Help4Mood system for 4 weeks followed by an exit interview containing questions to assess the acceptability of the system's components. Regarding the assessment of the VA's acceptability, six (Likert-based scale) questions were designed to collect the feedback from the participants (see Table 1). The first three questions are directly related with the observed emotional behaviour of the VA. These questions will help to assess whether the users perceive an adequate empathic behaviour from the VA and analyse if in the long run it could contribute to a better engagement and long-term use of the whole system as part of the treatment.

A minimum of 15 participants are expected to be enroled in the final pilot which is already ongoing. At the moment, the feedback from the first three patients has been received. All three participants were female aged 38(P1), 42(P2), 58(P3) and used to the use of technology (laptops, smartphones). Two of the three participants (P2 and P3) rated as *disagree* Q1 stating that they did not consider the VA as cold and aloof; P1 rated Q1 as *agree*. Regarding Q2, P2 and P3 rated *agree* while P3 rated *neither agree or disagree*. The responses to Q3 were similar while P2 and P3 rated *agree*, P1 rated it as *disagree*. Similar responses were obtained in Q4, Q5 and Q6, while P2 and P3 consider the VA as trustworthy, reported that they like to continue the interaction with the VA and

---

[2] Measured through standardised questionnaires such as the Beck Depression Inventory II.

with the daily use of the system, P1 responded more negative to these questions (and it was confirmed that she did not logged into the system on daily basis during the two weeks). Moreover, during the exit interview it was found that the low level of acceptance from P1 to the VA was related not only to the VA's behaviour but also to its appearance. This is an important consideration due that a negative view of the VA's appearance would influence also negatively in the perception of its behaviour (and vice-versa). Although the design of the VA's different appearances (male and female characters wearing formal and informal clothes) was performed following suggestions, preferences and recommendations from users and clinicians, it is important to study to what extent how much of the positive/negative ratings on VA's behaviour is related with positive/negative rating on VA's appearance once all the feedback from the pilot's participants is collected. Despite the different ratings about the VA from the first three participants, all of them rated as positive the use of the whole Help4Mood system as a tool to complement the clinicians with the remote follow-up of the treatment.

Although these initial results are interesting, the small number of participants that already provided the feedback is not relevant to get definite conclusions. These initial results will be complemented with the rest of the participants in the final pilot that is currently ongoing. Nevertheless, what is interesting is that with the inclusion of the emotion regulation model, the participants in the second pilot noted better the emotional reactions from the VA than the participants in the first pilot. This suggests that the inclusion of negative (but regulated) emotional reactions in the VA to the reported adverse events in patient's wellbeing contributes to better convey *adequate* empathic reactions.

6   Conclusions and Further Work

The combination of the two—reappraisal and suppression—emotion regulation strategies produce more varied emotional responses in the Help4Mod's VA. In particular, the emotional reactions of the VA in front of *adverse situations* have been improved and facilitates the provision of a more empathic feedback according to the detected events. Initial tests have been performed to analyse the different reactions and feedback produced during the reappraisal of some negative events. These new emotional reactions has facilitated the inclusion of more specific dialogues during the session which in turn would facilitate a better level of acceptability in the users.

Nevertheless, the significant evaluation of the model is expected at the end of the final pilot where the feedback from all the participants will be collected. Similarly to the first pilot, an interview to all the participants will be administered to acquire relevant findings that help with the improvement of the system in a next development phase of the project. It is expected that the feedback obtained from the participants in the final pilot will support to better assess whether the believability and acceptability of the virtual agent has increased.

In terms of further work, the current presented model can be extended in at least one interesting direction: the inclusion of a mechanism to select the specific emotion regulation strategy depending on the personality modelled in the virtual agent. During the user and system requirements stage of the Help4Mood project, some of the people in the group of potential users identified the importance to get two different styles of interaction in the virtual agent. While a group of users prefer a closer and friendly virtual agent, some others suggest that the virtual agent should adopt a more formal or professional stance.

At the moment, these two different *personalities* have been modelled by authoring different thresholds and decay rates in the modelled emotions. The thresholds for the activation of the positive emotions in the *friendly* virtual agent are smaller than in the *formal* version of the agent. Moreover, the decay rates for these positive emotions in the friendly agent are also smaller than in the formal agent which produce more positive emotional reactions in the first one and a more neutral attitude in the second one. What it is interesting to model in terms of emotion regulation, is the selection of the specific emotion regulation strategy and its frequency of use based on the different personalities. There is an evidence that the emotion regulation strategies habitually adopted by people are related with some individual differences characterised by different personalities [25]. The behaviours produced in the agent through the selection and frequency of the particular emotion regulation strategy would help to clearly differentiate the two personalities and provide the users with their preferred style of interaction.

An additional interesting further work is to investigate whether the regulation of negative emotions is enough to produce useful therapeutic empathy responses. At the moment, and following clinicians recommendations, we have concentrated on the regulation of negative emotions. Depending on the results collected from the final pilot, we would assess if there would be situations where even when the user is reporting a good input to a specific question, the VA should regulate its positive emotional responses reflecting on a more general assessment of current patient's condition.

Acknowledgements. This paper reflects only the author's views. The European Community is not liable for any use that may be made of the information contained herein. This research is carried out within the EU-FP7 Project "Help4Mood—A Computational Distributed System to Support the Treatment of Patients with Major Depression" (ICT-248765).

References

1. Armony, J.L., Servan-Schreiber, D., Cohen, J.D., LeDoux, J.E.: Computational modeling of emotion: explorations through the anatomy and physiology of fear conditioning. Trends Cogn. Sci. **1**, 28–34 (1997)
2. Becker-Asano, C.: WASABI: affect simulation for agents with believable interactivity. Ph.D. thesis for the Faculty of Technology, University of Bielefeld, Bielefeld, Germany (2008)
3. Bickmore, T., Puskar, K., Schlenk, E., Pfeifer, L., Sereika, S.: Maintaining reality: relational agents for antipsychotic medication adherence. Interact. Comput. **22**(4), 276–288 (2010)

4. Bohart, A., Elliott, R., Greenberg, L.S., Watson, J.C.: Empathy. In: Norcross, J.C. (ed.) Psychotherapy Relationships that Work, pp. 89–108. Oxford University Press, New York (2002)

5. Bosse, T., de Lange, F.P.J.: Development of virtual agents with a theory of emotion regulation. In: Proceedings of IEEE/WIC/ACM International Conference on Web Intelligence and Intelligent Agent Technology, WI-IAT'08, vol. 2, pp. 461–468 (2008)

6. Bosse, T., Pontier, M., Siddiqui, G.F., Treur, J.: Incorporating emotion regulation into virtual stories. In: Pelachaud, C., Martin, J.-C., André, E., Chollet, G., Karpouzis, K., Pelé, D. (eds.) IVA 2007. LNCS (LNAI), vol. 4722, pp. 339–347. Springer, Heidelberg (2007)

7. Bosse, T., Pontier, M., Treur, J.: A computational model based on Gross' emotion regulation theory. Cogn. Syst. Res. **11**, 211–230 (2010)

8. Burleson, W., Picard, R.: Affective agents: sustaining motivation to learn through failure and state of stuck. In: Proceedings of workshop of Social and Emotional Intelligence in Learning Environments, Brazil (2004)

9. Campos, J.J., Frankel, C.B., Camras, L.: On the nature of emotion regulation. Child Dev. **75**, 377–394 (2004)

10. Campos, J.J., Campos, R.G., Barrett, K.C.: Emergent themes in the study of emotional development and emotion regulation. Dev. Psychol. **25**, 394–402 (1989)

11. Clark, A.J.: Empathy in Counseling and Psychotherapy: Perspectives and Practices. Lawrence Erlbaum Associates, Mahwah (2007)

12. Davidson, R.J., Fox, A., Kalin, N.H.: Neural bases of emotion regulation in nonhuman primates and humans. In: Gross, J.J. (ed.) Handbook of Emotion Regulation, pp. 47–68. The Guilford Press, New York (2007)

13. Dias, J., Mascarenhas, S., Paiva, A.: FAtiMA modular: towards an agent architecture with a generic appraisal framework. In: Proceedings of the International Workshop on Standards for Emotion Modeling (2011)

14. Dias, J., Paiva, A.C.R.: Feeling and reasoning: a computational model for emotional characters. In: Bento, C., Cardoso, A., Dias, G. (eds.) EPIA 2005. LNCS (LNAI), vol. 3808, pp. 127–140. Springer, Heidelberg (2005)

15. Ekman, P.: Emotions Revealed: Recognizing Faces and Feelings to Improve Communication and Emotional Life. Times Books, New York (2003)

16. El Nasr, M.S., Yen, J., Iorger, T.: FLAME: fuzzy logic adaptive model of emotions. Auton. Agent Multi-Agent Syst. **3**(3), 219–257 (2000)

17. Frijda, N.H.: The Emotions. Cambridge University Press, Cambridge (1986)

18. Gross, J.J.: Emotion regulation in adulthood: timing is everything. Curr. Dir. Psychol. Sci. **10**(6), 214–219 (2001)

19. Gross, J.J., Richards, J.M., John, O.P.: Emotion regulation in everyday life. In: Snyder, D.K., Simpson, J.A., Hughes, J.N. (eds.) Emotion Regulation in Couples and Families: Pathways to Dysfunction and Health, pp. 13–35. American Psychological Association, Washington DC (2006)

20. Gross, J.J. (ed.): Handbook of Emotion Regulation. The Guilford Press, New York (2007)

21. Gross, J.J., Thompson, R.A.: Emotion regulation: conceptual foundations. In: Gross, J.J. (ed.) Handbook of Emotion Regulation, pp. 3–24. The Guilford Press, New York (2007)

22. Hoorn, J.F., Pontier, M., Siddiqui, G.F.: When the user is instrumental to robot goals. First try: agent uses agent. In: Proceedings of IEEE/WIC/ACM Web Intelligence and Intelligent Agent Technology WI-IAT 2008, vol. 2, pp. 296–301 (2008)

23. Hoorn, J.F., Pontier, M., Siddiqui, G.F.: Coppélius' concoction: similarity and complementarity among three affect-related agent models. Cogn. Syst. Res. **15–16**, 33–49 (2012)

24. Hudlicka, E., Lisetti, C., Hodge, D., Paiva, A., Rizzo, A., Wagner, E.: Panel on artificial agents for psychotherapy. In: Proceedings of AAAI Spring Symposium: Emotion, Personality, and Social Behavior'08, pp. 60–64 (2008)

25. John, O.P., Gross, J.J.: Individual differences in emotion regulation. In: Gross, J.J. (ed.) Handbook of Emotion Regulation, pp. 351–372. The Guilford Press, New York (2007)

26. Kroenke, K., Spitzer, L., Williams, J.: The PHQ-9: validity of a brief depression severity measure. J. Gen. Intern. Med. **16**(9), 606–613 (2001)

27. Marsella, S., Gratch, J.: EMA: a model of emotional dynamics. Cogn. Syst. Res. **10**(1), 70–90 (2009)

28. Marsella, S., Gratch, J.: Modeling coping behavior in virtual humans don't worry, be happy. In: Proceedings of the 2nd International Joint Conference on Autonomous Agents and Multiagent Systems - AAMAS'03 (2003)

29. Marsella, S., Gratch, J., Petta, P.: Computational models of emotion. In: Scherer, K.R., Bänziger, T., Roesch, E.B. (eds.) Blueprint for Affective Computing: A Sourcebook, Chap. 1.2, pp. 21–46. Oxford University Press, Oxford (2010)

30. Moullec, G., Maïano, C., Morin, A.J.S., Monthuy-Blanc, J., Rosello, L., Ninot, G.: A very short visual analog form of the Center for Epidemiologic Studies Depression Scale (CES-D) for the idiographic measurement of depression. J. Affect. Disord. **128**(3), 220–234 (2010)

31. Ortony, A., Clore, G., Collins, A.: The Cognitive Structure of Emotions. Cambridge University Press, Cambridge (1988)

32. Picard, R.: Affective Computing. MIT Press, Cambridge (1997)

33. Preece, J., Rogers, Y., Sharp, H.: Interaction Design: Beyond Human-Computer Interaction. Wiley, New York (2002)

34. Prendinger, H., Ishizuka, M.: The empathic companion: a character-based interface that addresses users' affective states. Appl. Artif. Intell. **19**, 267–285 (2005)

35. Rogers, C.: Your body language speaks loudly: nonverbal communication makes patient more comfortable. In: Academy News of The American Academy of Orthopaedic Surgeons. http://www2.aaos.org/acadnews/2002news/b16-7.htm

36. Rogers, C.R.: On Becoming a Person: a therapist's view of psychotherapy. Constable and Company, London (1967)

37. Soleimani, A., Kobti, Z.: A mood driven computational model for gross emotion regulation paradigm. In: Proceedings of the 5th International C* Conference on Computer Science and Software Engineering, pp. 9–17. ACM, New York (2012)

38. Thwaites, R., Bennett-Levy, J.: Conceptualizing empathy in cognitive behaviour therapy: making the implicit explicit. Behav. Cogn. Psychother. **35**, 291–612 (2007)

39. Vanaerschot, G.: The process of empathy: Holding and letting go. In: Liataer, G., Rombauts, J., Van Balen, R. (eds.) Client-Centered and Experiential Psychotherapy in the Nineties, pp. 269–293. Leuven University Press, Leuven (1990)

Social Support Strategies for Embodied Conversational Agents

Janneke M. van der Zwaan[(⊠)], Virginia Dignum, and Catholijn M. Jonker

Delft University of Technology, Delft, The Netherlands
jannekevdzwaan@gmail.com

Abstract. There is a growing interest in employing conversational agents as companions and coaches. An important skill for this type of agents is providing social support to users after they have an experienced upsetting event. In order to provide social support, conversational agents need to be empathic to the user. In this paper, we specify strategies for conversational agents to provide social support to users. The main contribution of this paper is a mapping between OCC emotion types and support types that can be used to generate emotional behavior in a largely domain-independent way.

1   Introduction

Social support refers to communicative attempts to alleviate the emotional distress of another person [1]. To alleviate emotional distress different techniques are available to support providers, including giving advice and providing emotional support [2]. For social support to be found effective, it is crucial that the support giver is empathic with the receiver [3]. Empathy can be defined as 'the capacity to (a) be affected by and share the emotional state of another, (b) assess the reasons for the other's state, and (c) identify with the other, adopting his or her perspective' [4].

In our research, we are investigating how and to what extent Embodied Conversational Agents (ECAs) can provide social support to users. The definition of social support used in our work specifies that a context of emotional distress is required in order to be able to provide social support. The context of emotional distress we selected for our work is cyberbullying, that is, bullying through electronic communication devices [5]. Rather than aiming to reduce or 'solve' the problem of cyberbullying, our research is focussed on creating supportive interactions between ECAs and users. We are particularly interested in endowing ECAs with the emotional skills required to comfort users.

In previous work, we proposed a design for an empathic virtual buddy against cyberbullying [6], that was subsequently implemented in a prototype. The virtual buddy prototype combines a conversation and emotional model in order to understand, comfort and suggest actions to the user. The conversation model specifies the contents and structure of social support conversations [7]. This paper specifies the virtual buddy's strategies for providing social support. The buddy

© Springer International Publishing Switzerland 2014
T. Bosse et al. (Eds.): Emotion Modeling, LNAI 8750, pp. 134–147, 2014.
DOI: 10.1007/978-3-319-12973-0_8

expresses different types of social support, including information support (advice and teaching), emotional (sympathy and encouragement), and esteem support (compliment). While the provision of information support is directly linked to the conversation model, expressions of emotional and esteem support are generated by the virtual buddy's emotion model. This emotion model is a simplification of the OCC model of emotions [8]. The main contribution of this paper is a mapping between OCC emotion types and support types that can be used to generate emotional behavior in a largely domain-independent way.

This paper is organized as follows. In Sect. 2, we discuss related work on (embodied) conversational agents. Section 3 provides a background on social support. Section 4 presents the virtual buddy prototype, including the conversation model and the emotion model. Section 5 specifies the virtual buddy's different supportive strategies. In Sect. 6, we briefly discuss the results of user studies on the virtual buddy's supportive behavior. We also discuss some limitations of the simple emotion model. Finally, in Sect. 7, we present our conclusions.

2   Related Work

Early work on affective computing demonstrated that agents are able to reduce negative emotions in users by addressing them [9]. Since then, emotional agents have been applied predominantly in task oriented systems, i.e. systems that support users in performing concrete tasks, such as finding information. Examples include museum guide MAX that provides users with information about the museum and exhibitions [10], and agent GRETA that presents health information to the user [11]. Another popular application of emotional agents is responding to user emotions in e-learning and tutoring systems [12–14]. These so called pedagogical agents use different (emotional) strategies, such as displaying active listening behavior, encouragement and praise, to motivate the user and to make learning more engaging.

Because looking for social support after experiencing an upsetting event does not necessarily involve concrete tasks for the user to perform, the virtual buddy is not a task oriented system. Another example of a non-task oriented ECA is the 'How was your day' (HWYD) system, that allows users to talk about their day at the office [15,16]. The system tries to influence the user's attitudes as a part of a free conversation on work related topics, such as office mergers, promotion and workloads. The system alternates between employing clarification dialogue (asking questions to find out details) and generating appropriate affective responses to the information gathered. The system allows users to speak uninterrupted for longer periods of time (utterances of >30 words). In addition to short sympathetic responses to the user's input, the system may start a longer utterance to provides advice and support. These longer utterances are called comforting tirades. Comforting tirades are aimed at encouraging, comforting or warning the user. An important difference between the HWYD system and the virtual buddy for social support is the structure of the conversation. While the HWYD system incorporates social support into free conversation, the virtual buddy imposes a structure on the conversation. This structure facilitates giving support, because the buddy's verbal support actions are directly linked to this structure (see Sect. 3).

Existing ECAs mainly express support in response to user input. In that respect, expressing social support is similar to small talk (i.e. talk that is not used for content exchange, but that has a social function in the conversation), as specified in Schneider's small talk model [17]:

1. A query from the dominant conversation partner (in our case, this is the virtual buddy),
2. An answer to the query (from the other conversation partner),
3. A response to the answer (from the dominant conversation partner), consisting of one of the following possibilities: echo-question, check-back, acknowledgement, confirming an unexpected response, positive evaluation,
4. An unrestricted number of null steps or idling behavior.

This model shows that engaging in small talk or, in our case, expressing social support, consists of a response to input from the user (e.g., virtual buddy responds sympathetically to the user's answer to a query). The model does not specify when it is appropriate to express social support. In Sect. 4, we show how emotional responses to user input can be used to trigger expressions of social support. Schneider's model is used as a template for expressing support.

3   Social Support

In this section, we provide a background on social support. The virtual buddy's social support actions are based on a typology of social support in online settings [2]. This typology is relevant for the virtual buddy, because online communication is mostly textual and does not depend on additional communication channels (such as non-verbal behavior and auditory information). The typology consist of five main support categories [2]:

– Information support (messages that convey instructions),
– Tangible assistance (offers to take concrete, physical action in support of the recipient),
– Network support (messages that appear to broaden the recipient's social network),
– Esteem support (messages that validate the recipient's self-concept, importance, competence, and rights as a person), and
– Emotional support (attempts by the sender to express empathy, support the emotional expressions of the recipient or reciprocate emotion)

Each category breaks down into multiple subtypes. From these subtypes, 5 that occur frequently in counseling conversations by chat [18] were selected to be implemented in the virtual buddy, that is sympathy (emotional support), compliment (esteem support), encouragement (emotional support), advice (information support) and teaching (information support). This initial selection of social support types can be extended later on. Table 1 lists descriptions and examples of the selected support types.

Table 1. The types of social support implemented in the virtual buddy prototype.

Support type	Description	Example
Sympathy	Express feelings of compassion or concern	*How awful that you are being bullied!*
Encouragement	Provide recipient with hope and confidence	*There is no easy solution for bullying, but there are some things you can do to try to make it stop*
Compliment	Positive assessments of the recipient and his or her abilities	*Blocking the bully was a smart thing to do!*
Advice	Suggestions for coping with a problem	*Give your contact information only to people you know and trust*
Teaching	Factual or technical information	*You can block a contact by clicking the 'block' button*

4   The Virtual Buddy Prototype

Figure 1 shows a screen shot of virtual buddy prototype system. Because we are interested in understanding the principles that enable ECAs to provide social support, the design and implementation of the prototype is focused on these principles and other aspects have been kept simple. The reasoning behind this approach is that it is easier to determine why behavioral strategies of a simple ECA prototype trigger certain responses in users than it is to explain responses to ECAs using complex reasoning processes and/or collections of (advanced) behavioral strategies.

In this section, we first present the design decisions that guided the implementation of the prototype. Next, we briefly discuss the structure and contents of conversations between the virtual buddy and the user. The conversation is scripted and social support types advice and teaching are directly incorporated in the script. Finally, we explain the virtual buddy's emotion model and show how it triggers social support types sympathy, compliment, and encouragement.

4.1   Design Decisions

Table 2 lists the design decisions made for the prototype. Most of these are simplifications. In order to keep the prototype as simple as possible, the first design decision is that we assume the user has a single conversation with the virtual buddy. The virtual buddy prototype presented in this chapter is the first step in the development of a virtual buddy that provides social support to cyberbullying victims. It is unlikely that a single conversation with the virtual buddy solves a bullying situation. However, allowing users to have multiple conversations requires a complex prototype. For example, the virtual buddy needs to

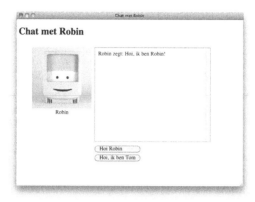

Fig. 1. Screen shot of Robin, the empathic virtual buddy prototype.

store information between conversations and incorporate this information in subsequent conversations. If a simple prototype is not able to provide social support, it is unlikely that a more complex prototype will be successful. Therefore, we focus on the provision of support during a single conversation.

Table 2. Design decisions for the virtual buddy prototype.

Design decision
1. Single conversation
2. Scripted dialogue
3. Pre-defined response options
4. Pre-defined text messages for verbal output
5. Static pictures for nonverbal behavior

The design decision we made regarding conversation management is that we use a finite model. This means that the structure and contents of conversations are fixed in advance (i.e., scripted) and that there is little variation between conversations. The design decision to script conversations between the user and the virtual buddy is a simplification that results from the design decision to model a single conversation; because the user only has a single conversation with the virtual buddy, there is no need to make the conversation flexible or adaptive.

In order to interact with a conversational agent, users must be able to communicate with ECAs. To keep managing turn taking, and input interpretation simple, we decided to use predefined response options as the means for the user to communicate with the virtual buddy. In addition to being able to 'listen' to users, ECAs need to be able to convey messages to users. Again, to avoid unnecessary complexity, we decided that the virtual buddy uses predefined text messages to convey verbal messages to the user.

An ECA's nonverbal behavior is displayed by its embodiment. The appearance of embodiments and the quality of nonverbal behavior vary between ECA systems, and range from static cartoon-like representations to highly realistic human-like appearances and animated nonverbal behavior. From the options available, we selected static pictures of different facial expressions to generate the virtual buddy's nonverbal behavior. This is the most simple alternative.

4.2   Conversation Model

As mentioned in the introduction, the structure and contents of the conversation between the virtual buddy and the user is based on a conversation model [7]. The structure of the conversation is based on the 5-phase model [19]. The 5-phase model was developed as a methodology to structure counseling conversations via telephone and chat. The five phases of a conversation are:

1. Warm welcome: the counselor connects with the child and invites him to explain what he wants to talk about
2. Clarify the question: the counselor asks questions to try to establish the problem of the child
3. Determine the objective of the session: the counselor and the child determine the goal of the conversation (e.g., getting tips on how to deal with bullying)
4. Work out the objective: the counselor stimulates the child to come up with a solution
5. Round up: the counselor actively rounds off the conversation

The 5-phase model thus provides a template for the conversation. Using this template ensures that the conversation progresses and that the user does not get stuck on discussing his problem. The 5-phase model assumes the child itself can come up with a solution. Since our goal is to demonstrate how a conversational agent can give social support, we relax this responsibility and have the virtual buddy take the lead in phase 4. Additionally, to simplify the model, we assume certain types of support only occur in certain phases: sympathy, compliment and encouragement can occur in phase 2; advice and teaching only occur in phase 4.

4.3   Emotion Model

The emotion model determines when the virtual buddy expresses sympathy, compliments or encourages the user. It is based on the OCC model of emotions [8]. In OCC, emotions are conceptualized as responses to events, agents, and objects. The OCC model specifies eliciting conditions for all emotion types. The implementation of the virtual buddy's emotion model is based on the implementation of the OCC model in domain-independent agent architecture FAtiMA [20]. In particular, it closely resembles FAtiMA's reactive layer. The virtual buddy's emotion model is depicted in Fig. 2. In the model, response options are interpreted as actions or events. An action or event triggers an OCC emotion type,

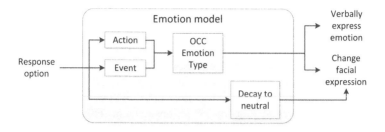

Fig. 2. The virtual buddy's emotion model.

that is expressed both verbally and nonverbally. Although OCC also specifies emotional responses to objects, emotional responses to objects are not included in the current emotion model.

A response option triggers zero or one emotion types. Emotions are expressed verbally and nonverbally. If an emotion is triggered, the virtual buddy sets the next speech act to be an *expressive* (i.e., a verbal expression of emotions [21]). The mapping between OCC emotion types and speech acts is discussed later. The emotion triggered by the emotion model replaces the virtual buddy's current emotional state. After the current emotional state is updated, the virtual buddy's facial expression is changed to reflect its current emotional state. In the current prototype, the virtual buddy's emotional state ranges from sad to happy. Figure 3 shows the facial expressions the virtual buddy displays for each emotional state it is capable of expressing (left to right: sadness, medium sadness, neutral, medium happiness, happiness). If a response option triggers a negative emotion, the buddy's facial expression changes to sadness, and if a response option triggers a positive emotion, the buddy facial expression changes to happiness.

Fig. 3. The virtual buddy's emotional states (left to right: sadness, medium sadness, neutral, medium happiness, happiness).

If a response option does not trigger an emotion, the virtual buddy's current emotional state decays to neutral; from sadness to medium sadness to neutral, and from happiness to medium happiness to neutral.

There is a fixed mapping between OCC emotion types and social support types. This mapping is listed in Table 3. Sympathy is triggered by events that

Table 3. Mapping between OCC emotion types, social support types, and facial expressions.

OCC emotion type	Social support type	Facial expression
Sorry-for	Sympathy	Sadness
Admiration	Compliment	Happiness
Happy-for	Encouragement	Happiness

are unpleasant for the user (OCC emotion type sorry-for). Compliment is triggered by praiseworthy actions performed by the user (OCC emotion type admiration). Encouragement is triggered by events that are pleasant for the user (OCC emotion type happy-for).

As mentioned before, emotions are expressed both verbally and nonverbally. The verbal expression of emotions is explained in Sect. 5.

5   Specification of Social Support Types

To illustrate the different supportive strategies employed by the virtual buddy, this section specifies how the five different social support types are delivered during the conversation. As mentioned before, we assume that sympathy, compliment and encouragement only occur in the second conversation phase (gather information), and advice and teaching only in phase 4 (work out objective). Social support types sympathy, compliment, and encouragement are triggered by the virtual buddy's emotion model, whereas advice and teaching are incorporated in the conversation script.

5.1   Sympathy

Sympathy expresses feelings of compassion or concern. During the information gathering phase, the virtual buddy may respond sympathetically to answers given by the user. For example,

Virtual buddy: *Can you tell me what happened?*
User: *Someone is calling me names on MSN[1]...*
Virtual buddy: *That's awful!* (sympathy)

5.2   Compliment

Compliments are positive assessments of the recipient and his abilities. In the context of a social support conversation about an upsetting event, there are two possibilities for the support provider to give compliments: (1) the support recipient tells the support provider he performed a constructive, positive or otherwise

---

[1] MSN Messenger was an Instant Messaging service provided by Microsoft. It was discontinued in 2013 [22].

positive action (e.g., in response to being bullied, the support recipient did not retaliate), and (2) the support recipient performs well as a dialogue partner (e.g., the support recipient gives a clear explanation of something). Currently, only the first type of compliment is included in the conversation. The following example illustrates giving compliments.

Virtual buddy: *How did you respond when you were being called names on msn?*
User: *I told the bully to stop, but he didn't listen...*
Virtual buddy: *That was very brave of you!* (compliment)

5.3   Encouragement

Encouragement concerns providing the recipient with hope and confidence. The process of encouraging the user closely resembles the way in which compliments are given. Again, the conversation model assumes that encouragement is always provided in response to a user utterance. Encouragement is triggered by events that are pleasant for the user. The following conversation snippet illustrates encouragement:

Virtual buddy: *Did standing up to the bully help?*
User: *Yes, I felt better after I did that*
Virtual buddy: *I'm glad you felt better!* (encouragement)

5.4   Advice

In phase 4 of the conversation model, the user is provided with advice. Which advice is given depends on domain knowledge and the specific situation of the user (i.e., the information that was gathered during conversation phase 2). The conversation model assumes the user confirms all advice:

Virtual buddy: *Do not respond to abusive messages. Many bullies bully to provoke a response.* (advice)
User: *OK*

5.5   Teaching

In the domain of cyberbullying, many measures the user can take to protect himself require technical know-how, such as blocking users, changing accounts, and reporting inappropriate content. Since the user may not possess the knowledge on how to perform these actions, the conversation model includes teaching of this information. Teaching concerns conveying factual or technical information. The implementation of teaching is based on the work by Vergunst [23]. The virtual buddy uses a list of instructions to explain how to perform the task. After the explanation of a step, the virtual buddy waits for confirmation from the user before moving on to the next step. For example,

Virtual buddy: *Block the bully on MSN, so he can't harass you anymore.* (advice)
User: *OK*
Virtual buddy: *Do you want me to explain to you how to do that?* (teaching)
User: *Yes, please!*
Virtual buddy: *First, you login to MSN.* (teaching)
User: *Yes*
Virtual buddy: *Next, locate the contact you want to block in your contact list.* (teaching)
User: *OK*
...
Virtual buddy: *Okay, now you know how to block a contact on MSN.* (teaching)

6   Discussion

This paper presented supportive strategies of a virtual empathic buddy that provides emotional support and practical advice to cyberbullying victims by guiding them through a supportive conversation. In order to determine to what extent the virtual buddy's behavior was experienced as being supportive, three user studies were conducted. The first study was designed to quantitively assess the effect of variations in the virtual buddy's emotional expressiveness (i.e., verbal and non-verbal expression of emotions) on the effectiveness of support, and perceptions of social support [24]. The results show that the virtual buddy is effective at providing support. However, we found no statistically significant effects of increased emotional expressiveness on the effectiveness of support or perceptions of support. In order to gain more detailed insight as to why the virtual buddy's behavior is experienced as supportive, we subsequently conducted two qualitative studies of the virtual buddy's supportive behavior. The first qualitative study was a focus group discussion among pedagogical and bullying experts [25]. The results demonstrate that the experts recognized all five selected social support types employed by the virtual buddy. The experience of being supported was contributed to the virtual buddy's supportive verbal utterances, the different facial expressions, and the combination of verbal utterances and facial expressions. The second qualitative study consisted of 12 one-on-one interviews among children between the ages of 10 and 14, the virtual buddy's target age group [26]. The results from the interviews correspond to the results from the focus group; participants asserted they felt supported and contributed this experience to the advice provided and the changing facial expressions.

The results from our studies of the virtual buddy's supportive behavior indicate that the expression of emotions is essential to the experience of support. To some extent, the virtual buddy appears empathic to the user. In order to appear empathic to the user's situation, the virtual buddy expresses emotions generated by its emotion model. Compared to other models of computerized emotions, such as FAtiMA [20][2], and PLEIAD [27], the virtual buddy's emotion model is simple. Simplifications include only a limited subset of OCC emotion types generated, for each user utterance exactly zero or one emotions are generated, and generated emotions are not 'added' to the virtual buddy's current emotional state, but replace it. In this section these characteristics, and underlying assumptions and consequences of these characteristics are discussed. In addition, we briefly discuss the validity of the emotion model.

First of all, the emotion model only generates OCC emotion types that are relevant for expressing sympathy, giving compliments, and encouraging the user. The virtual buddy only uses its emotion model to express emotional and esteem support. This use of emotions corresponds to the social function of emotions (cf. [28]), whereas existing emotion models typically focus on the role of emotions to mediate cognitive processes, i.e., the virtual agent's behavior is driven by its emotions, that are generated in a psychologically plausible way. Because the virtual buddy uses its emotions only to provide emotional and esteem support, and not, for example, to determine the course of the conversation, a simple emotion model suffices. Additionally, design decisions made for the virtual buddy prototype ensure that at most a single emotion is generated in response to a user utterance. This simplification is enabled by the fact that the virtual buddy guides the user through a structured conversation, and that the user communicates with the virtual buddy by selecting pre-defined response options.

Because a response option selected by the user generates at most one emotion, and all user utterances are followed by an utterance from the virtual buddy during which the virtual buddy's emotional state decays towards neutral, it is also unnecessary to combine multiple emotions into a single emotional state. Instead, to calculate the virtual buddy's current emotional state, it is sufficient to replace it with the generated emotion. A consequence of this strategy for updating the emotional state is that the emotion model does not prevent the virtual buddy from expressing one emotion in response to a user utterance, and expressing an opposite emotion in response to the next. The results from the user studies show that participants noticed some inconsistent expressions of emotions, for example:

> *First Robin* [the virtual buddy] *says that you are not allowed to retaliate, but then he is glad it helped!* (Expert 1)

In addition, participants felt that the virtual buddy's emotions decay too quickly back to neutral, and that its neutral facial expression was too cheerful. Although, according to the participants of the evaluation studies, the emotions generated by the emotion model are generally appropriate, a more complex model is required to fine-tune emotional expressions and solve emotion mismatches.

In order to validate the emotional model we must assess (1) whether emotional responses are expressed at appropriate moments in the conversation, and (2) whether the type of supportive response (i.e., sympathy, compliment, or

---

[2] The virtual buddy's emotion model is based on FAtiMa's reactive layer (see [20] for more details).

encouragement) is appropriate at that moment. In spite of the fact that the user studies conducted with the virtual buddy prototype focussed on the supportive behavior in general (emotional support and practical advice) and not on the validation of the emotion model per se, the results show that the emotion model is not valid. For example, the experts that participated in the focus group identified both emotion mismatches and emotional inconsistency. Additionally, they agreed that the virtual buddy misses opportunities to express emotional or esteem support.

7   Conclusion

This paper specified social support strategies for embodied conversational agents; in particular, sympathy, compliment, encouragement, advice, and teaching. We also showed how, inspired by a model of small talk, these strategies were implemented in a prototype of a virtual buddy that provides social support to cyberbullying victims. Social support types advice and teaching are scripted in the conversation, while sympathy, compliment and encouragement are generated by a simple emotion model that is based on the OCC model of emotions. The main contribution of this paper is a mapping between OCC emotion types and social support types that can be used to generate supportive emotional behavior in a largely domain-independent way. We show that a relatively simple emotional model is sufficient behavior that is experienced as being supportive by different types of users, including pedagogical and bullying experts, and children between the ages of 10 and 14.

As the results from our evaluation studies show, the simple emotion model produces inconsistent emotions and emotion mismatches. Therefore, the next step is to fine-tune the emotion model. This requires adding more complexity. After improving the emotion model, it should be validated. We propose to explore the validity of the emotion model by having pedagogical and bullying experts judge conversation fragments generated for different cyberbullying situations with and without supportive statements generated by the emotional model. Another line of future work is to expand our initial selection of social support type and explore ways in which they can be incorporated in conversations. We are particularly interested in more cognitive forms of empathy. This requires reasoning about the user's emotional state.

Acknowledgements. This work is funded by the Netherlands Organization for Scientific Research (NWO) under the Responsible Innovation (RI) program via the project 'Empowering and Protecting Children and Adolescents Against Cyberbullying'.

References

1. Burleson, B., Goldsmith, D.: How the comforting process works: alleviating emotional distress through conversationally induced reappraisals. In: Andersen, P., Guerrero, L. (eds.) Handbook of Communication and Emotion: Research, Theory, Applications, and Contexts, pp. 245–280. Academic Press, Orlando (1998)

2. Braithwaite, D., Waldron, V., Finn, J.: Communication of social support in computer-mediated groups for people with disabilities. Health Commun. **11**(2), 123–151 (1999)
3. Thoits, P.: Social support as coping assistance. J. Consult. Clin. Psychol. **54**(4), 416–423 (1986)
4. de Waal, F.: Putting the altruism back into altruism: the evolution of empathy. Annu. Rev. Psychol. **59**, 279–300 (2008)
5. Li, Q.: New bottle but old wine: a research of cyberbullying in schools. Comput. Hum. Behav. **23**(4), 1777–1791 (2007)
6. van der Zwaan, J.M., Dignum, V., Jonker, C.M.: Simulating peer support for victims of cyberbullying. In: Proceedings of the 22st Benelux Conference on Artificial Intelligence (BNAIC 2010) (2010)
7. van der Zwaan, J.M., Dignum, V., Jonker, C.M.: A conversation model enabling intelligent agents to give emotional support. In: Ding, W., Jiang, H., Ali, M., Li, M. (eds.) Modern Advances in Intelligent Systems and Tools. SCI, vol. 431, pp. 47–52. Springer, Heidelberg (2012)
8. Ortony, A., Clore, G., Collins, A.: The Cognitive Structure of Emotions. Cambridge University Press, Cambridge (1988)
9. Hone, K.: Empathic agents to reduce user frustration: The effects of varying agent characteristics. Interact. Comput. **18**(2), 227–245 (2006)
10. Kopp, S., Gesellensetter, L., Krämer, N.C., Wachsmuth, I.: A conversational agent as museum guide – design and evaluation of a real-world application. In: Panayiotopoulos, T., Gratch, J., Aylett, R.S., Ballin, D., Olivier, P., Rist, T. (eds.) IVA 2005. LNCS (LNAI), vol. 3661, pp. 329–343. Springer, Heidelberg (2005)
11. Pelachaud, C., Carofiglio, V., De Carolis, B., de Rosis, F., Poggi, I.: Embodied contextual agent in information delivering application. In: Proceedings of the First International Joint Conference on Autonomous Agents and Multiagent Systems: Part 2, pp. 758–765. ACM (2002)
12. D'Mello, S., Lehman, B., Sullins, J., Daigle, R., Combs, R., Vogt, K., Perkins, L., Graesser, A.: A time for emoting: when affect-sensitivity is and isn't effective at promoting deep learning. In: Aleven, V., Kay, J., Mostow, J. (eds.) ITS 2010, Part I. LNCS, vol. 6094, pp. 245–254. Springer, Heidelberg (2010)
13. Lee, T.Y., Chang, C.W., Chen, G.D.: Building an interactive caring agent for students in computer-based learning environments. In: Proceedings of the 7th IEEE International Conference on Advanced Learning Technologies, ICALT 2007, pp. 300–304 (2007)
14. Zakharov, K., Mitrovic, A., Johnston, L.: Towards emotionally-intelligent pedagogical agents. In: Woolf, B.P., Aïmeur, E., Nkambou, R., Lajoie, S. (eds.) ITS 2008. LNCS, vol. 5091, pp. 19–28. Springer, Heidelberg (2008)
15. Cavazza, M., et al.: Persuasive dialogue based on a narrative theory: an ECA implementation. In: Ploug, T., Hasle, P., Oinas-Kukkonen, H. (eds.) PERSUASIVE 2010. LNCS, vol. 6137, pp. 250–261. Springer, Heidelberg (2010)
16. Smith, C., et al.: Interaction strategies for an affective conversational agent. In: Safonova, A. (ed.) IVA 2010. LNCS(LNAI), vol. 6356, pp. 301–314. Springer, Heidelberg (2010)
17. Schneider, K.: Small Talk: Analyzing Phatic Discourse. Hitzeroth, Marburg (1988)
18. Fukkink, R.: Peer counseling in an online chat service: a content analysis of social support. Cyberpsychology Behav. Soc. Netw. **14**(4), 247–251 (2011)
19. de Beyn, A.: In gesprek met kinderen:de methodiek van de kindertelefoon. SWP, Amsterdam (2003)

20. Dias, J., Paiva, A.C.R.: Feeling and reasoning: a computational model for emotional characters. In: Bento, C., Cardoso, A., Dias, G. (eds.) EPIA 2005. LNCS (LNAI), vol. 3808, pp. 127–140. Springer, Heidelberg (2005)
21. Searle, J.R.: A taxonomy of illocutionary acts. In: Gunderson, K. (ed.) Language, Mind, and Knowledge. University of Minnesota Press, Minneapolis (1975)
22. Wilhelm, A.: Confirmed: microsoft to retire its messenger im service in q1 2013, moving 100m+ users to skype in single act (2012). http://thenextweb.com/microsoft/2012/11/06/microsoft-to-retire-its-messenger-im-service-in-q1-2013-moving-100mm-users-to-skype-in-single-move/. Accessed 3 June 2013
23. Vergunst, N.: BDI-based Generation of Robust Task-Oriented Dialogues. Ph.D. Thesis, Utrecht University (2011)
24. van der Zwaan, J.M., Dignum, V., Jonker, C.M.: The effect of variations in emotional expressiveness on social support. In: Conci, M., Dignum, V., Funk, M., Heylen, D. (eds.) Proceedings of the 2013 Workshop on Computers as Social Actors, pp. 9–20 (2014)
25. van der Zwaan, J.M., Dignum, V., Jonker, C.M.: A qualitative evaluation of social support by an empathic agent. In: Aylett, R., Krenn, B., Pelachaud, C., Shimodaira, H. (eds.) IVA 2013. LNCS, vol. 8108, pp. 358–367. Springer, Heidelberg (2013)
26. van der Zwaan, J.M.: An Empathic Virtual Buddy for Social Support. Ph.D. Thesis, Delft University of Technology (2014)
27. Adam, C.: The Emotions: From Psychological Theories to Logical Formalization and Implementation in a BDI Agent. Ph.D. Thesis (2007)
28. Gratch, J., Marsella, S.: Lessons from emotion psychology for the design of lifelike characters. Appl. Artif. Intell. **19**(3), 215–234 (2005)

Affective Processes as Network Hubs

David Gibson[(✉)]

Curtin University, Kent St, Bentley, WA 6102, Australia
david.c.gibson@curtin.edu.au

Abstract. The practical problems of designing and coding a web-based flight simulator for teachers has led to a 'three-tier plus environment' model (COVE model) for a software agent's cognition (C), psychological (O), physical (V) processes and responses to tasks and interpersonal relationships within a learning environment (E). The purpose of this article is to introduce how some of the COVE model layers represent preconscious processing hubs in an AI human-agent's representation of learning in a serious game, and how an application of the Five Factor Model of psychology in the O layer determines the scope of dimensions for a practical computational model of affective processes. The article illustrates the model with the classroom-learning context of the simSchool application (www.simschool.org); presents details of the COVE model of an agent's reactions to academic tasks; discusses the theoretical foundations; and outlines the research-based real world impacts from external validation studies as well as new testable hypotheses of simSchool.

Keywords: Affective processing models · Cognitive models · Five factor model of psychology · Teacher education · Game-based learning · Simulation

1 Affective Processes in a Serious Game for Training Teachers

A web-based training simulation – simSchool - has been built to improve teacher education because what teachers do in the classroom matters a great deal and is part of a causal network that brings about student learning as evidenced in the teacher's skill- and knowledge-based performances [1–3]. Teacher decisions can be thought of as independent variables in an ongoing experiment that builds expertise over time [4, 5]. A major challenge facing beginning as well as experienced teachers is how to juggle a number of parameters in an often-overwhelming complex setting where learner psychological characteristics, cultural and family backgrounds, content requirements, school routines, state and national policies, and community expectations intersect. For example, teachers must learn to constantly negotiate a balance between content, pedagogy, and technology in ways that are appropriate to the specific parameters of their content area and an ever-changing educational context [6]. They must learn to differentiate instruction to meet the needs of mixed ability groups [7]. And they must develop the ability to self-assess and plan for their own professional growth while encountering a variety of pedagogical approaches in teacher education [8].

© Springer International Publishing Switzerland 2014
T. Bosse et al. (Eds.): Emotion Modeling, LNAI 8750, pp. 148–166, 2014.
DOI: 10.1007/978-3-319-12973-0_9

Normally, these capacities are developed through a combination of teacher education experiences followed by student teaching in real classrooms and then honed further during their first job as a schoolteacher and subsequent years on the job. However, two major problems with this situation are evident; 1. Governments experience low retention rates from teacher preparation to lifelong teaching and 2. There are ill impacts of inexperienced teachers on student learning that are known to harm some students and prevent many of them from reaching their potential.

The possibility of using a simulation to help develop and assess the performance of teachers has arisen in concert with a growing appreciation of the potential for games and simulation-based learning [9–11]. Using simulations in teacher education has at least two broad goals; producing better teachers and building operational models of physical, affective processing, cognitive, social and organizational theories involved in teaching and learning [12], to which we will turn in the following sections. The broad goals are situated in the context of using technology to improve field experiences for preservice teachers and in ongoing professional development of inservice teachers, where simulations can provide learning and training opportunities with unique characteristics such as repeatability, automated analysis, representations that spark reflection, and the potential to transfer lessons learned and higher teaching skill levels to the real classroom [13]. In addition, the significance of using a digital simulation as an assessment environment includes more authentic item and response types, scalability, safety and usability for formative assessment and learning, and production of rich data; and when combined with an evidence-centered assessment, can provide high-resolution performance data linked to a standards-based model [14, 15].

In this context, simSchool was created to develop capacities needed for teaching and to also address the major problems of field-based experience, reasoning that a scalable simulation would have far fewer ill impacts on real students while a candidate was developing skills and the confidence to become an effective teacher. Previous research has indicated that teacher development via simSchool does indeed lead to increased self-efficacy, improved teaching skills and a positive shift in the locus of control of classroom learning in preservice teachers [16, 17]. In addition, a recent study indicates that exposure may also impact teacher retention [18].

It is important to point out at the outset that the computational model underlying simSchool described here treats affective states as a relatively undifferentiated continuum from unexpressed, sometimes inexpressible, states that might transform into recognized and relatively persistent states of mind. This contrasts with affective states seen as a small number of expressible states such as grief, love, frustration, boredom, and joy. The affective continuum stance is supported by both cognitive disequilibrium theory [19, 20] which dynamically links affect and cognition during learning and the requirement of a fine-grained analysis of the rapid dynamics of processes that naturally occur during learning, for modeling cognitive-affective dynamics [21]. The fine-grained preconscious continuum model may not be appropriate for understanding sustained affective states, or the end points of continua of affect (e.g. love, anger) that have become conscious, but it is critical to negotiating the dynamic change during a learner's experience, for example a learner's state of engagement with a task or a conversation changing to confusion then to frustration during a learning process.

A second important issue of the model that requires additional introductory explanation is the foundation of the fine-grained continuum in the Five Factor Model or OCEAN model of psychology [22]. The OCEAN model is typically used as a 'trait' theory [23], but here it is used as scope for the dimensionality of a large but finite number of 'states' of preconscious processes (e.g. affects and emotions if made conscious), so additional explanation is needed. State-trait distinctions can be analyzed as having four overlapping but distinct dimensions: duration, continuous vs reactive manifestation, concreteness vs abstractness and situational vs personal causality [24].

To illustrate, consider the face validity of a learner who is facing a performance challenge, such as singing one's national anthem in front of an audience. Even if the person is normally 'open' to new ideas (e.g. the 'O' in the OCEAN theory), the singing task calls upon memory of words, remembering a melody and the production of sound in a musical context, in front of an audience. So the person will need psychological and mental resources related to the repetition of familiar tasks, which will cause disequilibrium and send the person through a range of preconscious states to deal with the gap between a current state and the one needed to perform the required task. Using the four state-trait distinctions in this example, the song will be over soon (duration) as opposed to a trait set point of openness, which remains after the song is over; the disequilibrium will change to equilibrium when the performance requirement is removed or the performance concludes (reactive manifestation returning to continuous manifestation); the context will shift during and after the performance as the audience turns attention to something else other than the person (moving from concreteness on self to abstractness of the group, from the person's perspective); and the personal causal role will subside back into the general contextual situation. It seems natural to infer that a state interpretation of variables operating dynamically over time within the five continua of OCEAN dimensions is feasible for illustrating the change in state from the condition prior to the challenge to sing, to the states experienced during the performance, and those experienced afterwards, when the person returns to a resting state that is more trait-like.

The theory outlined below and used to drive the AI of the simSchool application asserts that a person's current state settings on variables of openness, conscientiousness, extraversion, agreeableness and neuroticism (OCEAN) will shift positions many times before, during and after a required performance. Accompanying these positions will be preconscious passages of partial or fuzzy affective states with a large number of barely differentiated positions within those dimensions driving and being driven by interpersonal interactions [25] as well as driving and being driven by key physical processes [26]. The model has been designed for learning, task performance and interpersonal interaction contexts and may not be valuable or practical for other contexts.

2   The simSchool Simulation

In order to simulate learning, simSchool had to exhibit physical, psychological and cognitive features of classroom learning and allow a user to exercise and test a variety of learning theories. The broad interaction rules thus embody several well-known educational mechanisms including the zone of proximal development [27], mastery and performance goals [28], multiple intelligences [29], differentiation of instruction [7], and culturally responsive teaching [30]. For the focus of this paper, we concentrate on the physical, psychological and cognitive features of an individual learner, which will set the stage to discuss how pre-conscious processing reactions impact the AI representation of the ability to learn. The model of individual learning in simSchool contains ten variables or factors that are organized into three bundles or hubs of physical (visual, auditory, kinesthetic) psychological (openness, conscientiouness, extraversion, agreeableness, neuroticism) and cognitive variables (academic performance capability, and language capability).

A simplifying assumption of the model is that the variables are independent of each other in their responsiveness to the external environment and are grouped together for the display of behavior. So for example, the visual component of a task only impacts the visual capability of the learner (not capabilities in hearing, or thinking or feeling) but the overall affective state computed from the combined impact of all variables leads to a behavior based on all the physical variables as a bundle.

Three hubs (physical, psychological, cognitive) comprised of ten variables hold a past and current state for each individual learner in the simulated classroom. Hillclimbing algorithms (e.g. computing the distance from a goal state to a current state and then reducing that distance) take time to raise or lower the ten variables simultaneously and in relation to the environment (classroom tasks given by the user and conversational interactions). The environment drives the evolution of the variables and the distance-reducing algorithm gives rise to momentary and transitory affective psychological stances of the agents. Those stances, in conjunction with the physical and cognitive challenges of classroom learning, impact the agent's behavior and academic performance.

Together the (V) visceral physical factors, (O) OCEAN-based Five Factor psychological factors and (C) cognitive factors are thus used to represent salient elements of individual emotional response to the (E) environment of classroom learning challenges, in the COVE model [31]. Aspiring teachers interact with simSchool over several sessions, which often take place over several weeks, with microteaching interactions lasting from 10 to 30 min. The teacher candidates attempt to negotiate the simulated classroom environment while adapting their teaching to the diversity of students they face.

With this brief background and context, the next section discusses the theoretical framework that guided the design decisions for the model of preconscious processes, including both physical and affective states, in the COVE agent model.

3   Design Decisions

The COVE model treats emotions and other affective states as arising from hubs of regulatory networks of non-cognitive as well as cognitive processing. These networks specifically span from unconscious to conscious processing in order to fulfill a causative and evolving role in shaping values that lead to behavior. Affect and emotions are viewed as participating in an interstitial space between preconscious and fully conscious processing in order to provide a dynamic bridge as well as a structure for the orchestration of subconscious processes to arise into recognizable conscious states which become tagged with emotion and affect terms such as anger, fear and joy. The model differs from the notion of affective processes as "valenced reactions to events, agents or objects" [32] and in particular subjective-based appraisal theory [33] because it does not contain the concept of conscious personal significance. Instead, it uses a metric distance between task requirements and the current state of a person's COVE variables to represent a 'multidimensional gap closing' as the primary mechanism of transitory as well as sustained preconscious and conscious states. The model combines undifferentiated precursor states arising prior to as well as simultaneously with observable reactions and behavior and makes operational a complex landscape of flexible networks of processing centers that give rise via combinatorial interactions to a great number of physical, pre-conscious and conscious states (e.g. approximately 10^{20} states).

3.1 Multidimensional and Multileveled Homeostasis

Considered during the design decisions of the COVE model, emotion has most often been defined as *an affective state of consciousness*, distinct from volitional (deciding and committing) and cognition (acquiring knowledge and understanding through thought, experience, and the senses) [34]. In this definition, feeling (emotion), willing (volition), and knowing (cognition) are distinguished from one another as separate aspects of reality, all of which require consciousness. However, in other literature the emotions are also generally understood as representing a synthesis of subjective experience, expressive behavior, and subconscious neurochemical activity. It is this synthesis of physiology with experience and adaptive behavior in particular that opens the door to unconscious and preconscious activity-shaping precursor affective states leading to emotions. For example the homeostasis of underlying physiological processes gives rise to cyclic regimes that alternate between promoting and inhibiting particular emotional responses [35]. *This leads to a design decision for the computational model of affective processes to include a multidimensional and multileveled homeostatic relationship with the external world – the agent emotes in a complex adaptive relationship to its context, which is not limited to rational thought or cognitively prescient appraisal.*

3.2 Balance of Control and Flexibility

Emotions arose in evolution in order to provide a superordinate coordinating system for potentially competing preconscious subprograms of the mind [27, 28]. An animal could not have survived, for example, if simultaneous cues for sleep and escaping an approaching lion had sent ambiguous signals; emotional reactions help sort things out. Emotions play a shaping role in focusing attention, increasing the prominence of memories, affecting cognitive style and performance, and influencing judgments [12]. As a result of these shaping forces, emotions also play a part in personality development; and of equal importance, one's personality shapes one's emotional life.

This aspect is particularly important in relation to learning and classroom performance. *This leads to a design decision for the computational model to have the capability of controlling subsystems while maintaining a flexible, adaptive capability.*

3.3 Experience-Based Learning

Emotions have been properly viewed as a form of intelligence involved in learning [38]. In fact, a common ground between non-cognitive (e.g. physical, emotional, psychological) and cognitive (thinking, rationalizing) forms of intelligence is learning. Whether it is the adaptive physical and behavioral structures arising in a survival context, or how linked emotional and behavioral repertoires of a male and female of a species ensures courtship followed by reproductive and parental roles, or how a flushed face projects an internal state to others in a social setting, something has been learned via evolution if not during one's lifetime. *This leads to a design decision for the computational model to be able to learn from experience, allowing the development and expression of intelligence.*

3.4 Affective Processes as Pre-conscious Processes

The literature on emotional intelligence has for the most part focused on conscious processes that are seen as syndromes of conscious thoughts, feelings and actions [39]. This may be due to the fact that the study of human intelligence is in general, reliant upon psychometric methods that observe or poll people behaving in a social or testing setting. However, alternative theories of intelligence assert that consciousness is not required, for example the intelligence of lower forms of life [40], artificial life [41], the intelligence that is distributed across both the world and evolutionarily determined bodies [42], and the group intelligence of social animals that individually lack consciousness [43]. This evidence *influenced the design decision to treat affective processes as primarily pre-conscious and secondarily as conscious processes.*

3.5 Time-Based Learning

Since learning needed to be explicitly integrated into the simSchool model of agent emotions, the COVE model includes the layered characteristics of human learning. Typologies have arisen to describe those layers to account for a wide variety of learners in terms of physiological Cognitive models and psychological factors, and to explain how differing forms of intelligence arise in cultures and communities of practice [35, 36]. Integrated with these conceptions and refining them, layered approaches to cognition have been discussed by neuroscientists [37, 38], psychometricians [48], cognitive scientists [49] and computer scientists [32, 41, 42]. For example, Bruner [49] discussed cognitive development using a three-stratum framework of "enactive, iconic and symbolic" and Carroll's [52] factor-analytic model defined three layers as "narrow, broad, and general." These layered models have in common the idea that learning progresses from specifics negotiated at a "lowest level" active layer interfacing with the environment, to generalities synthesized from abstractions at higher levels. *This leads to a design decision that enables the model to develop over time both in evolutionary timescales and during an individual's lifetime through a layered process of learning.*

3.6 Design Decisions Summary

These design considerations set the stage for a computational model of affective processes that (1) traverses and operates across several levels: from physical, through pre-conscious processing layers, to higher cognitive areas that are capable of labeling experience; (2) maintains a critical balance between flexibility and control; (3) maintains a homeostatic dynamic equilibrium with both internal and external world features; and (4) learns from experience.

4 The COVE Model

COVE uses three layers to organize the internal variables of an AI student in simSchool and one layer to represent the external context of learning (Figs. 1 and 2). The E layer is the external environment, which in a classroom includes the task set before a student by the teacher and things the teacher might say to the student, as well as what others in the class say and do in reaction to the same stimuli. The V layer is the visceral, early-stage physical and pre-emotional processing stratum. The O layer contains the emotions and other pre-conscious processing, and the C layer contains conscious processing. The full COVE model uses a modified psychometric approach based on the factor-analytic model (sixteen factors) proposed by Cattell-Horn-Carroll (the CHC theory of intelligence), which has been validated and is widely used to understand cognitive abilities. simSchool uses ten of the sixteen factors and also uses a blend of structural-functional learning theories, which are needed to fully model the holistic context of a classroom learning context.

For each factor, the model adopts a representation as either a bipolar continuum of qualitatively different capabilities or a combination of a threshold with a qualitative continuum. For example, the skill of mathematical computation can be represented on a continuum with low positions on the scale representing basic arithmetic skills and high positions representing abstract or symbolic computations of higher orders. The number of positions on each continuum is selected to balance computational flexibility with representational accuracy (e.g. typically from five to twenty). The choice of number of

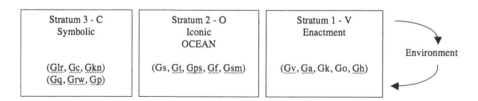

Fig. 1. COVE model of cognition integrating the CHC theory of intelligence

levels and factors increases the computational possibilities and challenges for modeling. A fully connected 16 factor cognitive model with 5 levels on each factor, for example would have 5^16 connection possibilities.

Evidence for simplifying the number of relationships through layering and hierarchical networks is available from intercorrelation data among the broad factors [53]. For example, for people aged 14–19 who took part in the development and standardization of the Woodcock-Johnson III, comprehensive knowledge (Gc) was .62 correlated with fluid reasoning (Gf) but only .37 with processing speed (Gs). This suggests that there may be a closer relationship between Gc and Gf. In addition, structural and functional considerations suggest a narrowing and channeling of the factors. For example, perception usually precedes cognition and the consolidation of long-term memory is facilitated by emotional arousal [54] implying that the layers handling perception (V) must link with emotional and psychological layers (O) before linking with long-term memory and crystallized knowledge (C). These kinds of considerations lead to a layered model (Fig. 2) consistent with Hawkin's ideas about hierarchical and time-based memory that is stored as sparse dynamic patterns changing over time [55].

4.1   The C Layer

The "C" layer of the COVE model utilizes 6 of the 16 CHC factors to model conceptual knowledge (Fig. 1): general storage and retrieval (Gc, Glr, Gkn); and specific storage and retrieval abilities (Gq, Grw, Gp). In the simSchool application, two of these six are directly represented in explicit variables (Gc and Gkn). Processes and relations in the algorithms function as the remaining factors. As higher cognitive functions, Gc is used to represent generalized academic capability and a specific type of Gkn (language) represents the degree to which the simulated student's language is the majority language of the classroom.

4.2   The O Layer

The "O" layer of the COVE model utilizes CHC factors involved in processing and reasoning (Gf, Gs, Gt, Gps, Gsm). The "O" layer is an interface between intelligence and personality in which one's psychological make-up is dominant and involved in basic central information processing mediated by emotions. In addition, the psychological model – that we assert is the crucible of affect and emotions – utilizes the Five-Factor (or OCEAN) Model of psychology [56] as the foundation of the student personality spectrum. The factors are treated as states (not traits) to allow evolution over short time spans during a single class session. Theoretical justification for the state-trait distinction was introduced above. For each of the five variables a continuum from negative one to positive one (increments of .1) is used to situate the learner's specific pre-conscious processing propensities, which shift as the context of the classroom changes.

Following Ortony, Clore, and Collins [32] but extending into subconscious processes, the "O" layer assumes that reactions developing during the appraisal of a situation influence performance. Appraisal in the COVE model can be physical (e.g. hair standing up on the back of the neck), subconscious (e.g. a smell and time of day triggering a nondiscursive association), conscious (e.g. a feeling clearly associated with a linguistic label such as shame, fear or attraction), or any combination. With continuous factor subcomponents, the COVE model treats affective states as a large number and wide range of states from preconscious to conscious that result from factor interactions as the variable settings on OCEAN ascend and descend around their set points; similar in spirit to Russell's continuous two-factor model [57].

Individual psychology is represented in COVE by the "Five Factor Model of Personality," "Big Five," or OCEAN model [58, 59]. OCEAN stands for Openness, Conscientiousness, Extroversion, Agreeableness and Neuroticism. Each factor has an opposite (e.g. the opposite of Extroversion is Intraversion). The OCEAN taxonomy encompasses several important psychological characteristics of learners and is represented by a continuum on each factor. The end of each continuum has maximum value in a variable or its opposite. The link of OCEAN to affect is established, for example by well-known affective disorders that are known to have OCEAN model correlates [60, 61] with certain maxima and minima.

In simSchool (www.simschool.org), the OCEAN variables are set on a scale from -1 to 1, with 0 at the midpoint, which allows the software agent to possess a 21^5 mix of valences upon which to base its observable behavior. SimSchool divides the scale into .1 units, giving 21 positions from -1 to 1 (e.g. -1, $-.9$, $-.8$ ... .8, .9, 1). This provides the "O" layer of the agent-learning model with over 4 million OCEAN-related states. The application narrows the observable descriptions of these possibilities by grouping the factors into 5-position narratives, representing clusters near -1, $-.5$, 0, .5 and 1. This creates a space of 5^5 or 3125 narrative descriptions that act as clues about the underlying 4 million actual states, in "student records" that a user can read in the role of playing the teacher of a simSchool class. The narratives are dynamically assembled from a database to create each unique personality and are presented to the user on demand as well as during the course of a simulation. Affective states (a concept that is proposed to apply to some of the 4 million OCEAN-based states) affect the overall behavior of the agent as one of the three hubs of data in the current state space of the agent, which is then mapped to a much smaller behavior space.

Linking OCEAN to the CHC model of intelligence (Figs. 1 and 2) has been proposed based on correlation evidence from studies of subjectively assessed intelligence (SAI) [62]. An example of SAI is a student who has often failed tests, which leads the student to an expectation to fail a future test, and thus lowered performance on the future test influenced by his or her appraisal. Citing a number of studies, it has been proposed that SAI mediates between personality, intelligence and performance, with a number of correlations noted by researchers, including:

- Personality traits are significant predictors of academic achievement.
- (Gf) and (Gc) are both positively correlated with performance.
- Openness (O) is positively correlated with intelligence.
- Conscientiousness (C) is a positive predictor of performance.

- Extraversion (E) is positively correlated with intelligence which is assumed to be due to higher speed of response (Gs, Gt, Gps) and lower arousal (N−).
- Neuroticism (N) is a negative predictor.

The COVE model links OCEAN to CHC at the "O" layer reasoning that OCEAN is more complex than receptor-based perception at layer "V", and more immediate but less complex than conceptualization and long term memory at layer "C." In addition, following Eysenck and Eysenck [26] who suggested that SAI should be considered a part of personality rather than intelligence and Chamorro-Premuzic and Furnham [62] who note the "considerable conceptual overlap between the concept of SAI and Openness" (p. 256), the COVE model layer "O" situates psychology, emotions, and reasoning fluidity (Gf) to fulfill the non-cognitive appraisal function.

The correlation evidence and structural-functional considerations lead to a model of "O" that includes causal precedence in the incoming signals from the environment (Fig. 2). Intercorrelation of Neuroticism and Extroversion with Openness, Conscientiousness and Agreeableness is suggested based on neurophysiological evidence from animal and human studies that posits two large clusters: (1) Extraversion, Exploration, Novelty seeking, Sensation Seeking, Positive Affectivity and Impulsiveness, versus (2) Neuroticism, Anxiety, Fearfulness and Negative Affectivity [24]. The two large E & N clusters are mediated by independent neurobiological mechanisms (e.g. catecholamines, dopamine and norepinephrine for E; and the amygdala and the benzodiazepine/ GABA receptor system for N). The arrows in Fig. 2 all represent positive correlations.

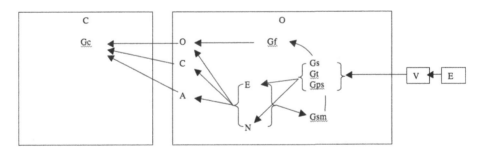

Fig. 2. Linking CHC to OCEAN variables

The COVE model is an attempt to describe the contents and the mechanisms of environmental responsiveness, information processes, affect, emotions and thought, but much work remains to be done. For example, the pathways in Fig. 2 focus on the "incoming" signals leading to crystallized knowledge; however, returning pathways from pattern formation, recognition, beliefs, and decisions to intentions and action exist at every level too. The simSchool application creates a simple mapping of current state to the mechanisms that update the state over time and the externally supplied goal of responding to the environment. Appraisal of a situation is an unconscious process that in simSchool takes place in eight of the ten dimensions (3 V-layer, 5 O-layer) and results in behaviors that become visible to the player. The simSchool model of today narrows the focus of appraisal to that of learning-task performance (objects in the environment), teacher conversations (agents in the environment) and the evolution of both of those influences in sequences (internal as well as external events in all layers).

The arrow in Fig. 2 from the E to N subcomponent sends a reentrant signal within the O layer via short term memory (Gsm) to the (Gs, Gt, Gps) cluster dealing with processing and leading to flexibility (Gf) and Openness. This mapping allows for reinforcement learning as well as cyclic reappraisal [63]. In addition, with the returning pathways that provide internal situational content [64], the mechanism described by Lahnstein [65] can be supported, where the onset and decay of an emotive episode is shaped by dynamics of interactions with previous states. Finally, the reentrant loop also introduces time and time delay into the mapping, without which Fig. 2 would be a primarily feed-forward network.

4.3   The V Layer

The "V" layer of the COVE model includes the five factors related to sensory perception (Gv, Ga, Gk, Go, Gh). The physiological characteristics involved in learning entail both sensory (afferent) and motor (efferent) neural pathways. While learning is sometimes thought of as primarily the organization of incoming sensory signals, recent work in artificial intelligence and robotics as well as constructivist learning theories suggests that pre-motor and motor systems - the body's exploration and action in the world - plays a major role in the development of intelligence [42]. The "V" layer concentrates on the sensory components of learning. In the simSchool engine, only (Gv, Ga, Gk) are used since those are more typical in classroom learning.

In these physiological or "V" variables, unlike the bipolar "O" psychological variables, there is the possibility of a complete absence of an input pathway, such as in blindness or deafness, thus the use of a threshold level in addition to a range of ability or preference. The physical sensory model thus utilizes a quasi-continuous scale from zero to one (increments of .1) to represent the simulated student's strength and preference (e.g. a setting of zero means that the simulated student cannot see and has no preference for visual information; a setting of one indicates that the student can both see and has the highest possible preference for visual information).

4.4   The E Layer

The "E" layer of environment variables in the COVE model includes learning tasks that involve the nature of knowledge (objects), interpersonal relationships and expectations states theory [66, 67] (agents) and the effects of sequences of interactions (events). In a recent review of learning theory [68], environment also includes "community," which reflects the social context of learning and the feedback role of external "assessment." In addition, some aspects of the nature of knowledge itself are external to the individual learner, namely objective reality. The COVE model is thus evolving to contextualize cognition as a social, cultural, and psychological interaction of internal and external factors, not solely as an "information processing" or "knowledge acquisition" problem of an individual.

In simSchool, signals from the environment are of two types: tasks have duration and influence continuously, conversations are point-like events with a pulse of influence that decays over time. The user can control which tasks are impacting which simulated students, so a high degree of differentiation is possible. Instances of talking are likewise controllable to impact a single student or the group as a whole.

5   Agent Learning Process

At its simplest, the process of learning in the model is represented by the complete acquisition of each of the ten variable targets set by any task assigned or talking behavior of the user. The process takes variable amounts of time because of the role of the O layer emotional reactions within the rest of the complex of other variables. In practice, the targets are almost never fully attained because either time runs out when the user changes the task or quits the simulation, or the simulated student begins to act out because a threshold level of task completion is reached, slowing the pace of additional progress. In simSchool, the appearance of learning is knowable via the performance of the agent in relation to the characteristics of a task, as the task attractors (or repellors) for the ten variables in the COVE model of each simulated student shapes each performance. Affects are envisioned as the transitory and momentary states passed through as the agent integrates the environmental triggers of the tasks and talking with their current internal state. The ten-dimensional model provides numerous states with specific implications for externally observable behaviors; for example, a student who is highly extraverted when given a task that is highly introverted, has a clear trajectory on that variable, while another student may be highly introverted and will have almost none. The learning process and any related affective states for each of these agents will be different. These differences give rise to roughly $20^{\wedge}10$ internal states (as opposed to 6 to 8 labeled affective states) in the possibility space for agent behavior.

6   Validation Studies

No formal studies have yet validated the computational modeling of either subjective affective states or the larger field of preconscious states traversed by a learner during a process of learning. However, internal model validation of simSchool has been achieved in incremental stages using expert and literature review, and controlled testing with the platform. To facilitate validation by any user, visualizations of the transitions of the ten variables in the model have been built as part of the user interface, so that all the actions of the variables are transparent, allowing a user, for example, to hold nine variables constant while testing for the directionality of a tenth test variable. The magnitude and speed of changes have not been verified in the model at this stage of development, but the directionality of all variables has been verified by experiment and can be replicated by any user.

For example, consider the expected direction of variables in the user described earlier who needs to sing the national anthem in front of an audience. If the person is highly 'open' (distractible) and 'neurotic' (fearful) and the singing task requires a high degree of 'repetition from memory' (focus) and 'steeled nerves to face an audience' (emotional stability) compared to a completely similar AI person but with less openness and less neuroticism, then the result will show a noticeable difference in the time and shape of the variable trajectories needed for successful performance. A person with the requisite openness and lack of neuroticism will succeed at the task quicker than otherwise, and the trajectories of all variables will be noticeably different via visual inspection (Fig. 3) giving insight into the model's causal explanation of the dynamics. Remembering the theoretical foundation of cognitive dissonance [20] and the need for high resolution rendering of affective and cognitive transitions [21], the visual inspection method of validation has succeeded in supporting judgments of the model's validity, which has also later been shown to be effective in impacting a user's intuition and judgments in externally validated contexts described next.

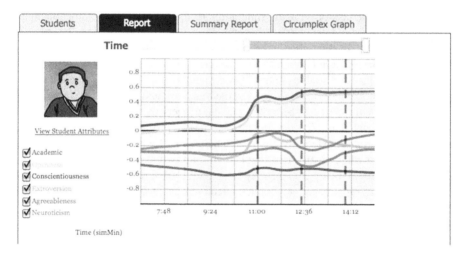

Fig. 3. Trajectories of OCEAN variables during a task in simSchool

Since the mapping of a dynamic set of internal mental states (e.g. physical, psychological and cognitive) to observable behavior (e.g. student records, grades, sitting, speaking and evidencing academic progress) in a classroom context is the whole point of the COVE model and the model was created in order to stimulate a user's insight into teaching and learning processes, several external validation studies have been conducted on the real world impacts of the simulation in its intended use context. These studies indicate that the COVE model adequately represents classroom learning differences [69, 70], and facilitates positive changes in teacher confidence, skills, and attitudes [16, 71].

One study used the Teacher Preparation Survey (TPS) a 25-item, Likert-based instrument divided into two sections, one about perceptions of teaching situations, and the other about teaching skills. It was adapted from [72]. The instrument was found to have both content validity as well as construct validity as determined through factor analysis [16]. In 2007 the instrument was found to have acceptable internal consistency reliability (Cronbach's Alpha) for Instructional Self-Efficacy (Alpha = .72) but not as high for Learning Locus of Control (Alpha = .57). Post hoc internal consistency reliability analysis for one 15-item factor produced a Cronbach's Alpha value of .97. These pedagogical scales were reconfirmed on an additional set of data. The 25 items from the TPS were resubmitted to a single exploratory factor analysis (Principal Components, Varimax rotation). The three-factor solution converged in four iterations and all items loaded on the anticipated factors. Cronbach's Alpha values for these scales were: Instructional Self-Efficacy = .77 (5 items); Learning Locus of Control = .68 (5 items); and Teaching Skill = .95 (15 items). Internal consistency reliability estimates were all in the range of "acceptable" to "very good" according to standard guidelines [73]. Items composing Teaching Skills, Instructional Self-Efficacy, and Learning Locus of Control scales are listed in an earlier publication featuring development of these indices [71].

Two studies in subsequent years found similar results, leading the research team to conclude that pre-post data gathered at three points in time across five years indicates that simSchool in a preservice teacher candidate environment measurably increases Instructional Self-Efficacy (confidence in one's competence), Learner Locus of Control, and Self-Reported Teaching Skills [74].

These studies show that the COVE model's map of the preconscious processes to classroom behavior and academic performance are adequate for training teachers and conducting practical educational psychology experiments. The contexts for validation studies thus far have included:

- Expert evaluation of the content, construct and face validity of real psychological profiles compared with simulation-based profiles of learners.
- Experienced teachers create simulated students that mirror real students they are working with, and conduct parallel instructional and interactional interventions for comparison.
- Pre and post-tests of knowledge, skills and attitudes of people who are training to become teachers; these tests indicate impacts of the simulation on users.
- Treatment-comparison group impact differences.
- Survey of users three years after treatment indicating higher retention in service compared to national averages in the U.S. This suggests that the simulation better prepares people to teach than other methods.
- Test-retest reliability of repeated measures.
- Internal reliability of measures regarding major constructs of experience versus confidence, resulting in a new measure of "pedagogical balance" in self-reports.

Additional replication and extension studies are needed. The model will need revision if empirical findings indicate gaps between learning theory and instructional practice that are unexplainable by, or missing in, the model's algorithms. Some future research findings are anticipated that will require an extension of the model either in its overall scope of defining learning as a physical-pre-conscious-cognitive complex (hubs) co-evolving with an environment, or for further elaboration of key factors within the hubs (e.g. "decoding" as a sub-element of "reading" as a sub element of "language ability"), or for the introduction of new processing layers and linkages among the factors, some of which might be keyed to engage only in certain contexts or domains of performance.

6.1 Testable Hypotheses

The testable hypotheses (exploratory as well as confirmatory) within educationally-focused studies of simSchool include a wide range of possibilities that span from individualized learning to classroom social processes and include the choices and behaviors of the teacher as a primary actor in a network of relationships, as well as the further validation of the COVE model instantiated in simSchool. For example, questions such as the following are a sampling of those that can be can be raised, for which data can automatically be collected by simSchool to provide visualizations and an analytic basis for insights into learning processes as well as some of the epistemological issues of teaching and learning:

1. Q: How does psychological differentiation among students impact group performance on academic tasks and on verbal interactions with a teacher? (The confirmatory hypothesis has been shown – psychological differentiation among students does impact academic performance and classroom interactions).
2. Q: How do teacher decisions about sequencing tasks differentially impact student learning? (The confirmatory hypothesis has been shown – teacher decisions do differentially impact student learning).
3. Q: How does the emotional stance of students impact their ability to learn?
4. Q: Are there linkages between physical, pre-conscious and cognitive factors that are empirically based and needed for accurate simulation of learning?
5. Q: Does a teacher have a preferred pattern of approaching students? Does that pattern differ by student, differ over time, and differ on other dimensions?
6. Q: How does the structure of an environment shape a student's emotional responses to teacher interactions and task requirements?
7. Q: Is the COVE model of affective processes sufficient for certain purposes at its current level of description, and under what conditions are other descriptive levels needed?

The range of testable hypotheses will be increased by the addition of new parts of the simSchool model that are needed for classroom simulation; most particularly, social interactions among the students, and short and long term memory with specific domain contents. With these extensions of the modeling space, the testable questions will expand further into social-constructivist theories of learning.

7 Summary

This article presented a practical and operational framework for a cognitive, psychological, physical and environmental (COVE) model of learning, including a transient preconscious-processing layer in an AI agent's representation of learning in a serious game. The model organizes a hierarchy of cognitive (C), psychological (O) and physical (V) functioning of agents in an environment (E). The classroom-learning context of the simSchool application and its model of an AI student's reactions to academic tasks and teacher talk were utilized to discuss the theoretical foundations, design decisions, assumptions and implications of the model.

References

1. Darling-Hammond, L.: Quality teaching: The critical key to learning. Principal **77**, 5–6 (1997)
2. Darling-Hammond, L., Youngs, P.: Defining 'Highly qualified teachers': What does 'Scientifically-based research' actually tell us? Educ. Res. **31**(9), 13–25 (2002)
3. Rice, J.: Teacher Quality: Understanding the Effectiveness of Teacher Attributes. Economic Policy Institute, Washington, DC (2003)
4. Girod, G., Girod, M., Denton, J.: Lessons learned modeling 'connecting teaching and learning'. In: Gibson, D., Aldrich, C., Prensky, M. (eds.) Games and simulations in online learning: Research and development frameworks, pp. 206–222. Idea Group, Hershey (2007)
5. Girod, M., Girod, J.: Simulation and the need for quality practice in teacher preparation. American Association of Colleges for Teacher Education (2006)
6. Mishra, P., Koehler, M.J.: Technological pedagogical content knowledge: A framework for teacher knowledge. Teach. Coll. Rec. **108**(6), 1017–1054 (2006)
7. Tomlinson, C.A.: How to differentiate instruction in mixed-ability classrooms, p. iv, p. 80. Association for Supervision and Curriculum Development, Alexandria (1995)
8. Grossman, P.: Research on pedagogical approaches in teacher education. In: Cochran-Smith, M. (ed.) Studying Teacher Education, pp. 425–476. American Educational Research Association, Washington DC (2005)
9. Aldrich, C.: Simulations and the Future of Learning: An Innovative (and perhaps revolutionary) Approach to e-Learning. Wiley, San Francisco (2004)
10. Foreman, J., Gee, J., Herz, J., Hinrichs, R., Prensky, M., Sawyer, B.: Game-based learning: How to delight and instruct in the 21st century. Educ. Rev. **39**(5), 50–66 (2004)
11. Prensky, M.: Digital Game-Based Learning. McGraw-Hill, New York (2001)
12. Brave, S., Hass, C.: Emotion in human-computer interaction. In: Jacko, J., Sears, A. (eds.) The human-computer interaction handbook: Fundamentals, evolving technologies and emergine applications, pp. 81–96. Lawrence Erlbaum Associates Inc, Mahwah (2003)
13. Mayrath, M., Clarke-Midura, J., Robinson, D.: Introduction to Technology-based assessments for 21st Centry skills. In: Mayrath, M., Clarke-Midura, J., Robinson, D., Schraw, G. (eds.) Technology-Based Assessments for 21st Century Skills: Theoretical and Practical Implications from Modern Research, p. 386. Information Age Publishers, Charlotte (2012)
14. Clarke-Midura, J., Code, J., Dede, C., Mayrath, M., Zap, N.: Thinking outside the bubble: Virtual performance assessments for measuring complex learning. In: Technology-Based Assessments for 21st Century Skills: Theoretical and Practical Implications from Modern Research, pp. 125–148. Information Age Publishers, Charlotte (2012)
15. Mislevy, R., Steinberg, L., Almond, R.: Evidence-Centered Assessment Design. Educational Testing Service, Princeton (1999)
16. Christensen, R., Tyler-Wood, T., Knezek, G., Gibson, D.: simSchool: An online dynamic simulator for enhancing teacher preparation. Int. J. Learn. Technol. **6**(2), 201–220 (2011)
17. Knezek, G., Vandersall, K.: simMentoring Results. In: simZine, vol. 2008, p. 3. CurveShift, Stowe (2008)
18. Knezek, G., Fisser, P., Gibson, D., Christensen, R., Tyler-Wood, T.: simSchool: Research outcomes from simulated classrooms. In: Society for Information Technology and Teacher Education International Conference 2012 (2012)
19. Festinger, L.: A Theory of Cognitive Dissonance. Standford University Press, Standford (1957)

20. Piaget, J.: The Equilibration of Cognitive Structures: The Central Problem of Intellectual Development. University of Chicago Press, Chicago (1985)
21. D'Mello, S., Graesser, A.: Modeling cognitive-affective dynamics with hidden markov models. In: Annual Meeting of the Cognitive Science Society, pp. 2721–2726 (2010)
22. McCrae, R., Costa, P.: Validation of the five-factor model of personality across instruments and observers. J. Pers. Soc. Psychol. **52**(1), 81–90 (1987)
23. John, O., Srivastava, S.: The Big Five trait taxonomy: History, measurement, and theoretical perspectives. In: Pervin, L. (ed.) Handbook of Personality: Theory and Research, pp. 102–138. Guilford Press, New York (1999)
24. Fridhandler, B.M.: Conceptual note on state, trait, and the state trait distinction. J. Pers. Soc. Psychol. **50**, 169–174 (1986)
25. Hofstee, W., de Raad, B., Goldberg, L.: Integration of the Big Five and Circumplex approaches to trait structure. J. Pers. Soc. Psychol. **63**(1), 146–163 (1992)
26. Eysenck, H., Eysenck, M.: Personality and Individual Differences. Plenum, New York (1985)
27. Vygotsky, L.S.: Mind in Society: The Development of Higher Psychological Processes. Harvard University Press, Cambridge (1978)
28. Elliot, A.: Approach and avoidance motivation and achievement goals. Educ. Psychol. **32**, 1–19 (1999). (34, 149–169)
29. Gardner, H.: Multiple Intelligences: The Theory in Practice. Basic Books, HarperCollins, New York (1993)
30. Gay, G.: Culturally Responsive Teaching Theory, Research, and Practice. Teachers College Press, New York (2000). (Variation: Multicultural education series)
31. Gibson, D.: simSchool-A complex systems framework for modeling teaching and learning. In: National Educational Computing Conference, Atlanta, GA (2007)
32. Ortony, A., Clore, G., Collins, A.: The Cognitive Structure of Emotions. Cambridge University Press, Cambridge (1988)
33. Scherer, K.R.: Appraisal theory. In: Dalgleish, T., Power, M. (eds.) Handbook of Cognition and Emotion, pp. 637–663. Wiley, Chichester (1999)
34. Merriam-Webster: Merriam-Webster Online Dictionary, vol. 2006 (2008)
35. Cooper, S.J.: From claude bernard to walter cannon. Emergence of the concept of homeostasis. Appetite **51**(3), 419–427 (2008)
36. Cosmides, L., Tooby, J.: Evolutionary Psychology: A Primer. University of California, Santa Barbara, Santa Barbara (2007)
37. Cosmides, L., Tooby, J.: Evolutionary psychology and the emotions. Handb. Emot. **2**(1), 91–115 (2000)
38. Goleman, D.: Emotional Intelligence: Why It Can Matter More Than IQ. Bantam Books, New York (1995)
39. Averill, J.: Together again: Emotions and intelligence reconciled. In: Matthews, G., Zeidner, M., Roberts, R. (eds.) The Science of Emotional Intelligence: Knowns and Unknowns, pp. 49–71. Oxford University Press, New York (2007)
40. Budaev, S.: The Dimensions of Personality in Humans and Other Animals: A Comparative and Evolutionary Perspective. Moscow (2000)
41. Braitenberg, V.: Vehicles, Experiments in Synthetic Psychology. MIT Press, Cambridge (1984)
42. Pfeifer, R., Bongard, J.: How the Body Shapes the Way We Think: A New View of Intelligence. MIT Press, Cambridge (2007)
43. Wilson, E.O.: What is sociobiology? Society **15**(6), 10–14 (1978)
44. Bloom, B., Engelhart, M., Furst, E., Hill, W., Krathwohl, D.: Taxonomy of Educational Objectives: The Classification of Educational Goals. David McKay, New York (1956)

45. Gardner, H.: Frames of Mind: the Theory of Multiple Intelligences, p. xiii, 440 p. Basic Books, New York (1983)
46. Edelman, G., Tononi, G.: Neural darwinism: The brain as a selectional system. In: Cornwell, J.J. (ed.) Nature's Imagination: The Frontiers of Scientific Vision, pp. 148–160. Oxford University Press, New York (1995)
47. McGrew, K.: Cattell-Horn-Carroll CHC (Gf-Gc) Theory: Past, Present and Future, vol. 2007. Institute for Applied Psychometrics (2003)
48. Cattell, R.: Personality and Motivation: Structure and Measurement. Harcourt, Brace and World, New York (1957)
49. Bruner, J., Oliver, R., Greenfield, P.: Studies in Cognitive Growth. Wiley, New York (1966)
50. Baum, E.: What is Thought?. MIT Press, Cambridge (2004)
51. Brooks, R.: A robust layered control system for a mobile robot. J. Robot. Autom. 2(April), 14–23 (1986)
52. Carroll, J.B.: The three-stratum theory of cognitive abilities. In: Flanagan, D., Genshaft, J., Harrison, P. (eds.) Contemporary Intellecual Assessment: Theories, Tests, and Issues, pp. 122–130. Guilford Press, New York (1996)
53. McGrew, K., Woodcock, R.: Technical Manual. Riverside Publishing, Itasca (2001)
54. LaBar, K., Phelps, E.: Arousal-mediated memory consolidation: Role of the medial temporal lobe in humans. Psychol. Sci. 9, 490–493 (1998)
55. Hawkins, J., Blakeslee, S.: On Intelligence. Henry Holt and Company, New York (2004)
56. McCrae, R., Costa, P.: Toward a new generation of personality theories: Theoretical contexts for the five-factor model. In: Wiggins, J.S. (ed.) The Five-Factor Model of Personality: Theoretical Perspectives, pp. 51–87. Guilford, New York (1996)
57. Russell, J.: Core affect and the psychological construction of emotion. Psychol. Rev. 110(1), 145–172 (2003)
58. Ewen, R.: Personality: A Topical Approach. Erlbaum, Mahweh (1998)
59. Digman, J.: Personality structure: Emergence of the five-factor model. Annu. Rev. Psychol. 41, 417–440 (1990)
60. Bagby, R.M., Costa, P.T., Widiger, T.A., Ryder, A.G., Marshall, M.: DSM-IV personality disorders and the five-factor model of personality: A multi-method examination of domain- and facet-level predictions. Eur. J. Pers. 19, 307–324 (2005)
61. Nestadt, G., Costa, P.T., Hsu, F.C., Samuels, J., Bienvenu, O.J., Eaton, W.W.: The relationship between the five-factor model and latent Diagnostic and Statistical Manual of Mental Disorders, Fourth Edition personality disorder dimensions. Compr. Psychiatry 49, 98–105 (2008)
62. Chamorro-Premuzic, T., Furnham, A.: A possible model for understanding the personality-intelligence interface. Br. J. Psychol. 95, 249–264 (2004)
63. Marsella, S., Gratch, J.: EMA: A process model of appraisal dynamics. Cogn. Syst. Res. 10 (1), 70–90 (2009)
64. Broekens, J.: Modeling the experience of emotion. Int. J. Synth. Emot. 1, 1–17 (2010)
65. Lahnstein, M.: The Emotive Episode is a Composition of Anticipatory and Reactive Evaluations. AISB Press, Edinburgh (2005)
66. Berger, J., Cohen, E., Zelditch Jr., M.: Status characteristics and expectation states. In: Berger, J., Zelditch Jr., M. (eds.) Sociological Theories in Progress, vol. 1, pp. 29–46. Houghton-Mifflin, Boston (1966)
67. Kalkhoff, W., Thye, S.: Expectation states theory and research: New observations from meta-analysis. Sociol. Methods Res. 35(2), 219–249 (2006)
68. Bransford, J., Brown, A., Cocking, R.: How People Learn: Brain, Mind, Experience and School. National Academy Press, Washington DC (2000)

69. Mcpherson, R., Tyler-wood, T., Ellison, A., Peak, P.: Using a computerized classroom simulation to prepare pre-service teachers. J. Technol. Teach. Educ. **19**(1), 93–110 (2011)
70. Ellison, A.M., Tyler-Wood, T.L., Periathiruvadi, S., Sayler, M., Barrio, B., Lim, O.: Preservice Teacher Experiences with a Computerized Classroom Simulation: A Content Analysis of Discussion Postings. AERA, New Orleans (2011)
71. Knezek, G., Christensen, R.: Preservice educator learning in a simulated teaching environment. Res. Highlights Technol. Teacher Educ. **1**(1), 161–170 (2009)
72. Reidel, E.: Teacher Beliefs and Preparation Survey. University of Minnesota, Minneapolis (2000)
73. DeVellis, R.: Scale Development. Sage Publications, Newbury Park (1991)
74. Knezek, G., Christensen, R., Tyler-Wood, T., Fisser, P., Gibson, D.: simSchool: Research outcomes from simulated classrooms. In: Society for Information Technology and Teacher Education International Conference 2012 (2012)

Author Index

Printed in the United States
By Bookmasters